FOR DUMMIES

COMPUTER
BOOK SERIES
FROM IDG

Visual Basic® 4 For Windows® For Dummies®

Object Naming Conventions

Object	Prefix	Example
Check box	chk	chkInTheMail
Combo box	cbo	cboSandwich
Command button	cmd	cmdSit
Directory list box	dir	dirTree
Drive list box	drv	drvMyCar
File list box	fil	filThisBox
Form	frm	frmMainMenu
Frame	fra	fraToolbar
Horizontal scroll bar	hsb	hsbRange
Image	img	imgPrettyPicture
Label	lbl	lblGraffiti
Line	lin	linBorder
List box	lst	lstPotentialDates
Menu	mnu	mnuFileExit
Radio button	opt	optRock101
Picture box	pic	picAndShovel
Shape (circle, square, oval, etc.)	shp	shpUpOrShipOut
Text box	txt	txtNotes
Vertical scroll bar	vsb	vsbTemperature

Editing in the Code Window

Key	Description
Backspace	Deletes one character to the left of the cursor
Delete	Deletes one character to the right of the cursor
Ctrl+X	Cuts selected text
Ctrl+C	Copies selected text
Ctrl+V	Pastes previously copied or cut text
Ctrl+Y	Cuts the current line
Ctrl+N	Inserts a blank line
Ctrl+Delete	Clears to the end of a line
Shift+Ctrl+Delete	Cuts to the end of a line
Ctrl+F	Finds text
F3	Finds next occurrence of text
Ctrl+R	Replaces text

Opening Windows

Which Window	Keystroke	Use for Window
Code	F7	Edits and examines BASIC code
Debug	Ctrl+Break	Examines the values of variables and expressions; tests procedure and function calls
Menu Editor	Ctrl+E	Creates and edits pull-down menus
Object Browser	F2	Lists all the procedures stored in each file of an entire Visual Basic program
Project	Ctrl+R	Lists all the files that make up your entire Visual Basic program
Properties	F4	Examines and changes the value of an object's properties

Visual Basic File Name Extensions

Extension	Description	Contents
FRM	Form file	Forms and event procedures
BAS	Module file	General procedures
VBP	Project file	List of all files (FRM, BAS, etc.) that make up a single Visual Basic program
OCX	Custom control	An object that extends the capability of Visual Basic

Visual Basic® 4 For Windows® For Dummies®

COMPUTER
BOOK SERIES
FROM IDG

Cheat Sheet

Control Structures

```
If Condition Then In-
structions

If Condition Then
    Instructions1
    Instructions2
End If

If Condition Then
    Instructions1
Else
        Instructions2
End If

If Condition1 Then
    Instructions1
ElseIf Condition2 Then
    Instructions2
End If

Select Case VariableName
```

```
    Case X
        Instructions1
    Case Y
        Instructions2
    Case Z
        Instructions3
End Select

Select Case VariableName
    Case X
        Instructions1
    Case Y
        Instructions2
    Case Z
        Instructions3
    Case Else
        InstructionsDefault
End Select
```

Loop Structures

```
Do While Condition
    Instructions
Loop

Do
    Instructions
Loop While Condition

Do Until Condition
    Instructions
Loop

Do
    Instructions
Loop Until Condition

For Counter = Start To
End
    Instructions
Next Counter

For Counter = Start To
End Step Increment
    Instructions

Next Counter
```

Objects That Get Data from the User Interface

Object	Data	Object Property
Check box	0 (Unchecked) 1 (Checked) 2 (Grayed)	Value
Combo box	String	Text
Directory list box	String	Path
Drive list box	String	Drive
File list box	String	FileName
List box	String	Text
Radio button	0 (False) 1 (True)	Value
Scroll bars	Number	Value
Text box	String	Text

Moving the Cursor in the Code Window

Key	What It Does
Ctrl+Home	Moves to the beginning of a procedure
Ctrl+End	Moves to the end of a procedure
Ctrl+right arrow	Moves one word to the right
Ctrl+left arrow	Moves one word to the left
Ctrl+PgDn	Displays the next procedure, organized alphabetically by object
Ctrl+PgUp	Displays the previous procedure, organized alphabetically by object

IDG
BOOKS
WORLDWIDE™

...For Dummies: #1 Computer Book Series for Beginners

VISUAL BASIC® 4
FOR
WINDOWS®
FOR
DUMMIES®

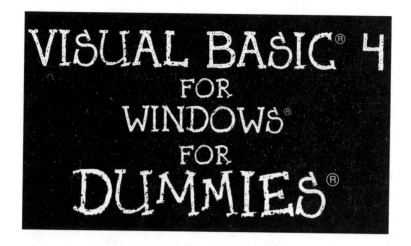

VISUAL BASIC® 4
FOR
WINDOWS®
FOR
DUMMIES®

by Wallace Wang

Foreword by
Sam Patterson
General Manager, Component Products Division
MicroHelp, Inc.

IDG Books Worldwide, Inc.
An International Data Group Company

Foster City, CA ◆ Chicago, IL ◆ Indianapolis, IN ◆ Southlake, TX

Visual Basic® 4 For Windows® For Dummies®

Published by
IDG Books Worldwide, Inc.
An International Data Group Company
919 E. Hillsdale Blvd.
Suite 400
Foster City, CA 94404
http://www.idgbooks.com (IDG Books Worldwide Web site)
http://www.dummies.com (Dummies Press Web site)

Library of Congress Catalog Card No.: 95-79913

ISBN: 1-56884-230-9

Printed in the United States of America

10 9 8 7 6 5 4 3

1B/RT/RR/ZW/IN

Distributed in the United States by IDG Books Worldwide, Inc.

Distributed by Macmillan Canada for Canada; by Transworld Publishers Limited in the United Kingdom and Europe; by WoodsLane Pty. Ltd. for Australia; by WoodsLane Enterprises Ltd. for New Zealand; by Longman Singapore Publishers Ltd. for Singapore, Malaysia, Thailand, and Indonesia; by Simron Pty. Ltd. for South Africa; by Toppan Company Ltd. for Japan; by Distribuidora Cuspide for Argentina; by Livraria Cultura for Brazil; by Ediciencia S.A. for Ecuador; by Addison-Wesley Publishing Company for Korea; by Ediciones ZETA S.C.R. Ltda. for Peru; by WS Computer Publishing Company, Inc., for the Philippines; by Unalis Corporation for Taiwan; by Contemporanea de Ediciones for Venezuela. Authorized Sales Agent: Anthony Rudkin Associates for the Middle East and North Africa.

For general information on IDG Books Worldwide's books in the U.S., please call our Consumer Customer Service department at 800-762-2974. For reseller information, including discounts and premium sales, please call our Reseller Customer Service department at 800-434-3422.

For information on where to purchase IDG Books Worldwide's books outside the U.S., please contact our International Sales department at 415-655-3172 or fax 415-655-3295.

For information on foreign language translations, please contact our Foreign & Subsidiary Rights department at 415-655-3021 or fax 415-655-3281.

For sales inquiries and special prices for bulk quantities, please contact our Sales department at 415-655-3200 or write to the address above.

For information on using IDG Books Worldwide's books in the classroom or for ordering examination copies, please contact our Educational Sales department at 800-434-2086 or fax 817-251-8174.

For press review copies, author interviews, or other publicity information, please contact our Public Relations department at 415-655-3000 or fax 415-655-3299.

For authorization to photocopy items for corporate, personal, or educational use, please contact Copyright Clearance Center, 222 Rosewood Drive, Danvers, MA 01923, or fax 508-750-4470.

 is a trademark under exclusive license to IDG Books Worldwide, Inc., from International Data Group, Inc.

About the Author

Wallace Wang, the author of *CompuServe For Dummies* and coauthor of the *Illustrated Computer Dictionary For Dummies,* writes a monthly column in *Boardwatch* magazine, and writes software reviews for stand-up comedians and comedy writers in a monthly comedy newsletter. He also performs stand-up comedy at night, teaches computer classes during the day, and once taught at the University of Zimbabwe, where he slept in a hut and wild monkeys stole his breakfast. When he's not writing computer books and magazine articles, Wallace is busy running a BBS, writing jokes, and infecting an old 386 with computer viruses just to see what will happen next.

ABOUT IDG BOOKS WORLDWIDE

Welcome to the world of IDG Books Worldwide.

IDG Books Worldwide, Inc., is a subsidiary of International Data Group, the world's largest publisher of computer-related information and the leading global provider of information services on information technology. IDG was founded more than 25 years ago and now employs more than 8,500 people worldwide. IDG publishes more than 275 computer publications in over 75 countries (see listing below). More than 60 million people read one or more IDG publications each month.

Launched in 1990, IDG Books Worldwide is today the #1 publisher of best-selling computer books in the United States. We are proud to have received eight awards from the Computer Press Association in recognition of editorial excellence and three from *Computer Currents'* First Annual Readers' Choice Awards. Our best-selling *...For Dummies*® series has more than 30 million copies in print with translations in 30 languages. IDG Books Worldwide, through a joint venture with IDG's Hi-Tech Beijing, became the first U.S. publisher to publish a computer book in the People's Republic of China. In record time, IDG Books Worldwide has become the first choice for millions of readers around the world who want to learn how to better manage their businesses.

Our mission is simple: Every one of our books is designed to bring extra value and skill-building instructions to the reader. Our books are written by experts who understand and care about our readers. The knowledge base of our editorial staff comes from years of experience in publishing, education, and journalism — experience we use to produce books for the '90s. In short, we care about books, so we attract the best people. We devote special attention to details such as audience, interior design, use of icons, and illustrations. And because we use an efficient process of authoring, editing, and desktop publishing our books electronically, we can spend more time ensuring superior content and spend less time on the technicalities of making books.

You can count on our commitment to deliver high-quality books at competitive prices on topics you want to read about. At IDG Books Worldwide, we continue in the IDG tradition of delivering quality for more than 25 years. You'll find no better book on a subject than one from IDG Books Worldwide.

John Kilcullen
President and CEO
IDG Books Worldwide, Inc.

Eighth Annual
Computer Press
Awards ≥1992

Ninth Annual
Computer Press
Awards ≥1993

Tenth Annual
Computer Press
Awards ≥1994

Eleventh Annual
Computer Press
Awards ≥1995

IDG Books Worldwide, Inc., is a subsidiary of International Data Group, the world's largest publisher of computer-related information and the leading global provider of information services on information technology. International Data Group publishes over 275 computer publications in over 75 countries. Sixty million people read one or more International Data Group publications each month. International Data Group's publications include: **ARGENTINA:** Buyer's Guide, Computerworld Argentina, PC World Argentina; **AUSTRALIA:** Australian Macworld, Australian PC World, Australian Reseller News, Computerworld, IT Casebook, Network World, Publish, Webmaster; **AUSTRIA:** Computerwelt Osterreich, Networks Austria, PC Tip Austria; **BANGLADESH:** PC World Bangladesh; **BELARUS:** PC World Belarus; **BELGIUM:** Data News; **BRAZIL:** Annuário de Informática, Computerworld, Connections, Macworld, PC Player, PC World, Publish, Reseller News, Supergamepower; **BULGARIA:** Computerworld Bulgaria, Network World Bulgaria, PC & MacWorld Bulgaria; **CANADA:** CIO Canada, Client/Server World, ComputerWorld Canada, InfoWorld Canada, NetworkWorld Canada, WebWorld; **CHILE:** Computerworld Chile, PC World Chile; **COLOMBIA:** Computerworld Colombia, PC World Colombia; **COSTA RICA:** PC World Centro America; **THE CZECH AND SLOVAK REPUBLICS:** Computerworld Czechoslovakia, Macworld Czech Republic, PC World Czechoslovakia; **DENMARK:** Communications World Danmark, Computerworld Danmark, Macworld Danmark, PC World Danmark, Techworld Denmark; **DOMINICAN REPUBLIC:** PC World Republica Dominicana; **ECUADOR:** PC World Ecuador; **EGYPT:** Computerworld Middle East, PC World Middle East; **EL SALVADOR:** PC World Centro America; **FINLAND:** MikroPC, Tietoverkko, Tietoviikko; **FRANCE:** Distributique, Hebdo, Info PC, Le Monde Informatique, Macworld, Reseaux & Telecoms, WebMaster France; **GERMANY:** Computer Partner, Computerwoche, Computerwoche Extra, Computerwoche FOCUS, Global Online, Macwelt, PC Welt; **GREECE:** Amiga Computing, GamePro Greece, Multimedia World; **GUATEMALA:** PC World Centro America; **HONDURAS:** PC World Centro America; **HONG KONG:** Computerworld Hong Kong, PC World Hong Kong, Publish in Asia; **HUNGARY:** ABCD CD-ROM, Computerworld Szamitastechnika, Interneto online Magazine, PC World Hungary, PC-X Magazin Hungary; **ICELAND:** Tolvuheimur PC World Island; **INDIA:** Information Communications World, Information Systems Computerworld, PC World India, Publish in Asia; **INDONESIA:** InfoKomputer PC World, Komputek Computerworld, Publish in Asia; **IRELAND:** ComputerScope, PC Live!; **ISRAEL:** Macworld Israel, People & Computers/Computerworld; **ITALY:** Computerworld Italia, Macworld Italia, Networking Italia, PC World Italia; **JAPAN:** DTP World, Macworld Japan, Nikkei Personal Computing, OS/2 World Japan, SunWorld Japan, Windows NT World, Windows World Japan; **KENYA:** PC World East African; **KOREA:** Hi-Tech Information, Macworld Korea, PC World Korea; **MACEDONIA:** PC World Macedonia; **MALAYSIA:** Computerworld Malaysia, PC World Malaysia, Publish in Asia; **MALTA:** PC World Malta; **MEXICO:** Computerworld Mexico, PC World Mexico; **MYANMAR:** PC World Myanmar; **NETHERLANDS:** Computer! Totaal, LAN Internetworking Magazine, LAN World Buyers Guide, Macworld Netherlands, Net, WebWereld; **NEW ZEALAND:** Absolute Beginners Guide and Plain & Simple Series, Computer Buyer, Computer Industry Directory, Computerworld New Zealand, MTB, Network World, PC World New Zealand; **NICARAGUA:** PC World Centro America; **NORWAY:** Computerworld Norge, CW Rapport, Datamagasinet, Financial Rapport, Kursguide Norge, Macworld Norge, Multimediaworld Norge, PC World Ekspress Norge, PC World Nettverk, PC World Norge, PC World ProduktGuide Norge; **PAKISTAN:** Computerworld Pakistan; **PANAMA:** PC World Panama; **PEOPLE'S REPUBLIC OF CHINA:** China Computer Users, China Computerworld, China InfoWorld, China Telecom Weekly, Computer & Communication, Electronic Design China, Electronics Today, Electronics Weekly, Game Software, PC World China, Popular Computer Week, Software Weekly, Software World, Telecom World; **PERU:** Computerworld Peru, PC World Profesional Peru, PC World SoHo Peru; **PHILIPPINES:** Click!, Computerworld Philippines, PC World Philippines, Publish in Asia; **POLAND:** Computerworld Poland, Computerworld Special Report Poland, Cyber, Macworld Poland, Networld Poland, PC World Komputer; **PORTUGAL:** Cerebro/PC World, Computerworld/Correio Informatico, Dealer World Portugal, Mac*In/PC*In Portugal, Multimedia World; **PUERTO RICO:** PC World Puerto Rico; **ROMANIA:** Computerworld Romania, PC World Romania, Telecom Romania; **RUSSIA:** Computerworld Russia, Mir PK, Publish, Seti; **SINGAPORE:** Computerworld Singapore, PC World Singapore, Publish in Asia; **SLOVENIA:** Monitor; **SOUTH AFRICA:** Computing SA, Network World SA, Software World SA; **SPAIN:** Communicaciones World España, Computerworld España, Dealer World España, Macworld España, PC World España; **SRI LANKA:** Infolink PC World; **SWEDEN:** CAP&Design, Computer Sweden, Corporate Computing Sweden, Internetworld Sweden, it.branschen, Macworld Sweden, MaxiData Sweden, MikroDatorn, Natverk & Kommunikation, PC World Sweden, PCaktiv, Windows World Sweden; **SWITZERLAND:** Computerworld Schweiz, Macworld Schweiz, PCtip; **TAIWAN:** Computerworld Taiwan, Macworld Taiwan, NEW ViSiON/Publish, PC World Taiwan, Windows World Taiwan; **THAILAND:** Publish in Asia, Thai Computerworld; **TURKEY:** Computerworld Turkiye, Macworld Turkiye, Network World Turkiye, PC World Turkiye; **UKRAINE:** Computerworld Kiev, Multimedia World Ukraine, PC World Ukraine; **UNITED KINGDOM:** Acorn User UK, Amiga Action UK, Amiga Computing UK, Apple Talk UK, Computing, Macworld, Parents and Computers UK, PC Advisor, PC Home, PSX Pro, The WEB; **UNITED STATES:** Cable in the Classroom, CIO Magazine, Computerworld, DOS World, Federal Computer Week, GamePro Magazine, InfoWorld, I-Way, Macworld, Network World, PC Games, PC World, Publish, Video Event, THE WEB Magazine, and WebMaster; online webzines: JavaWorld, NetscapeWorld, and SunWorld Online; **URUGUAY:** InfoWorld Uruguay; **VENEZUELA:** Computerworld Venezuela, PC World Venezuela; and **VIETNAM:** PC World Vietnam.
10/22/96

Dedication

This book is dedicated to my parents, Herbert and Ruth Wang, my wife, Cassandra, and Bo and Scraps, my cats.

Publisher's Acknowledgments

We're proud of this book; please send us your comments about it by using the Reader Response Card at the back of the book or by e-mailing us at feedback/dummies@idgbooks.com. Some of the people who helped bring this book to market include the following:

Acquisitions, Development, and Editorial

Project Editors: Susan Pink, Mary Corder, Kristin A. Cocks

Assistant Acquisitions Editor: Gareth Hancock

Product Development Manager: Mary Bednarek

Permissions Editor: Joyce Pepple

Editors: Colleen Rainsberger, Barb Terry

Technical Editor: Jeff Bankston

Editorial Assistants: Constance Carlisle, Chris Collins

Production

Project Coordinator: Valery Bourke

Layout and Graphics: Megan Briscoe, Elizabeth Cárdenas-Nelson, Dominique DeFelice, Maridee V. Ennis, Lee Hubbard, Angela F. Hunckler, Carla C. Radzikinas, Anna Rohrer, Gina Scott, Michael Sullivan

Proofreaders: Henry Lazarek, Melissa D. Buddendeck, Dwight Ramsey, Robert Springer, Carrie Voorhis

Indexer: Alexandra Nickerson

Special Help

Editorial Executive Assistant: Richard Graves

General and Administrative

IDG Books Worldwide, Inc.: John Kilcullen, CEO; Steven Berkowitz, President and Publisher

Dummies, Inc.: Milissa Koloski, Executive Vice President and Publisher

Dummies Technology Press and Dummies Editorial: Diane Graves Steele, Vice President and Associate Publisher; Judith A. Taylor, Brand Manager

Dummies Trade Press: Kathleen A. Welton, Vice President and Publisher; Stacy S. Collins, Brand Manager

IDG Books Production for Dummies Press: Beth Jenkins, Production Director; Cindy L. Phipps, Supervisor of Project Coordination; Kathie S. Schutte, Supervisor of Page Layout; Shelley Lea, Supervisor of Graphics and Design; Debbie J. Gates, Production Systems Specialist; Tony Augsburger, Reprint Coordinator; Leslie Popplewell, Media Archive Coordinator

Dummies Packaging and Book Design: Patti Sandez, Packaging Assistant; Kavish+Kavish, Cover Design

◆

The publisher would like to give special thanks to Patrick J. McGovern, without whom this book would not have been possible.

◆

Acknowledgments

Nobody writes and publishes a book without the help of other people, and this book is no exception. It goes without saying (although I'm going to say it anyway) that two of the most important people responsible for this book are Matt Wagner and Bill Gladstone of Waterside Productions. Thanks guys. I'd give you more than your usual 15 percent cut but if I did, I wouldn't have anything left over to pay for my groceries.

Two other people who deserve thanks include Mary Corder of IDG Books Worldwide, Inc., and Susan Pink, who converted this book from a mass of Microsoft Word documents and shaped it into what you're now holding in your hands. After all the frantic CompuServe and Federal Express messages passed back and forth between us, I almost feel like I know you better than my own family.

Then there are the people who had an indirect influence on this book. First there's Dan Gookin, whom everybody already knows from *DOS For Dummies*, *WordPerfect For Dummies*, and so on. Then there are Tina and Andy Rathbone, whom everyone also knows from *PCs For Dummies, Windows For Dummies, Modems For Dummies*, and so on. There are many memories tied up with these people, and it's only proper to acknowledge their contribution to my life so that they won't think I've completely forgotten all about them.

Next, I have to acknowledge Cassandra, my wife, and Bo, my cat, for their support during the long hours I've spent glued in front of my computer instead of doing anything else around the house. I'd also like to thank Dante, the $10,000 winner of ABC's "America's Funniest People" show, just because I always promised to put his name in a book of mine one day. There's also Fred Burns and Ron Clark at The Comedy Store in La Jolla, CA who didn't mind my working on this book on my laptop computer in The Comedy Store lobby every night.

And lastly, for political reasons as well as an honest-to-goodness way of saying thanks, I'd like to acknowledge Mitzi Shore, the owner of The Comedy Store, who has given me a chance to practice telling jokes in front of hostile, drunk, rowdy people late at night when all decent folks have long since gone to bed. Thanks for starting The Comedy Store. We all need a second place that we can call our home.

Contents at a Glance

Cartoons at a Glance

By Rich Tennant

page 399

page 363

page 120

page 167

page 337

page 317

page 219

page 421

page 7

page 55

Table of Contents

· ·

Part VIII: Database Programs and Printing 399

Chapter 30: Using Files from Database
Programs You'd Rather Not Use 401

Chapter 31: Making Your Program Print Stuff 413

Foreword

● ●

*W*elcome to the exciting world of Visual Basic Programming! I've been using the BASIC language since the TRS-80 Model 1 in 1977. Later, on the PC platform, I moved on to GW-BASIC and then to the various Microsoft QuickBasic and PDS compiler products.

When I got my first look at "Thunder," which later became Visual Basic 1.0, I was amazed! In 1991 I joined up with MicroHelp, Inc. — first as a beta tester and then as a contractor writing custom controls — to help produce VBTools 1.0, the first add-on package of custom controls for Visual Basic. This, in my opinion, was the start of the prebuilt component revolution we are seeing today.

Since Visual Basic's inception, writing programs for Windows has never been easier — and the release of Version 4.0 makes this even more true. After you finish reading *Visual Basic 4 For Windows For Dummies*, I think you'll be as excited as I was when I began tinkering and then writing full applications with Visual Basic.

Visual Basic is by far the tool of choice for programming in the Windows environment. Microsoft has strategically leveraged its knowledge of the BASIC and Windows environments to create a language that will be embedded in all of its major retail products, including Microsoft Word, Excel, and Access. The concepts you'll learn in this book will build a foundation for using Visual Basic in all other Microsoft applications and many non-Microsoft applications.

Whether you program for fun, casually, or for a living, the time you take to learn to use this language will bring you many rewards. *Visual Basic 4 For Windows For Dummies* gives you a headstart, with practical examples and an easy-to-understand style that makes learning that much more fun! Wallace Wang's intimate understanding of and ability to express complex ideas in simple and often humorous language makes a sometimes dry subject matter as easy to read as a current novel. I hope you enjoy your foray into Visual Basic programming as much as I have! Good luck and happy programming!

Sam Patterson
General Manager, Component Products Division
MicroHelp

Introduction

. . . .

*W*elcome to computer programming using Visual Basic. If you've ever tried to program before but found it too complicated, relax. If you can doodle mindlessly on a scrap of paper, you can write a program in Visual Basic. (Seriously!)

While I wrote this book, I took an unconventional approach to talking about programming — I used English. Besides honest-to-goodness English explanations, I also provide interesting programming trivia, example programs, and step-by-step instructions for writing programs in Visual Basic.

Programming really doesn't have to be difficult and can actually be lots of fun. To remind you to enjoy yourself, this book keeps up a spirit of playfulness. After all, that's why most people bought a computer in the first place — to have fun. (Admit it. Does anyone *really* buy a computer just to balance a budget?)

About This Book

Think of this book as a friendly guide to Visual Basic programming. Although Visual Basic isn't hard to learn, it can be hard to remember all the petty details needed to write programs that do something interesting. Some sample topics you'll find in this book include the following:

- ✔ Saving your program
- ✔ Designing a user interface
- ✔ Creating pull-down menus
- ✔ Killing bugs in your program
- ✔ Printing stuff out

Although many people think that programming a computer requires years of advanced mathematics and technical training, relax. If you can tell someone how to get to your house from work, you can certainly tell a computer what you want it to do. The purpose of this book isn't to cram your brain full of technical details and explanations. The purpose of this book is to show you all the steps you need to write a Visual Basic program and give you the know-how and confidence to do it.

How to Use This Book

This book tells you step by step how to create a user interface and then tells you the BASIC code that your program needs to respond to any action taken on the user interface (such as clicking buttons and pressing certain keys.)

All code appears in monospaced type like this:

```
Printer.DrawWidth = Value
```

Type letter for letter anything that appears in **bold**. Any code that is not in bold is a placeholder, for which you enter your own information. In the preceding example, you would type **Printer.DrawWidth** and then you would enter a number corresponding to the width of the line you wanted.

Due to the margins in this book, some long lines of code wrap to the next line. On your computer, though, these wrapped lines appear as a single line of code, so do not insert a hard return when you see one of these wrapped lines. Each instance of wrapped code is noted as follows:

```
Sub Form_MouseUp(Button As Integer, Shift As Integer, X As
                 Single, Y As Single)
```

Visual Basic doesn't care if you type everything in uppercase, lowercase, or both. But to make what appears on your screen correspond to the figures in this book, use uppercase and lowercase as shown throughout the book's examples.

To test your learning, there are also simple quizzes sprinkled throughout this book. But rather than focus on making people miserable, these quizzes emphasize boosting your self-esteem. Each quiz presents four possible choices for each question. Three choices will be so outrageously wrong that it will be easy for you to choose the right one. Not only will these questions teach you something, but you'll have a good chuckle reading the wrong choices as well.

Foolish Assumptions

This is what I'm assuming about you: You can turn a computer on and off, and you already know how to use a mouse and a keyboard. Plus, you want to write your own programs for fun, profit, or work (work isn't always fun or profitable).

In addition, you also have a copy of Visual Basic and a desire to learn how to use it. That's pretty much all you need to use this book. You don't need to be a wizard in math, you don't need a Ph.D. in computer science, and you don't need to know much about the internal guts of your computer or how it works.

In fact, Albert Einstein (the famous physicist who came up with the theory of relativity) once had an elementary school teacher who thought that Einstein was retarded. Perhaps in response to this, Albert Einstein said "Imagination is more important than knowledge." So if you have an imagination, you already have more than enough to get started writing programs in Visual Basic.

How This Book Is Organized

This book contains nine major parts. Each part contains several chapters, and each chapter contains several modular sections. Anytime you need help, just pick up this book and start reading.

Here is a breakdown of the nine parts and what you'll find in them.

Part I: A Beginner's Guide to Visual Basic

Part I contains a brief introduction to all the major features of Visual Basic. If the thought of programming a computer makes you break out in hives, this is the place to relieve your anxieties and boost your self-esteem.

Part II: Designing a User Interface

A user interface determines what your program looks like. This is the fun part, where you can make your program look as ugly or as beautiful as you want. In Part II, you'll be doodling circles, drawing lines, and scribbling all over the screen. In fact, if you tried doing this without a computer, people might think you had lost your mind and reverted to kindergarten fingerpainting.

Part III: Menus to Make Your Program Look Less Ugly

In Part III, you get to create fancy pull-down menus that you see all the expensive programs using these days. If you want your program to impress your friends and influence people, this is where you'll learn how to do it.

Part IV: The Basics of Writing Code

In Part IV, you learn how to write honest-to-goodness BASIC programs that the computer will understand and obey. Although you may already know how to tell your computer what to do (using four-letter words), this is where you learn how to tell your computer what to do using the BASIC language.

Part V: Making Decisions (Something You Stop Doing When You Get Married)

Part V is where you learn how to tell your computer to make up its own mind and do something useful instead of relying on you to do everything. For those of you raising children, you might find this idea of self-reliance particularly appealing.

Part VI: Loops and Loops (or "Do I Have to Repeat Myself?")

Loops are another way of telling your computer to do something until it gets it right. In Part VI, you learn different ways to make your computer repeat itself.

Part VII: Writing Subprograms (So You Don't Go Crazy All at Once)

Many people panic at the thought of writing a large program. In Part VII, you learn the secrets to maintaining your sanity while writing many little programs that work together to create one huge program.

Part VIII: Database Programs and Printing

Part VIII is called "Database Programs and Printing," but don't let the title intimidate you. Database programs are nothing more than special ways that computers organize information. People store their information in drawers, folders, and closets; computers use databases. No big deal. You also learn how to print all your valuable programs on paper for the whole world to see and admire.

Part IX: The Part of Tens

Part IX contains several chapters of miscellaneous information that you may find useful and interesting, including tips about add-ons for Visual Basic and where to find more information about Visual Basic programming.

Icons Used in This Book

This icon signals technical details that are informative (and sometimes interesting) but not necessary. Skip these if you want.

This icon flags useful or helpful information that makes programming even less complicated.

Don't pass these gentle reminders — they signify important information.

Be cautious when you encounter this icon. It warns you of things you shouldn't do.

Step-by-step instructions and explanations follow this icon.

This icon indicates information that you may find useful or interesting, but is by no means necessary to clutter your mind with it.

Where to Go from Here

This is the part where you step onto the Yellow Brick Road and get moving! Computer programming in Visual Basic is as fun as playing with an Etch-A-Sketch (except you can draw circles in Visual Basic). If someone accuses you of doodling when you should be working, you can impress them with all your new knowledge about Visual Basic programming!

Part I
A Beginner's Guide to Visual Basic

In this part . . .

1f you have always been interested in computer
programming but were intimidated because it seemed
too advanced and complicated looking, or if your boss
"suggested" that you learn how and you don't know where
to begin, this book is for you.

You won't be required to learn volumes of computer code,
and you just might have fun in the process. So grab some
Twinkies and read on. . . .

Chapter 1
How Visual Basic Works

*T*he whole purpose of writing a program is to make the computer do something useful. Before you start writing a Visual Basic program, turn off your computer, sit down with paper and pencil, and decide exactly what you want to make your computer do.

You can make your computer do almost anything you want, short of doing your homework or launching nuclear missiles at your neighbors. A program can be as simple as a display of your name on the screen or as complicated as a word processor specially designed for writing screenplays.

After you've decided what you want your computer to do, the next step is to use a programming language (such as Visual Basic) to tell your computer, step-by-step, exactly how to do what you want.

Writing Your Program

There's no single correct way to write a program. Theoretically, there are a million different ways to write a program correctly, just as there are a million different ways to travel from New York to Los Angeles. Some people prefer airplanes for speed, some prefer trains for sightseeing, and some prefer buses for cost-effectiveness. Similarly, there are millions of ways to write the same program, but no matter how you write it, the result can always be the same.

As a programmer, your job is to write a program that works correctly and is easy to use. If your program doesn't work, nobody can use it (although you can often sell a few thousand copies to unsuspecting individuals first). If your program isn't easy to use, nobody will want it, even if it works perfectly.

Testing whether your program works is usually simple enough. If your program is supposed to print mailing labels but erases all the files from your hard disk instead, it's obvious that it doesn't work. (Then again, you can always market your program as a quick hard-disk eraser.)

However, determining whether your program is easy to use is more difficult. What you consider easy to use may be almost impossible for someone else to understand.

To help you create programs that everyone agrees are easy to use, Visual Basic provides common items that are found in other Windows-based programs, such as pull-down menus, check boxes, and command buttons. The idea is that if all programs work the same way, people will have less trouble learning how to use different programs.

For example, most people can drive a Toyota and a Ford without any problems. The steering wheel and brakes are always in the same places, even if the windshield wipers and horn may not be. The same goes for programs. Commands are usually stored in pull-down menus at the top of the screen, and the mouse can always be used to point at and highlight objects. Although each program may offer slightly different commands, the overall structure remains familiar.

The Visual Basic development cycle

Here are the nine steps necessary to create a Visual Basic program — three steps fewer than those required to overcome an addictive habit. The first eight steps are what programmers call the *development cycle*. The ninth step is what programmers call *job security*.

1. Decide what you want the computer to do: the problem you most likely want to solve or the specific actions you want to occur.

2. Decide how your program will look on the screen. (How your program looks on the screen is its *user interface*.)

3. Draw your user interface using common parts, such as windows, menus, and command buttons. (These parts of a user interface are called *objects* or *controls*.)

4. Define the name, color, size, and appearance of your user interface objects. (An object's characteristics are its *properties*.)

5. Write instructions in BASIC to make each part of the program do something. (BASIC instructions are called *commands*.)

A quick (and incomplete) history of the BASIC language

Before you start writing Visual Basic programs, you may want to know where BASIC comes from and why it even exists.

Back in 1964, programming a computer was tedious, time-consuming, and a real pain in the neck. In an effort to make programming easier and more enjoyable, two Dartmouth professors, John G. Kemeny and Thomas E. Kurtz, developed the BASIC language.

BASIC (which is an acronym that stands for Beginner's All-Purpose Symbolic Instruction Code) was designed to make computer programming easy for people who weren't rocket scientists. Unlike other languages at the time, BASIC was interactive. That meant that the moment you typed a BASIC command into the computer, the computer would either obey the command or immediately tell you if you made a mistake.

Letting you know right away if you made a mistake was a big programming revolution at the time. In comparison, other languages forced you to write a complete program first. If you typed any mistakes, the computer wouldn't let you know until you finished. When your program refused to work, you had to find the mistake, which was like looking for the proverbial needle in a haystack. (This explains why most computer programmers are either geniuses or have completely lost their minds.)

Because BASIC was so friendly and easy to use, almost every computer offered this language. The early IBM PC computers came with a version called BASICA. IBM-compatible computers soon offered a similar version called GW-BASIC.

The release of MS-DOS 5.0 included a new version of BASIC called QBasic. But because BASIC was originally designed for beginners, serious programmers still considered BASIC a toy language.

Everything changed when Microsoft introduced Microsoft Windows. Not only did programmers have to write programs that worked, but they also had to write programs that offered pull-down menus, dialog boxes, and scrollable windows. Essentially, programming became twice as hard because of the more complicated Windows operating environment.

In 1991, Microsoft released Visual Basic. Now programmers could draw the appearance of their program first and concentrate on making the program work later. Because designing the way a program looks is half the battle, Visual Basic makes this part easy so that you can focus on making your program do something useful.

Because of these characteristics, Visual Basic is a lot easier to learn than Pascal or C++. Not only can you write programs faster, but it also takes less effort to create them.

6. Compile and run the program to see if it works.

7. Cry when your program doesn't work perfectly. (Required)

8. Look for errors (or *bugs*) in your program.

9. Start over. (Required)

Although you don't have to memorize these nine steps, you do have to follow them. There's never a shortcut, either. Trying to skip from step 1 to step 4 is like trying to start a car by using the gas pedal but forgetting to put the key in the ignition. You can try it, but you're not going to get anywhere.

Believe it or not, step 1 is actually the hardest and the most important. After you know what you want to do, it's just a matter of finding ways to do it. Persistence and creativity are helpful, as are lots of caffeine-laden beverages and take-out Chinese food.

Making a neat user interface

The user interface is what someone sees when your program is running. Every program has a user interface in one form or another. Some programs have elaborate, colorful windows that explode on the screen. Other programs have a sparse appearance, as if the programmer were afraid that screen phosphor might be in short supply one day.

A Visual Basic user interface consists of forms and objects. A *form* is nothing more than a window that appears on the screen. Every Visual Basic program has at least one form, although most programs use several forms.

Objects are items that appear in a form (see Figure 1-1), such as command buttons, scroll bars, and option buttons (sometimes called *radio buttons*). An object lets the user give commands to your program. If you really wanted to, you could create a program with only one form and no objects, but it wouldn't be very useful or interesting.

Properties make your user interface pretty

After you design your user interface, the next step is to define the properties of each form and object. An object's *properties* determine the object's name, color, size, location, and appearance on the screen.

Different objects have different properties. Each time you create a new object, Visual Basic assigns default property values to it. This is Visual Basic's way of saying that it knows what's best for you. You can use these default values, but you will have to modify some of them for your own particular program.

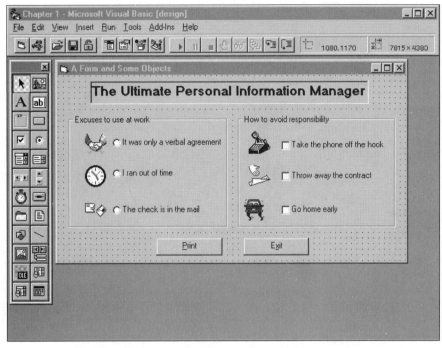

Figure 1-1:
A form and
objects.

After you finish designing your user interface, Visual Basic saves it in a file with an FRM file extension. If you look at an FRM file with a word processor, all you see is a bunch of meaningless words and symbols, much like the documentation that comes with Visual Basic.

Because your user interface can consist of one or more forms, your entire program's user interface may be stored in two or more separate FRM files, as shown in Figure 1-2.

Each time you create a new form, you have to give it a file name. (If you're using the 16-bit version of Visual Basic, you'll be limited to the typical DOS eight-letter file name maximum.)

Ideally, you want the file name to identify what the form does. If you write a sales reporting program, for example, naming your form SALES.FRM is smart. Naming your form X13P29.FRM may seem ingenious at the time, but it makes the file hard to find if you forget the file name.

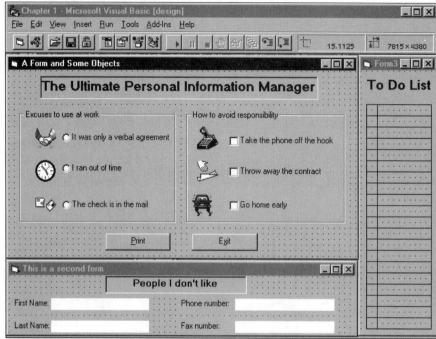

Figure 1-2:
A user
interface
divided into
multiple
forms and
FRM files.

Writing BASIC code

Until this point, writing a Visual Basic program has been completely unlike writing a C or Pascal program. C and Pascal programmers begin usually by writing code, whereas until now, Visual Basic programmers have just been doodling on their computer screens, creating their user interface.

When you're happy with the way your user interface looks, the final step involves writing BASIC commands (also known as *code*) to make your program work. (If you change your mind and want to edit the appearance of your user interface, you can go back and alter it at any time.)

✔ The whole purpose of Visual Basic code is to tell objects on a form what to do when the user does something. For example, if you use the mouse to click an OK or a Cancel command button, nothing happens unless you've written BASIC commands that state exactly what needs to occur.

✔ Any time a user presses a key, moves the mouse, or clicks the mouse button, it's called an *event*. Whenever an event occurs, your BASIC commands essentially tell the computer, "Hey, stupid, something just happened. Let's do something about it!"

✔ After you've written your BASIC commands, Visual Basic saves them as part of the form stored in the FRM file.

Stuff you don't need to know about programming languages

Computers really understand only *binary code*, which is nothing more than zeros and ones. Binary code, also known as *machine code*, is considered a low-level programming language.

But writing a program consisting of zeros and ones can be difficult, time-consuming, and tedious (much like using a computer). To make programming easier (because programmers are a notoriously lazy bunch), scientists invented *assembly language.*

Unfortunately, computers don't understand assembly language — only humans do. So before your computer can run a program written in assembly language, it first has to translate the assembly language program into an equivalent machine code program. Because this translation isn't 100-percent efficient (as reading the English translation of *The Three Musketeers* is slightly different from reading the original French version), assembly language programs are slightly slower and bigger than equivalent machine code programs.

In an effort to make programming easier than assembly language, scientists invented new languages starting with *A, B, C,* and eventually *C++,* which are all considered mid-level languages. Mid-level languages tend to mix ordinary English words with odd symbols. For example, a++ is a command that actually makes sense in C++.

C++ programs are much easier to write than assembly language programs. However, before your computer can run a C++ program, it first has to translate the C++ program into an equivalent machine code program. Because C++ is so different from machine code, the translation of

C++ code to machine code is even less efficient; therefore, C++ programs are slightly slower and bigger than equivalent machine code programs. (Think of the difficulties in translating *Tales of the Arabian Nights* from the original Arabic to English.)

Finally, the high-level languages, such as COBOL, Pascal, and BASIC, use English words and acronyms so that people can read and write them easily. Unfortunately, computers don't understand high-level languages either. Before a computer can run a high-level language program, it has to translate it into an equivalent machine code program.

Because English uses letters but computers understand only zeros and ones, the translation from a high-level language into zeros and ones is fairly inefficient, which means that high-level languages create slower and bigger programs than equivalent machine code programs. (Think of translating the great works of the Klingon Empire into English, and you can imagine the translation difficulties you'll face.)

Although programmers love to argue the merits of one language over another, there is no one *best* language to use for all your programming needs. You can use any language to write almost any type of program; it's just that some languages are better suited for certain purposes than others.

For sheer speed, programmers torture themselves into learning assembly language or C++. For those who are less masochistic, Pascal and BASIC work just fine, thank you.

Storing a Visual Basic program

A Visual Basic program always contains one or more FRM files, but how can you keep track of them all? Visual Basic's solution is to store all the names of your FRM files in (yet) another file called a *project file*, shown in Figure 1-3.

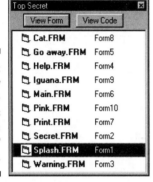

🗔 Cat.FRM	Form8
🗔 Go away.FRM	Form5
🗔 Help.FRM	Form4
🗔 Iguana.FRM	Form9
🗔 Main.FRM	Form6
🗔 Pink.FRM	Form10
🗔 Print.FRM	Form7
🗔 Secret.FRM	Form2
🗔 Splash.FRM	Form1
🗔 Warning.FRM	Form3

Figure 1-3:
How multiple FRM files make up a single VBP project file.

Here are some things to remember about project files:

- Project files always end with the VBP file extension (which stands for Visual Basic Project). If you look at this file with a word processor, you'll see that it contains a list of all the separate FRM files that make up a single Visual Basic program.

- You can choose any file name for your project file. For simplicity, you can even use the same file name that you used to name one of the forms in your program. The file name for a project file must still always end with VBP.

  For instance, if you write a sales reporting program, one form can be stored in the SALES.FRM file, and the entire project can be stored in the SALES.VBP file.

- When you save a Visual Basic program to a disk, you're actually saving the VBP project file plus all the files listed in the VBP project file. If you accidentally edit the VBP project file, Visual Basic won't know where to find all the necessary FRM files to load, even though the necessary FRM files still exist.

To load a Visual Basic program from a disk, you load the single project file. Visual Basic takes care of loading all the other files automatically.

Running a Visual Basic program

You can run your program without exiting Visual Basic. In fact, you should run it several times to make sure it works properly.

When you're satisfied that your program works the way it should (or if you've become impatient), you can compile it to an EXE file. Three reasons for compiling your program are as follows:

- ✔ If someone doesn't own a copy of Visual Basic, he or she can run your Visual Basic program only if you have compiled it to an EXE file.

- ✔ The EXE version of a Visual Basic program runs faster than the same program running from within Visual Basic.

- ✔ Compiling a program into an EXE file lets you keep the original FRM and VBP files to yourself. That way, others can never see (and possibly copy) how you've written your program.

Interesting (but not required) information about EXE files

Every language compiler converts a program from a string of commands into an executable file, called an EXE file. Traditional BASIC, Pascal, and C++ compilers create an EXE file that contains everything you need to run the program.

Visual Basic is different. When Visual Basic creates an EXE file, you can't use this EXE file unless you also have a special file called VB400xx.DLL. (Depending on which version of Visual Basic you're using at the time, this file may be called VB40032.DLL for the 32-bit version or VB40016.DLL for the 16-bit version.)

A Visual Basic EXE file contains the program's user interface and BASIC commands that make the program work. The VB400xx.DLL file contains the instructions that tell your computer how to run the Visual Basic EXE file.

You can't run a Visual Basic EXE file without the VB400xx.DLL file, no matter how hard you cry, plead, or scream at your computer. So if you give away or sell copies of your Visual Basic EXE programs, make sure that you include one copy of the VB400xx.DLL file as well.

Four Crucial Differences between Visual Basic and Other Languages

Because writing programs in Visual Basic requires a new *paradigm* (that's a hot and terribly overused word to describe any new way of thinking), here are some guidelines you need to remember. These guidelines are easy to forget, so they're printed in this book. That way, you'll know where to find them again.

Creating the user interface from scratch

With conventional languages, such as C++ and Pascal, you have to write code that does three things:

- ✔ First, your code has to tell the computer what to do. This task can be as simple as adding two numbers together or as complicated as balancing the national deficit.

- ✔ Second, your code has to create a user interface to display pretty menus, windows, and buttons on the screen. Without a user interface, there's no way anyone can use your program.

- ✔ Finally, your code has to tell the parts of your user interface how to work. Displaying menus on the screen may look nice, but if you click the mouse on a menu and nothing happens, the menu is worthless.

Essentially, when writing the same program in conventional programming languages (such as C or Pascal), you have to do three times as much work as a Visual Basic programmer, and a Visual Basic programmer can do the same work in half the amount of time. (Quick! Write a Visual Basic program to verify these calculations.)

What makes conventional languages even tougher to use is that any time you write code, it may be full of bugs. So now you have to look for bugs in the code that displays your user interface, in the code that tells the computer what to do, and in the code that tells your user interface how to work.

With Visual Basic, you draw your user interface on the screen until it looks exactly the way you want it to. From that point on, your user interface always works perfectly with no chance of bugs wrecking it at the last minute.

With C++ or Pascal, creating a user interface can be frustrating, tedious, and error-prone. With Visual Basic, it's simple.

Making the user interface do something

After you've written code for a user interface with C++ or Pascal (and debugged it so that it works correctly), guess what? Now you have to write more code to tell your user interface how to work.

Sound complicated? It is, which is why C++ and Pascal programmers spend most of their time writing code that creates their program's user interface instead of working on the part of their program that actually does something useful. (Now you know why so many programs from big-name companies don't always work the way they should.)

With Visual Basic, making your user interface do something is simple. After you draw the parts of your user interface, these parts automatically know how to behave. When you draw a menu in Visual Basic, the menu automatically knows to display menu commands if you click it with the mouse. If you draw a window on the screen, the window automatically knows how to move, close, or minimize itself at a click of the mouse button.

With C++ and Pascal, you have to specifically tell your user interface what to do if the user presses a key, clicks the mouse, types a command, and so on. With Visual Basic, every user interface object already knows what to do no matter what the user types, clicks, or presses. This kind of automation is part of what makes Visual Basic so much fun to use.

Displaying stuff on the user interface

A user interface communicates with a user in two ways. First, the user interface makes it easy for the user (that's you) to tell the computer what to do next. Second, a user interface enables the computer to display stuff on the screen in reply.

The user interface acts like a translator between you and the computer. You tell the user interface, "Hey, make the computer list all the people I owe money to." The user interface obeys and rushes off to tell the computer. Then the computer digs up all the names and says to the user interface, "Okay, here's a list of names. Show them on the screen so they look nice."

Once again, C++ and Pascal do everything the hard way. To display anything on your user interface, you have to write more code. Not only does this require time to write, it also requires time to debug the program to make sure it works properly. At this stage, most C++ and Pascal programmers are ready to throw away their computers in frustration and work for minimum wage at a fast-food restaurant.

To display stuff on the screen with Visual Basic, you modify the properties of objects already on the user interface. After you change an object's properties, the object takes care of displaying your information on the screen. So instead of wanting to throw away their computers, Visual Basic programmers are ready to order out for food (and maybe have it delivered to them by frustrated C++ and Pascal programmers).

Writing subprograms for fun and money

With C++ or Pascal, you write a program in a plain ASCII file called the *source code*. If your program is really large, you might store parts of it in separate files. Even though nothing in either C++ or Pascal forces you to do so, breaking your program into smaller files is simply good programming practice.

With either language, it's possible to write an entire program in one huge file. This would be like writing *War and Peace* on a long scroll of paper and then wondering why it's so hard to skip from Chapter 1 to Chapter 39 instantly.

In comparison, Visual Basic not only encourages you to write short programs, it forces you to do so. Although this may seem as liberating as having your mother tell you to clean up your room every day, you will appreciate it when you start writing large programs (and start living in your own place).

Visual Basic drawbacks (or why C++ programmers can still get work)

Lest you start thinking that C++ and Pascal are totally worthless languages that should be stomped out like an annoying habit, both offer several major advantages over Visual Basic.

First, C++ and Pascal give you more control over the computer (with the resulting drawback of requiring more time to learn the language). People have actually written entire operating systems in C and Pascal. Bell Laboratories wrote the UNIX operating system in C, and Apple Computer wrote the first Macintosh operating system in Pascal. Writing an operating system in Visual Basic is like trying to fly a hot-air balloon to the moon.

Second, C++ and Pascal create programs that run much faster than similar Visual Basic programs. Visual Basic lets you create programs faster, but they ultimately run slower than similar C++ or Pascal programs. If speed is crucial (you're designing a reentry program for the Space Shuttle, for example), Visual Basic is not a wise choice.

Third, C++ and Pascal offer *cross-platform portability*. Computers from the IBM, Macintosh, and Amiga all the way up to VAX minicomputers and Cray supercomputers can run C++ or Pascal programs. At the time of this writing, Visual Basic runs under only MS-DOS and Windows.

Microsoft has essentially killed all future development on the MS-DOS version of Visual Basic. They also keep promising, but never delivering, a Macintosh version of Visual Basic.

Of course, you'll never see a version of Visual Basic for OS/2 because Microsoft wants OS/2 to die a slow, painful death. And if you ever try writing a Visual Basic program to run on a Cray supercomputer, you'll be plain out of luck.

Microsoft's release of Visual Basic essentially stomped the living daylights out of Borland International's Turbo Pascal language. Borland has fought back by releasing a Visual Basic look-alike called Delphi.

Delphi works much like Visual Basic. First you draw your user interface on the screen; then you write code to make your user interface do something useful. Visual Basic uses BASIC commands, and Delphi uses Pascal commands.

If you want the advantage of creating user interfaces quickly and easily using Pascal, you should use Delphi. Otherwise, stick with Visual Basic and help line the pocketbooks of Microsoft and Bill Gates.

Writing programs for 16-bit versus 32-bit operating systems

Visual Basic comes in three versions: a Standard Edition, a Professional Edition and an Enterprise Edition. The Standard Edition of Visual Basic costs less but lets you write programs only for 32-bit operating systems (such as Windows 95).

The Professional Edition of Visual Basic costs more but gives you the option of writing programs for either 16-bit (Windows 3.1) or 32-bit operating systems (Windows 95). The Enterprise Edition of Visual Basic is the most expensive version of all and is designed for hard-core programmers working in teams, doing client/server work and other complicated stuff like that for either 16-bit or 32-bit operating systems.

So what's the difference between a 16-bit and a 32-bit operating system, and who really cares anyway? Good question.

Back in the early days, the brains of the first IBM computers consisted of a thin piece of silicon known as a *microprocessor*. The first microprocessors used in these early IBM PC computers were called the 8088 and the 8086.

The 8088 and 8086 could process 16 bits of data at any given time, which was like having a toll road with 16 open lanes available. As the science of developing microprocessors improved, later IBM computers used a variety of processors sporting similar names, such as the 80286.

Because these early microprocessors could handle only 16-bits of data, MS-DOS was designed to handle only 16 bits of data as well. As newer processors such as the 80386, 80486, and the Pentium appeared, guess what? They all continued to use MS-DOS.

Even though these newer processors could now handle 32 bits of data at any given time, MS-DOS still limited these microprocessors to 16 bits of data. This was like having a toll road with 32 lanes available, but only 16 lanes open at any given time.

So why did everyone keep using MS-DOS despite the fact that it was clearly holding up traffic? Easy — because so many programs had been written for MS-DOS, everyone still used MS-DOS to remain compatible with these earlier programs. The more that people used MS-DOS, the more people stuck with it; and the more they stuck with it, the more reluctant the computer industry was to change things.

Eventually, Microsoft and IBM teamed up to develop a new 32-bit operating system to take advantage of the 32-bit data capacity of the 80386 microprocessor. This operating system, dubbed OS/2, flopped in the marketplace because few people saw any advantages in switching to OS/2, even though OS/2 was technically superior to anything else available at the time.

Seeing the failure of OS/2 to completely dominate the computer industry, Microsoft decided to bring the advantages of OS/2 to the world of MS-DOS, so they released Microsoft Windows. Like OS/2, Windows gave programs a neat, graphical look (known as a *graphical user interface*, or *GUI*).

Because Windows needed MS-DOS, guess what? The combination of MS-DOS and Windows was still technically a 16-bit operating system. So for years, the world had 32-bit microprocessors (80386, 80486, and Pentiums) but crippled them by using the 16-bit data capabilities of MS-DOS and Windows 3.1.

To finally catch up with the technical capabilities of the newest microprocessors, Microsoft created Windows NT and Windows 95. Besides having the capability to run all existing MS-DOS and Windows programs, both Windows NT and Windows 95 finally took full advantage of the 32-bit capabilities of the 32-bit microprocessors. This idea was as revolutionary as putting four tires on a Ferrari and then being amazed that the Ferrari drives so much better with four tires instead of two.

As the world gradually shifts from ancient 16-bit operating systems (Windows 3.1) to modern 32-bit operating systems (Windows NT and Windows 95), programmers have to write programs to run on the newer 32-bit operating systems. That's why the Professional Edition of Visual Basic comes in a 16-bit version and a 32-bit version.

If you want to write a program for Windows 3.1, use the 16-bit version of Visual Basic. However, if you want to write a program for Windows NT or Windows 95, use the 32-bit version of Visual Basic.

(Of course, as the power of microprocessors takes another giant leap forward with the Pentium and its successors, we'll soon be stuck using a 32-bit operating system on a 64-bit microprocessor. Considering the fact that the latest $200 Nintendo and Sega Genesis video games use 64-bit processors, but $3,000 business computers will eventually be stuck running 32-bit operating systems on 64-bit microprocessors, we'll need yet another version of Visual Basic to help us write 64-bit programs. Aren't computers fun?)

Chapter 2

Designing Your First User Interface

● ●

In This Chapter

▶ Drawing your user interface

▶ Changing the property settings of the user interface

▶ Defining your user interface's properties

● ●

*T*o create any Visual Basic program, you have to perform each of the
following steps:

✔ Draw the user interface

✔ Define the user interface properties

✔ Write BASIC code

So before you can write your first program in Visual Basic, you need to know
how to draw a user interface.

A short history of user interfaces

In the old days of computers (back in the fifties), getting a computer to do anything useful meant opening it up and rearranging some wires. You had to know how to program a computer, and you had to know how to connect wires without electrocuting yourself in the process.

To use a computer in the sixties, you fed it a stack of punch cards. When the computer responded to your commands, it printed something on a piece of paper, a process that could take hours or even days. Therefore, using a computer was still slow, tedious, and boring.

The seventies connected a keyboard to a TV set and called the whole thing a computer terminal. For the first time, you could type a command directly into the computer and have the computer respond immediately. This capability should have made computers easier to use and actually fun for a change.

These first crude user interfaces consisted of nothing more than a blank screen and a blinking dot, called a cursor. To get the computer to do anything, you had to know the proper commands

(continued)

(continued)

to type. Programs using these ugly interfaces were called command-line interfaces. Unfortunately, if you didn't know the right commands to type or the proper keys to press, the computer would refuse to cooperate and would make you feel stupid. Once again, using a computer was slow, tedious, and boring.

To make computers easier to use (hah!), programs began listing available commands through menus on the screen. Instead of forcing people to type the right commands (and spell them correctly, too), menus let anyone choose the right command by pointing at the command using the keyboard or a mouse.

Soon every program offered menus. Unfortunately, none of these menus worked exactly alike, which meant that if you knew how to use one program, it didn't necessarily mean that you knew how to use another program. The menus would likely be totally different. At this point, most people threw their computers in the closet and hoped that computers would fade into obscurity the way 8-track tape players had.

To convince people that computers really were user-friendly (and to make money, which is what the computer industry is really all about),

programmers defined a standard way that all programs should work. Instead of displaying boring symbols and letters on the screen, such as `C:\DOS>`, this new standard used color, menus, and graphics. Now people could choose commands by pointing to a picture or an icon on the screen. Although this essentially destroyed the purpose of literacy, it did make computers much easier to use.

This new standard, dubbed *graphical user interface,* or *GUI* (pronounced "gooey"), soon appeared on every computer. Macintosh had the first popular GUI, but Microsoft quickly introduced a GUI for IBM computers and called it Microsoft Windows. Following the success of Microsoft Windows, IBM released another GUI called OS/2. In response to OS/2, Microsoft released Windows NT along with an improved version of Windows, dubbed Windows 95.

Naturally, each GUI is slightly different than the others, and programs designed to run under one GUI won't always run under another one. Until a single standard emerges, using different GUIs on a computer is likely to remain slow, tedious, and downright boring.

Common Parts of a User Interface

Despite their differences, graphical user interfaces tend to look the same because they use similar parts.

Every graphical user interface displays information in a *window*. A window can fill the entire screen or just part of it. Two or more windows can appear on the screen at the same time, either overlapping like cards or side by side like tiles. In Visual Basic, windows are called *forms*.

When you first start Visual Basic, it displays a blank form. To make your form useful, you have to put *objects* on the form. An object can be a picture, a box, a command button, or a check box. In Visual Basic, objects are sometimes called *controls*.

Objects make your form do something useful by letting the user perform some type of action.

A common object is a gray rectangular button called a *command button*. Clicking a command button can do anything from exiting a program to calculating the gross national product of Zimbabwe.

By themselves, objects do absolutely nothing. To make them do something, you have to write BASIC code (which you learn about in Chapter 3).

Visual Basic provides all the commonly used parts of a typical Windows user interface. As a Visual Basic programmer, your job is to paste these parts together to make a user interface that ordinary mortals can use and understand.

Drawing objects with Visual Basic

When you load Visual Basic, the program politely displays the Visual Basic Toolbox on the left side of the screen. This Toolbox contains little drawings that represent the various objects you can draw on a form (see Figure 2-1).

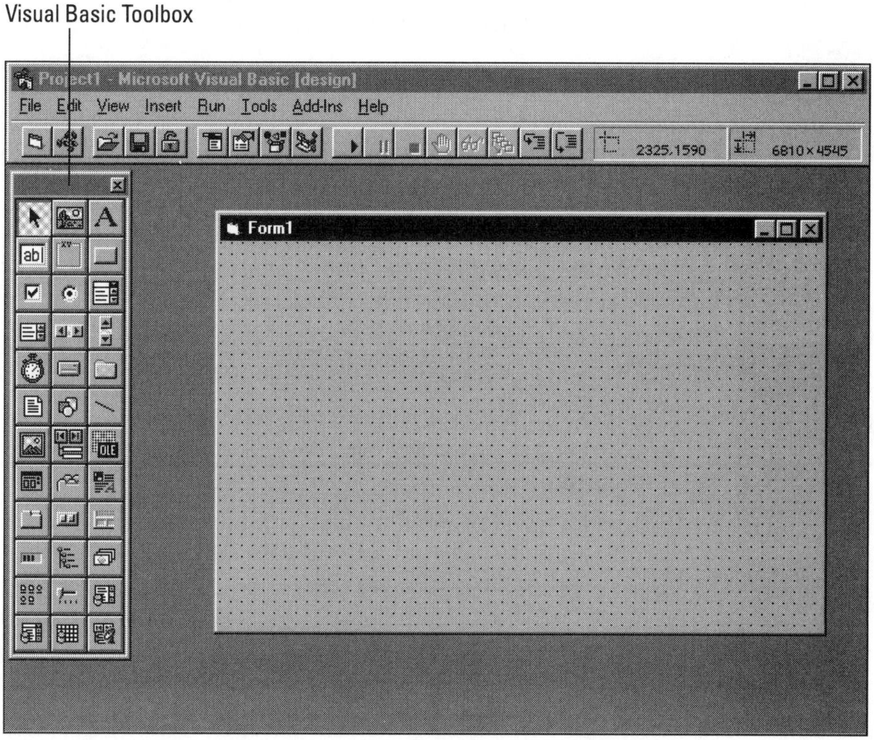

Visual Basic Toolbox

Figure 2-1:
The Visual
Basic
Toolbox.

To draw an object on a form, you always have to follow these steps:

1. Click the object in the Toolbox that you want to draw.

2. Position the mouse pointer on the form where you want to draw the object.

3. Hold down the left mouse button and drag the mouse. This action draws the object on the form.

Designing your user interface is a lot like doodling on an Etch-A-Sketch. The main difference between the two is that with Visual Basic, you can actually draw circles.

You learn more about specific objects and how and why to use them in Part II. For now, it's important for you to understand two things: All your programs need a user interface, and Visual Basic provides the parts for you to put a program together quickly and easily.

Drawing your first user interface

To get you acquainted with Visual Basic right away, here are some steps you can use to create a real-life user interface:

1. In Windows, start Microsoft Visual Basic if you haven't already. Visual Basic displays a blank form titled `Form1` (refer back to Figure 2-1).

2. Click the Command button icon in the Visual Basic Toolbox (see Figure 2-2.)

3. Drag the mouse so that the command button looks like Figure 2-3 on the form.

4. Click the Option button icon in the Visual Basic Toolbox, then drag the mouse so that the option button looks like Figure 2-4.

5. Click the Option button icon, and draw an option button. Repeat this process. You just created two more option buttons, and your form should look like Figure 2-5.

6. Click the Image icon in the Visual Basic Toolbox, then draw the image box on the form, as shown in Figure 2-6.

7. Click the Image icon, and draw an image box. Repeat this process. You just created two more image boxes, and your form should look like Figure 2-7.

Command button icon

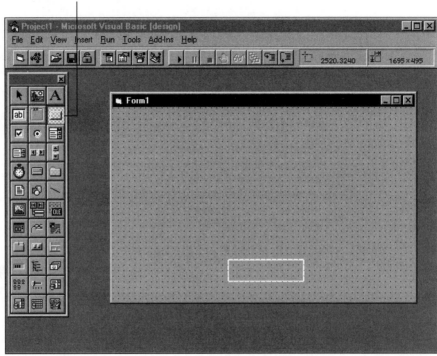

8. Click the Text box icon in the Visual Basic Toolbox, and then draw the text box on the form so that it looks like Figure 2-8.

9. Click the Text box icon, and draw a text box. Repeat this process. You just created two more text boxes, and your form should look like Figure 2-9.

10. From the File menu, select Save File or press Ctrl+S. A Save File As dialog box appears, asking what you want to name your file.

11. Type **HELLO** and select Save. This saves your form in a file called HELLO.FRM.

12. From the File menu, select Save Project. A Save Project As dialog box appears, asking what you want to name your project.

13. Type **HELLO** and click Save. This saves your entire Visual Basic project in a file called HELLO.VBP.

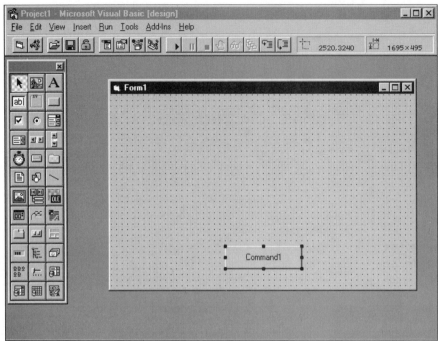

Figure 2-3:
The form
with the
command
button on it.

Option button icon

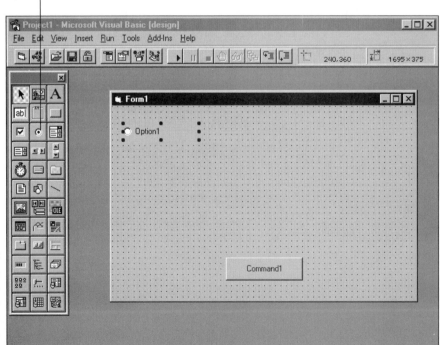

Figure 2-4:
The form
with the
option
button on it.

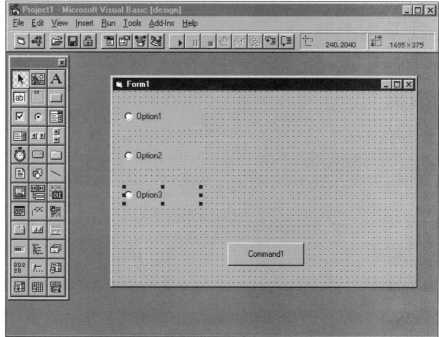

Figure 2-5:
The form
with all
three option
buttons
on it.

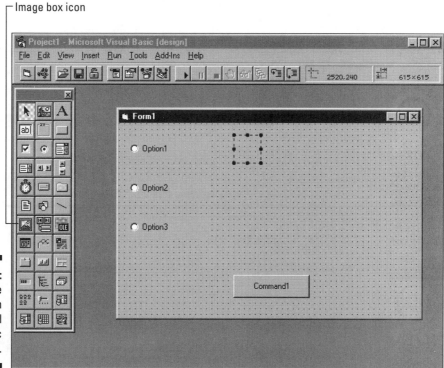

Figure 2-6:
The Image
box icon on
the Visual
Basic
Toolbox.

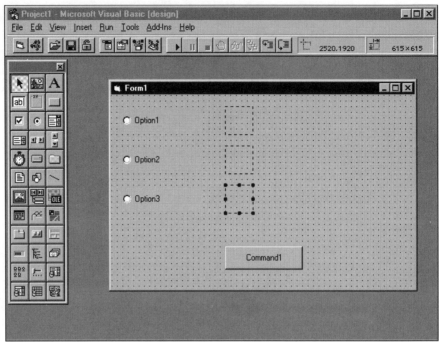

Figure 2-7:
The form with all three image boxes on it.

Text box icon

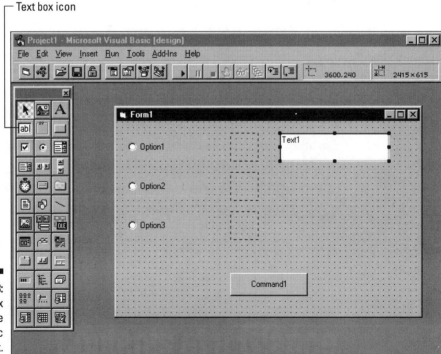

Figure 2-8:
The Text box icon on the Visual Basic Toolbox.

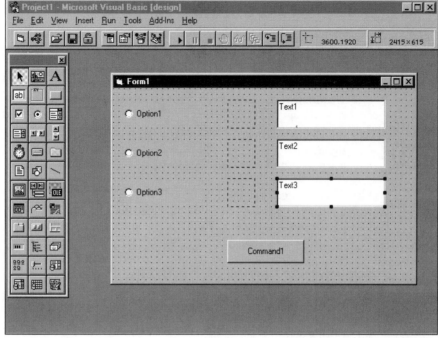

Figure 2-9:
The form
with all
three text
boxes on it.

Congratulations! You just created a generic Visual Basic user interface. If it looks a little less than impressive, it's because the user interface hasn't been customized for your program.

To customize a Visual Basic user interface, you have to define the *properties* for each object.

Defining the Properties of Your User Interface

Drawing your user interface is the first step in writing a Visual Basic program. The second step is defining the properties for each object in your user interface.

Is it really necessary to define properties? No. Visual Basic automatically sets default property values for all the objects in your user interface.

However, you may not want to use these default properties. You can customize your user interface by changing the property settings of your objects. Although each object has over twenty properties to modify, you won't have to change every single one. Most of the time, you'll just change one or two properties of each object.

What properties do

Before you change the properties of any object, you probably want to know what the heck properties do in the first place. Essentially, properties define an object's appearance on the screen and the object's name.

- ✔ The appearance of an object includes its size, color, and location on the screen. An object's appearance makes your user interface pretty.
- ✔ The name of an object is for your convenience only. When you're writing BASIC code, you need some way to identify the objects on the screen. (You learn to write BASIC code in Part IV.)

Visual Basic automatically gives objects boring names such as `Text1` or `Command3`. If you create descriptive names for each object, identifying your objects is a whole lot easier.

Changing property settings

You can change the property settings of an object in two ways:

- ✔ During design time
- ✔ During run time

Design time is when you're drawing your user interface but before you actually run your program.

Most of the time, you'll change your object's property settings at design time. If you're going to change the name of an object, you must do it at design time.

Run time is when your program uses BASIC code to change object properties with no help from you. Of course, before your program can change an object's properties, you have to write BASIC code telling your program exactly which object properties to change.

Changing a property during run time lets you create animation or display messages on the screen, such as error messages, program status messages, or messages reminding the user to pay for your program.

You need to change properties at run time if your program needs to respond to something the user does, such as repeatedly pushing the wrong key or holding down the mouse button indefinitely. Otherwise, change most of your property settings at design time.

Changing property settings at design time

Every object has twenty or more properties assigned to it, as shown in Figure 2-10. To change the property of an object, you must follow these steps:

1. Click the object whose properties you want to change.

2. Open the Properties window for that object by pressing F4 or by selecting Properties from the View menu.

3. Click the property you want to change.

4. Type a new setting for that property.

Simple, isn't it?

When it's time to change the property settings for one or more objects, this book will display a table similar to the following:

Object	*Property*	*Setting*
Form	Caption	Hello, World!
	Name	frmHello

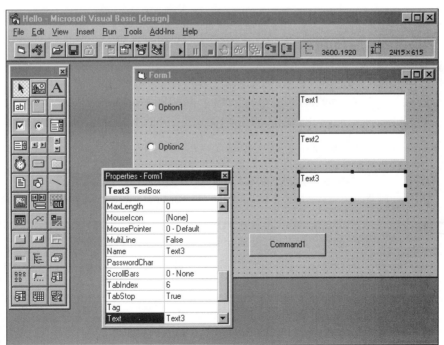

Figure 2-10: The Properties window showing some properties.

Test your newfound knowledge

1. What are the two common parts of almost every user interface?

   a. The easy-to-use interface and a 500-page manual that explains how easy the interface is to use.

   b. Menus that nobody can understand and a mouse that nobody can use.

   c. Useless icons that don't make any sense and text that doesn't explain a thing.

   d. Forms and objects.

2. How can you change property settings?

   a. You can't. The property settings have to want to change first.

   b. Through devout prayer and intense meditation.

   c. By sticking a magnet on the side of your screen and watching the images warp and wreck your monitor.

   d. By using the Property window after you've designed the user interface (known as *design time*) or writing BASIC code to change the settings while the program is running (known as *run time*).

Here's what this table is telling you:

1. Click the Form object.

2. Open the Properties window for the form by pressing F4 or by selecting Properties from the View menu.

3. Click the Caption property.

4. Change the setting by typing **Hello, World!**

5. Click the Name property.

6. Change the setting by typing **frmHello**.

Defining the properties of your first user interface

You can define the properties of your user interface by following these steps:

1. In Windows, start the Microsoft Visual Basic program if you haven't already. Visual Basic displays a blank form titled Form1.

2. From the File menu, select HELLO.VBP displayed at the bottom of the menu. Visual Basic loads your HELLO.FRM form on the screen. (You can skip this step if you already have the form displayed on the screen.)

3. From the View menu, choose Form or press Shift+F7. (Skip this step if the form is already displayed on your screen.)

4. Change the property settings of the objects listed in Figure 2-11. To select the Form window, click the title bar of the window.

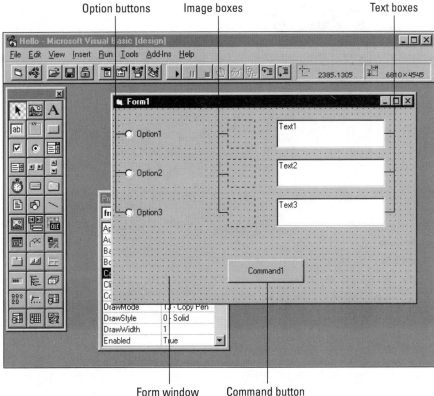

Figure 2-11:
The user
interface
with all the
objects
labeled.

Form window   Command button

5. Click Option1 to highlight it, which causes little black rectangles to appear around the edges.

6. Open the Properties window by pressing F4. (See Figure 2-12.)

7. Click the Caption property and type **I'm happy!** Click the Name property and type **optGrin**.

8. Click the Image1 box and open the Properties window by pressing F4.

9. Click the Name property and type **imgGrin.**

10. Click the Picture property. Click the three dots (...), which is an ellipsis, at the top of the Properties box. Visual Basic displays a Load Picture dialog box, as shown in Figure 2-13.

11. Open the icons folder. (You may have to dig through the folders in your Visual Basic folder to find it.) Then open the misc folder within the icons folder.

12. Choose the FACE03 icon. Visual Basic displays a really happy face in the picture box.

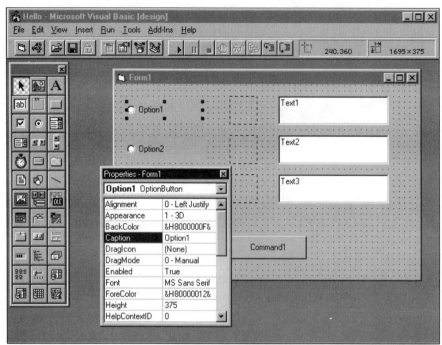

Figure 2-12:
The
Properties
window of
Option1.

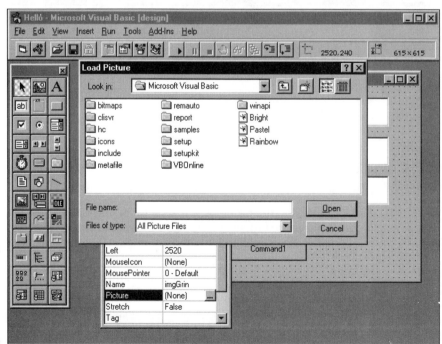

Figure 2-13:
The Load
Picture
dialog box of
Image1.

13. Click the Visible property. Then click the arrow in the settings box and choose False.

14. Click the Text1 box and open the Properties window by pressing F4.

15. Click the Border Style property. Click the arrow in the settings box and choose 0-None.

16. Click the Name property and type **txtGrin**.

17. Double-click the Text property. Press Backspace to set the Text property to a blank line.

18. Finish changing the properties for the rest of the objects according to Table 2-1.

19. From the File menu, choose Save Project to save all your changes.

Table 2-1	Properties to Change to Finish Designing Your User Interface	
Object	*Property*	*Setting*
Form	Caption	Hello, World!
	Name	frmHello
Option2	Caption	I'm okay.
	Name	optSmile
Option3	Caption	I'm sad.
	Name	optFrown
Image2	Name	imgSmile
	Picture	FACE02
	Visible	False
Image3	Name	imgFrown
	Picture	FACE01
	Visible	False
Text2	Border Style	0-None
	Name	txtSmile
	Text	(Empty)
Text3	Border Style	0-None
	Name	txtFrown
	Text	(Empty)
Command1	Caption	Exit
	Name	cmdBye

Congratulations! You just defined all the necessary properties for your first user interface. If this seems like a long way to go to create a trivial program, you're right.

Trivial programs may be tedious to write in Visual Basic, but hard programs are easy. It's just the opposite with languages like C++ or Pascal. These languages make trivial programs easy to write but writing hard programs really tough.

Chapter 3

Writing BASIC Code

● ●

● ●

*T*o have your computer do anything, you have to give it step-by-step instructions. If you skip a step or give unclear instructions, your computer won't know what to do. (Actually, it will know what to do — it just won't do what you wanted it to.)

✔ Programmers call a single instruction a *command*. A typical BASIC command might look like this:

```
Taxes = Income * TaxRate
```

✔ A series of commands is called *code*. A typical series of commands might look like this:

```
Income = 90000
TaxRate = .35
Taxes = Income * TaxRate
```

✔ A collection of code that makes your computer do something useful (such as play a game, calculate your taxes, or display flying toasters on your screen) is called a *program*.

If you want to speak the language of programmers (even though programmers are notorious for never saying much of anything), you have to learn programming etiquette.

You never write a *program*; you write *code*. Heaven forbid if you should say, "Let me look at your series of commands." Cool programmers will blush at your faux pas. Instead, you should say, "Let me look at your *code*."

What Is BASIC Code?

To get your computer to do anything, you have to give it instructions that it can understand. First you have to decide which language you want to use. When using Visual Basic, the language is BASIC.

Like all computer languages, BASIC has special commands called *reserved keywords*. Some examples of reserved keywords are as follows:

Loop	Function	Sub	End
Do	Integer	Case	If
Else	Select	Then	For

BASIC code consists of nothing more than BASIC reserved keywords creatively strung together to form a program. Whenever the computer sees a reserved keyword, it automatically thinks, "Oh, this is a special instruction that I already know how to obey."

A program can be as short as a single reserved keyword or as long as several million reserved keywords. Short programs generally don't do anything more interesting than display something like `Hello, world!` on the screen. Long programs usually do much more, but they're often as confusing to read as an IRS tax form.

Theoretically, you can write one long program consisting of a million or more reserved keywords. However, any programmer attempting to do so would likely go insane long before completing the task.

Writing a program one step at a time

To make programming easier, most programmers divide a large program into several smaller ones. After you finish writing each of the smaller programs, you paste the pieces together to make a complete program.

✔ When you divide a large program into several smaller ones, these smaller programs are called *subprograms*. In Visual Basic lingo, subprograms are called *procedures* (although some programmers may call them *subroutines*).

✔ Procedures tell each object on your form how to react to something the user does. Each object can have zero or more procedures that tell it how to respond to the user.

One procedure may tell the computer what to do if the user clicks an object with the mouse. Another procedure may tell the computer what to do if the user presses a certain key while the object is highlighted.

Not every object needs procedures. The only objects that need procedures are those that the user clicks or highlights in some way, such as command buttons, check boxes, or radio buttons.

Choosing objects and events

Before you can write a procedure, you have to tell Visual Basic which object you want to write a procedure for. There are two ways to do this:

✔ The simplest way is to click on an object on your form and open the Code window by pressing F7. Visual Basic then kindly displays the procedure for that object.

✔ The second way is almost as easy. Each time you draw an object on a form, Visual Basic stores the name of that object in a list called the *Object list*, as shown in Figure 3-1. The Object list appears at the top of the Code window, which you can open by pressing F7. You then scroll through the Object list until you find the object for which you want to write a procedure.

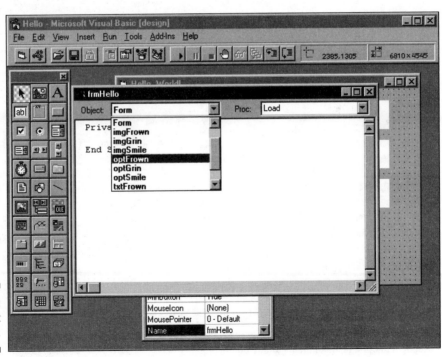

Figure 3-1:
The Object
list.

Another list, called the *Proc list*, also appears at the top of the Code window next to the Object list. The Proc list contains all possible events that you can write a procedure to respond to. Scroll through this list until you find the event that you need to write a procedure for. (English teachers are probably grinding their teeth over the previous two sentences ending in prepositions, but they could always write a subroutine to handle it.)

Spaghetti code and BASIC

One reason why BASIC has such a bad reputation among programmers is something known as *spaghetti code*. Spaghetti code refers to any program that is so poorly written that it's almost impossible to figure out how it works.

For example, in the old days, each line in a BASIC program was assigned a line number. A typical BASIC program could look something like the following:

```
10 PRINT "Hello, world!"
20 PRINT "Do it again? (Y/N)?"
30 INPUT I$
40 IF I$ = "Y" GOTO 10
50 END
```

In line 10, BASIC tells the computer to print Hello, world! on the screen. In line 20, the message, Do it again (Y/N)? appears. In line 30, BASIC waits for the user to type a reply. In line 40, the program checks to see whether the user typed Y. If so, BASIC GOes TO line 10. If the user typed anything else, BASIC goes to the next line, which is line 50. In line 50, BASIC stops the program.

The BASIC GOTO command tells the computer to jump to another line. Because this is a simple five-line program, it's easy to see why line 40 told the computer to GOTO line 10 to start all over again.

Here's an equivalent BASIC program that uses spaghetti code to make things totally confusing:

```
10 GOTO 110
20 END
30 INPUT I$
40 GOTO 80
50 PRINT "Do it again? (Y/N)?"
60 GOTO 30
70 GOTO 20
80 IF I$ = "Y" GOTO 130
90 GOTO 70
100 GOTO 60
110 Print "Hello, world!"
120 GOTO 50
130 GOTO 110
```

Although this program does the same thing as the first BASIC program, trying to follow all those GOTO commands is as frustrating as trying to untangle spaghetti (hence the spaghetti code nickname).

Spaghetti code isn't unique to BASIC. You can write spaghetti code in C++ and Pascal if you want to (and many people have). However, C++ and Pascal offer alternatives to the GOTO command, but early versions of BASIC did not. Consequently, the writing of spaghetti code was more likely to occur in BASIC than in other languages.

Fortunately, Visual Basic offers alternatives to the GOTO command so that you don't have to write spaghetti code unless you really want to.

After you choose an object from the Object list and an event from the Proc list, Visual Basic displays the first and last lines of the procedure. You're now ready to start writing code for this procedure.

Writing Visual Basic Procedures

Before you can write any Visual Basic procedures, you first have to draw some objects on your forms.

Then you have to change the properties of each object to give them unique names you can remember. If you don't do this, you're stuck with the generic names that Visual Basic provides by default for everything, such as `Option1` or `Text3`.

To write a Visual Basic procedure, click on the object that you want to write a procedure for and then open the Code window. (You can open the Code window by pressing F7, by selecting Code from the View menu, or by double-clicking on the object.) After the Code window appears, you can start typing your procedure or code. Figure 3-2 shows the Code window.

But wait! Visual Basic doesn't just display a blank window. Visual Basic automatically types `Private Sub`, which is followed by the object's name, an underscore, an event (such as `Click`), and an empty set of parentheses ().

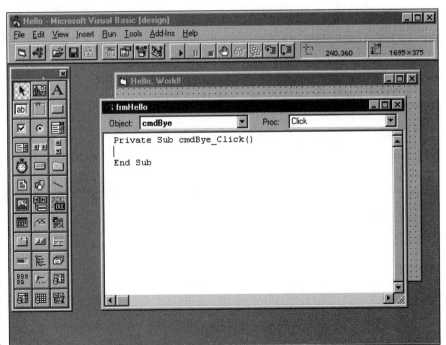

Figure 3-2:
The Code
window.

If you click the object named cmdBye and then open the Code window, Visual Basic displays the following:

```
Private Sub cmdBye_Click()
End Sub
```

- ✔ The first line of a Visual Basic procedure begins with Private Sub, which is short for a subprogram that belongs exclusively to a specific object. In this case, the subprogram belongs to the object named cmdBye.

- ✔ Next, Visual Basic types your object's name. If you forgot to change the name property of your object, Visual Basic uses a default name like Text2. Otherwise, Visual Basic displays your object's name (such as cmdBye).

- ✔ Following your object's name is an underscore, which separates your object's name from its event. An *event* is something the user does to communicate with the computer.

- ✔ Next comes an empty set of parentheses. Normally, the parentheses contain data that the subprogram uses from the routine that called this subroutine. An empty pair of parentheses says that this subprogram does not need any special data.

Translating this procedure into English, the first line means, "This is a subprogram for the object named cmdBye, and the subprogram tells the computer what to do if the user clicks the cmdBye object."

If this looks wordy, you're right. That's why Visual Basic shortens it to

```
Private Sub cmdBye_Click()
```

The last line of all Visual Basic procedures consists of two words: End and Sub. This line tells the computer, "This is the end of all the commands that belong in this subprogram." Rather than type all that, Visual Basic uses the simpler

```
End Sub
```

Right now, this Visual Basic procedure does nothing. To make the procedure do something, you have to add commands between the first line and the last line. Before you start adding commands, you need to know what BASIC commands (also known as code) can do.

Test your newfound knowledge

1. What are reserved keywords?

   a. Words you say when you have a reservation in a fancy restaurant where water costs $25 a glass.

   b. What shy people wish they could say.

   c. Special instructions that every programming language has.

   d. Words that you wish you could say to the face of someone you don't like.

2. How can you write a large program without losing your mind?

   a. Divide it into subprograms, otherwise known in Visual Basic as procedures.

   b. Watch others do it and then steal their homework.

   c. Just write a short program, make multiple copies, and hope that nobody notices.

   d. If you're thinking of writing a large program, you've probably already lost your mind.

What can BASIC code do?

BASIC code can do the following:

- Calculate a result
- Modify the properties (appearance) of another object

If you want to calculate the number of people who live in sailboats, subscribe to *The National Geographic*, and own cats, Visual Basic can calculate this as long as you provide all the necessary data.

After you calculate a result, you probably want to show it on the screen. To do so, you have to modify the properties of an object on your user interface. For example, if you want to display a message on the screen, you first need to draw a text box object on a Visual Basic form.

You then have to name this text box with something like `txtMessage`. Finally, to display anything in this text box, you have to modify the Text property of the `txtMessage` text box, such as:

```
txtMessage.Text = "This is hard to explain."
```

This command displays the message `This is hard to explain.` in the `txtMessage` text box on the screen, as shown in Figure 3-3.

txtMessage text box

Text property

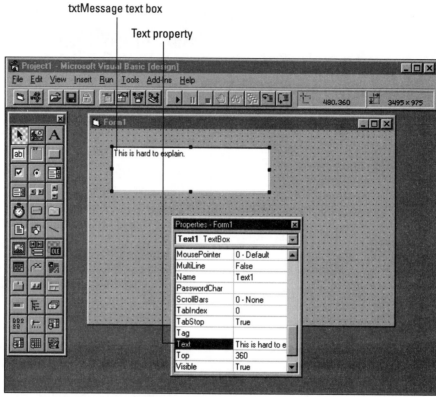

Of course, Visual Basic code can't change all the properties of an object. Some properties can be changed only during design time by using that object's property window. An example of this is an object's name, which you can change only by using its property window.

How a Visual Basic procedure works

After you've written a Visual Basic procedure, you may wonder when it actually does something. In ordinary BASIC, the computer follows each instruction line by line, from top to bottom, and when the computer reaches the bottom, it stops.

In Visual Basic, instructions run only when a specific event occurs, such as when the user clicks an object. The same set of instructions can run over and over again each time the user clicks an object. The only time a Visual Basic program ends is when an object's procedures specifically tell it to end.

As an example, look at the simplest Visual Basic procedure that is necessary for every program to stop completely. For a simple "Hello, world!" program, this procedure looks like the following:

```
Private Sub cmdBye_Click()
    End
End Sub
```

The code in this procedure is just a Visual Basic reserved keyword called End. The End reserved keyword tells Visual Basic, "Okay, you can stop this program now."

This procedure runs only when the user clicks the cmdBye object. If you look at the cmdBye object on your user interface, you see that it's a command button labeled Exit.

If you run this program, this is what happens:

1. Visual Basic displays your user interface on the screen, including the command button labeled Exit.

2. Clicking the Exit button causes Visual Basic to ask, "Hey, what's the name of this object that the user just clicked?"

3. In a huff, Visual Basic quickly notices that the Exit button's name is cmdBye.

4. Then Visual Basic asks, "Are there any instructions here that tell me what to do if the user clicks the cmdBye object?" Happily, Visual Basic finds the Private Sub cmdBye_Click() procedure.

5. Visual Basic then examines the first instruction of the cmdBye_Click() procedure. In this case, the instruction is End, which tells Visual Basic to stop running the program.

6. Visual Basic stops running the program and removes it from the screen.

Naturally, all this happens in the blink of an eye, and your computer looks as though it's responding instantly.

Writing Basic Code for Your First Visual Basic Program

Because experience is always the best teacher, the following steps show you how to write real-life BASIC code that you can use to impress your friends:

1. In Windows, start the Microsoft Visual Basic program if you haven't already done so. Visual Basic displays a blank form titled Form1.

2. From the File menu, select HELLO.VBP, which is displayed at the bottom of the menu. From the View menu, you may have to choose Form or press Shift+F7 to display the HELLO.FRM form on the screen. (You can skip this step if you already have the form displayed on the screen from Chapter 2.)

3. Click the `optGrin` option button displayed in the upper-left corner of the form. (It's the button that says "I'm happy!")

4. Open the Code window by pressing F7 or by selecting Code from the View menu.

5. Type in the `Private Sub optGrin_Click()` procedure so that it looks like the following:

```
Private Sub optGrin_Click()
   imgFrown.Visible = False
   imgSmile.Visible = False
   imgGrin.Visible = True
   txtSmile.TEXT = ""
   txtGrin.TEXT = "I'm going to DisneyWorld!"
   txtFrown.TEXT = ""
End Sub
```

6. Click the Object list at the top of the Code window and then choose the `optSmile` object. Visual Basic displays an empty `Private Sub optSmile_Click()` procedure.

7. Type in the `Private Sub optSmile_Click()` procedure so that it looks like the following:

```
Private Sub optSmile_Click()
   imgFrown.Visible = False
   imgSmile.Visible = True
   imgGrin.Visible = False
   txtSmile.TEXT = "Hello, world!"
   txtGrin.TEXT = ""
   txtFrown.TEXT = ""
End Sub
```

8. Click the Object list at the top of the Code window and then choose the `optFrown` object. Visual Basic displays an empty `Private Sub optFrown_Click()` procedure.

9. Type in the `Private Sub optFrown_Click()` procedure so that it looks like the following:

```
Sub optFrown_Click()
   imgFrown.Visible = True
   imgSmile.Visible = False
   imgGrin.Visible = False
   txtSmile.TEXT = ""
   txtGrin.TEXT = ""
   txtFrown.TEXT = "Good-bye, cruel world."
End Sub
```

10. Click the Object list at the top of the Code window and then choose the cmdBye object. Visual Basic displays an empty `Private Sub cmdBye_Click()` procedure.

11. Type in the `Private Sub cmdBye_Click()` procedure so that it looks like the following:

```
Private Sub cmdBye_Click()
   End
End Sub
```

12. Press F5 to run your program or select Start from the Run menu. If you typed everything correctly, Visual Basic displays your user interface on the screen, as shown in Figure 3-4.

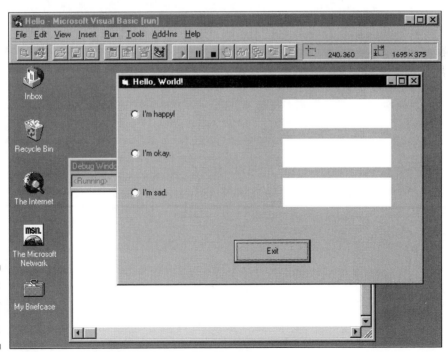

Figure 3-4: The Hello, World! program.

13. Click the option button next to the label "I'm sad." Visual Basic displays a face on the screen, along with the message "Good-bye, cruel world," as shown in Figure 3-5.

14. Click the option button next to the label "I'm okay." Visual Basic displays a smiley face on the screen, along with the message "Hello, world!", as shown in Figure 3-6.

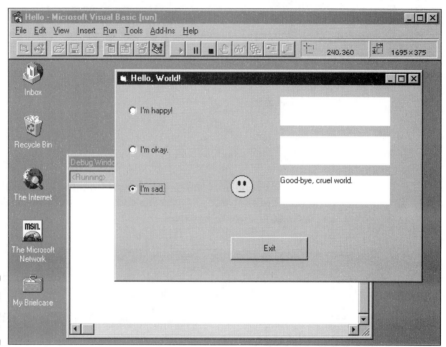

Figure 3-5:
Good-bye,
cruel world.

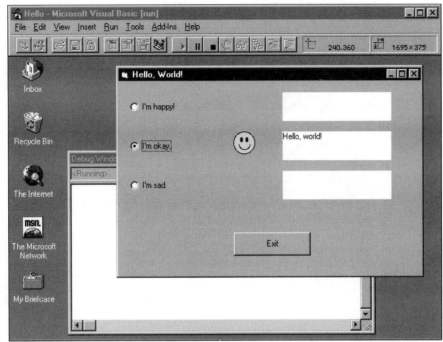

Figure 3-6:
Hello, world!

15. Click the option button next to the label "I'm happy." Visual Basic displays a really happy face on the screen, along with the message "I'm going to DisneyWorld!", as shown in Figure 3-7.

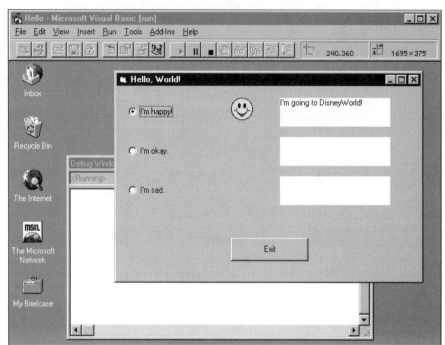

Figure 3-7:
I'm going to
DisneyWorld!

16. Click the command button labeled Exit. Visual Basic quits running your program and returns you to the Visual Basic program.

Congratulations! You finally completed the Hello, World! example. Although it took a few chapters just to get this far, you can see how you can use Visual Basic to create a friendly user interface quickly and easily.

Part II
Designing a User Interface

"I'M GONNA HAVE A LITTLE TROUBLE WITH THIS 'FULL MOON' ICON ON OUR GRAPHICAL USER INTERFACE."

In this part . . .

The purpose of a user interface is to let someone use your program. The clumsier the user interface, the harder your program will be to use. So if you make a good user interface, your program will be easier to use.

Just sit back, kick off your shoes, and relax. This is the fun part of the book. You won't have to write any code, learn any arcane commands, or memorize any bizarre keystrokes. In this part, you get to draw and doodle to your heart's content, under the guise of learning a programming language.

Chapter 4

User Interface Design 101

• •

In This Chapter

▶ Tips for creating a user interface

▶ Drawing objects on the user interface

▶ Moving, deleting, and copying objects

▶ Making objects unavailable

• •

To make oneself understood to the people, one must first speak to their eyes.

Napoleon Bonaparte

F irst of all, nobody really wants to use your program. Most people would rather be at the beach, watching TV, or making out. However, people do want the results that your program can produce. If they could get these same results by other means with less work, they would. But because they can't, they're willing to use your program.

This means that people really want your program to read their minds and then magically do whatever it is they need accomplished. Because that's not possible, the best you can hope for is to make your program as easy to use as possible. If a completely incompetent moron (your boss) can use your program, most other people will be able to use it as well.

Before You Create Your User Interface

Creating a user interface doesn't just mean slapping together some pretty pictures in a colorful window and hoping that the user will be able to figure out how your program works. Your program's user interface must make your program easy to use. To help you create a user interface, here are some points to keep in mind.

Know your user

Before designing your user interface, ask yourself who will be using your program. Will your typical users be data-entry clerks who understand computers, or managers who understand only paper procedures and have no idea how computers can help them?

When you decide who your users will be, design your user interface so that it mirrors the way the users already work, regardless of whether the user interface seems totally inefficient or alien to anyone else. Accountants readily accept spreadsheets because the row-and-column format mimics green sheets of ledger paper. Likewise, typists prefer word processors because a word processor mimics a blank sheet of paper.

But imagine if all word processors looked like spreadsheets with rows and columns. Any typist trying to use this kind of word processor would quickly feel lost and confused (although accountants might feel right at home with it).

The more a user interface mimics the way users currently work, the more likely it will be used and accepted. The only person the user interface really has to satisfy is the user.

Orient the user

It's no surprise that people get lost wandering through today's super malls, which contain multiple levels and two different time zones. How does it feel to have no idea where you are and no idea where you can go from your current position?

This feeling of helplessness is the reason why lost kids cry uncontrollably and confused computer users curse beneath their breath. (This is also the reason why malls install directories with the big red X that says, "You are here.")

A good user interface must orient people so they know where they are in your program and how to get out if they want to. Some user interfaces display a message at the bottom of the screen, such as "Page 2 of 5." In this case, the user knows exactly how many pages are available for viewing and which page currently appears on the screen.

Your user interface is a map to your program. Make sure that your user interface shows just enough information to orient users but not too much to confuse them.

Make the choices obvious

Besides letting users know where they are in a program, a good user interface must also make its choices obvious to the user. If your user interface displays "Page 4 of 25" at the bottom of the screen, how will the user know what to do to see the next or previous page? One solution may be to show forward- and backward-pointing arrows in each bottom corner of the page. Another solution may be buttons that say "Next Page" and "Previous Page." Figure 4-1 shows some possible solutions.

As long as your program shows the user which options are available next and which keys to press or where to click the mouse, the user will feel a sense of control and confidence when using your program.

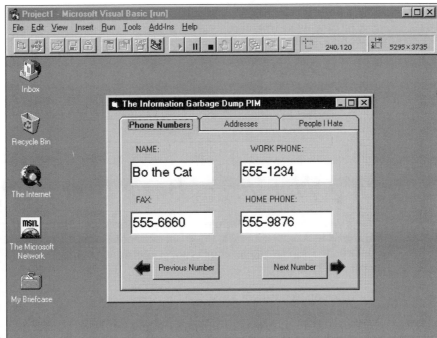

Figure 4-1:
Displaying choices to the user through icons and command buttons.

Be forgiving

The key here is feedback. If your program takes an arrogant attitude and displays scolding messages like "Command or file name not recognized" whenever the user presses the wrong key or clicks the mouse in the wrong area, the user will feel intimidated by your program.

So be kind. Have your program hide or dim any buttons or menu commands that are unavailable to the user. If the user does press the wrong key or click the mouse in the wrong area, have your program display a window and explain what the user's options are. Your users will love a program that guides them, and you'll have to spend a lot less time answering phone calls for technical support.

Keep it simple

Most programs offer users two or more ways to choose a specific command. You can click a button, choose a command from menus, or press certain keystroke combinations (Ctrl+F2, for example). Of these three methods, clicking directly on the screen is the easiest procedure to remember and pressing bizarre keystroke combinations is the hardest.

Make sure that commonly used commands can be accessed quickly through a button or a menu. Not all commands must be or should be accessed through a keystroke combination.

Although keystroke combination commands are faster to use, they're harder to learn initially. Make keystroke combinations easy to remember whenever possible. For a Save command, Ctrl+S is easier to remember than something totally abstract like Shift+F12. People can easily remember that *S* stands for Save, but who has any idea what F12 represents?

Designing Your Visual Basic User Interface

When you write a Visual Basic program, you first have to design its user interface. Essentially, a Visual Basic user interface consists of objects that you place on the screen and arrange in some semblance of organization so that the screen looks pretty.

The common elements of a Visual Basic user interface are shown in Figure 4-2 and consist of the following:

✔ Forms (also known as *windows*)
✔ Buttons
✔ Boxes
✔ Labels
✔ Pictures (and other decorative items)

Pictures   Text box   Label   Button   Form

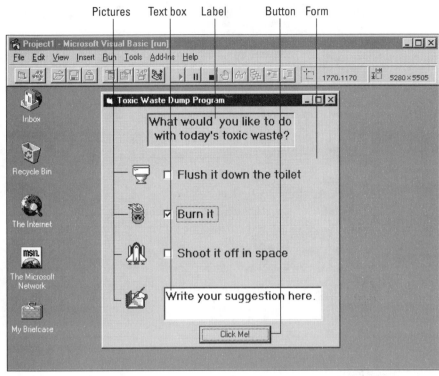

Figure 4-2:
The parts of
a typical
Visual Basic
user
interface.

To design your user interface, follow these steps:

1. Create a blank form.
2. Choose the object you want to draw from the Toolbox (see Figure 4-3).
3. Draw the object on the blank form.

Drawing objects

To draw any object, follow these steps:

1. Click the icon in the Visual Basic Toolbox that represents the object you want to draw (command button, picture box, label, and so on).
2. Move the mouse to the place on the form where you want to draw the object. The cursor will turn into a crosshair shape.
3. Click and drag the mouse where you want to draw your object. Then release the mouse button.

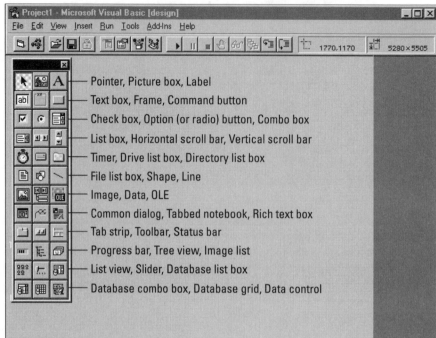

Figure 4-3:
Objects
labeled on
the Toolbox.

The toolbox items are labeled as follows:

— Pointer, Picture box, Label
— Text box, Frame, Command button
— Check box, Option (or radio) button, Combo box
— List box, Horizontal scroll bar, Vertical scroll bar
— Timer, Drive list box, Directory list box
— File list box, Shape, Line
— Image, Data, OLE
— Common dialog, Tabbed notebook, Rich text box
— Tab strip, Toolbar, Status bar
— Progress bar, Tree view, Image list
— List view, Slider, Database list box
— Database combo box, Database grid, Data control

Naming objects

Every object you draw has a Name property, which Visual Basic uses to identify the object. (That's the same reason your parents gave you a name — so people wouldn't be saying, "Hey you!" all the time to get your attention.)

Every Visual Basic object must have a unique name. If you try to give the same name to two different objects, Visual Basic complains and refuses to let you do it.

When you create an object, Visual Basic automatically gives it a boring, generic name. For example, the first time you create a command button, Visual Basic names it `Command1`. The second time you create a command button, Visual Basic names it `Command2`, and so on.

The name of an object never appears on the screen. Names can be up to 40 characters long, but they cannot contain punctuation marks or spaces. You can name your objects anything you want, but you should use Visual Basic's three-letter prefixes, as shown in Table 4-1.

Table 4-1	Suggested Prefixes When Naming Objects	
Object	*Suggested Prefix*	*Example Name*
Check box	chk	chkCareerChoice
Combo box	cbo	cboCrimesCommitted
Command button	cmd	cmdOpenSesame
Data	dat	datTopSecretInfo
Directory list box	dir	dirTree
Drive list box	drv	drvHardDisk
File list box	fil	filDocuments
Form	frm	frm1040Tax
Frame	fra	fraGroupedButtons
Horizontal scroll bar	hsb	hsbTemperature
Image	img	imgPrettyDrawing
Label	lbl	lblFakeName
Line	lin	linBorder
List box	lst	lstCandidates
Menu	mnu	mnuHamAndEggs
Picture box	pic	picPrettyPictures
Radio button	opt	optStation101
Shape (circle, square, oval, rectangle, rounded rectangle, and rounded square)	shp	shpUpOrShipOut
Text box	txt	txtWarning
Vertical scroll bar	vsb	vsbMoneyRaised

To change the name of an object, follow these steps:

1. Click anywhere on the object that you want to name. Black handles appear around the object. (To name a form, click anywhere on the form, but do *not* click any objects on the form.)

2. Open the Properties window by pressing F4 or by selecting Properties from the View menu.

3. Click the Name property and type a new name.

Captions for objects

In addition to a name, most (but not all) objects also have a caption. An object's caption is what you see on the screen. Some captions are shown in Figure 4-4.

By default, an object's caption and name are the same until you change them. So the moment you draw a check box on a form, the check box's caption will be something dull like Check1, and the check box's name will also be Check1.

The caption for a form appears in the title bar of that form. The caption for an object (such as a command button, label, check box, or text box) appears directly on that object.

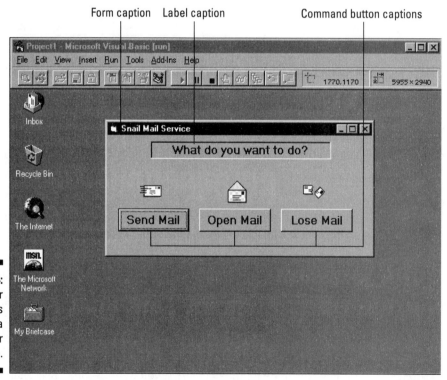

Figure 4-4:
Captions for
various
objects on a
user
interface.

Captions are for cosmetic purposes only, like blue eyeshadow or spiked purple hair. A caption can be blank or up to 255 characters long, including spaces, punctuation marks, and four-letter words. The following are valid captions:

```
Hello
Hello, jerk!
Do I really know what I'm doing?
```

To change the caption of an object, follow these steps:

1. Point and click the object whose caption you want to change so that black handles appear around it. (To select a form, click anywhere on the form but do *not* click any objects on the form.)

2. Open the Properties window by pressing F4 or by selecting Properties from the View menu.

3. Click the Caption property and type a new caption. Notice that Visual Basic displays your caption on the screen as you type.

Making captions into hot keys

Besides looking pretty and displaying information to the user, captions can also be used to create *hot keys* so that the user can choose an object without having to click it with the mouse.

To turn a caption into a hot key, you have to put the ampersand character (&) into an object's caption. You may be wondering, "Why the heck would I want to use an ugly symbol like that?" The answer is to give users yet another way to push your buttons.

There are two ways to push a button:

- Click the mouse.
- Press Tab until the button is highlighted and then press the spacebar or Enter (real obvious, huh?).

If you use the ampersand, the user can push a button by pressing Alt plus whatever letter the ampersand is in front of. For example, if a command button has a caption of &Exit, it appears in the command button with the E underlined, as in Exit. To push this button, you could simply press Alt+E. If the command button has a caption of E&xit, however, the caption appears in the command button with the *x* underlined, as in Exit, and you could use Alt+X to press this command button (see Figure 4-5).

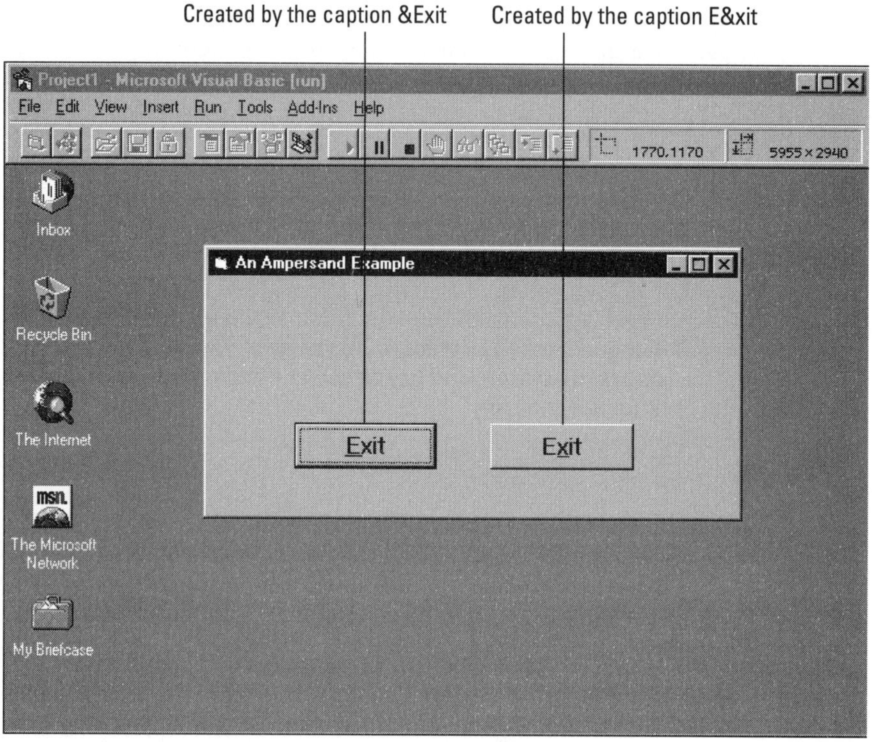

Created by the caption &Exit   Created by the caption E&xit

Figure 4-5:
Two
command
buttons
illustrating
the use of
the
ampersand.

Test your newfound knowledge

1. Why is it important to know the type of people who might use your program?

   a. So you can create false expectations and confuse your users.

   b. To customize your user interface to their expectations and experiences.

   c. Because someone might know friends in high places.

   d. It's not important, just as long as people pay for my program in cash.

2. A user interface must act like a map. Explain this sentence.

   a. Why should I explain it? You're the one who wrote it.

   b. Rand McNally is now writing software.

   c. This sentence is a simile, which is a creative way of expressing analogies.

   d. The user interface must always show the users where they are in your program.

Changing the font of an object's caption

When you create a caption, Visual Basic displays it on the screen in a plain type style. For you creative types who want to make your captions look spiffier, you can change the font, type style, and size of captions to give them more pizzazz.

Fonts are different ways to display text. Normally, Visual Basic uses the MS Sans Serif font, but you can use any font in your computer. (MS Sans Serif is similar to the Helvetica font, and the Visual Basic MS Serif font is similar to the Times Roman font.)

To change the font of a caption, follow these steps:

1. Click the object whose caption you want to modify.

2. Open the Properties window by pressing F4 or by selecting Properties from the View menu.

3. Click the Font property and click the ellipsis (...) that appears in the settings box. Visual Basic displays a dialog box of all the fonts you can use. This list is illustrated in Figure 4-6.

4. Click the font you want. Visual Basic immediately changes the font of the caption.

MS Sans Serif font

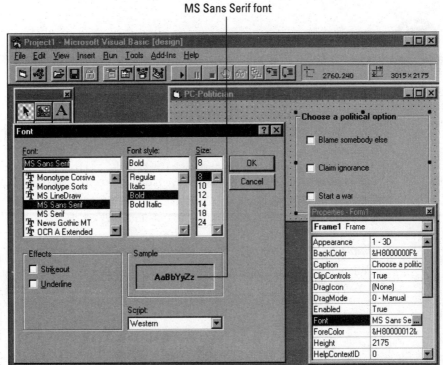

Figure 4-6:
Displaying
the Font
dialog box
for the Font
property.

Fonts give you a chance to be creative, but they can also disorient the user if you choose bizarre fonts that don't look like anything normally found in nature. To avoid confusion, let Visual Basic use its default font of MS Sans Serif, unless you have a really good reason to use a different font.

Changing the size of an object's caption

You can also change the size of your caption by making it smaller or larger to fit inside your object. Depending on the font you choose, Visual Basic gives you a variety of font sizes to choose from.

For example, if you choose the MS Sans Serif font, Visual Basic gives you the following choices of font sizes:

- 8
- 10
- 12
- 14
- 18
- 24

Obviously, the more font sizes you use, the odder your captions will look. It's best to use one size to avoid confusing the user any more than you have to.

To define the font size of your captions, follow these steps:

1. Click the object whose font size you want to modify.

2. Open the Properties window by pressing F4 or by selecting Properties from the <u>V</u>iew menu.

3. Click the Font property and click the ellipsis (...) that appears in the settings box. Visual Basic displays a dialog box like the one you saw in Figure 4-6.

4. Choose the font size you want to use and click OK.

Changing the type style of an object's caption

If changing the font and size of your captions isn't enough excitement for one day, Visual Basic also lets you change the type style of your captions. The number of available type styles depends on the font you are using for your caption.

For example, if you chose the MS Sans Serif font, Visual Basic gives you the following choices of type styles:

- ✔ Regular
- ✔ *Italic*
- ✔ **Bold**
- ✔ ***Bold Italic***
- ✔ <u>Underline</u>
- ✔ ~~Strikeout~~

These different type styles are shown in Figure 4-7. If you want, you can even combine two or more type styles for extra emphasis.

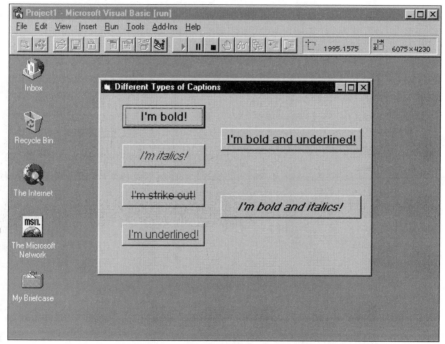

Figure 4-7:
Command
buttons
showing
different
type styles.

To set one or more of these font styles, follow these steps:

1. Click the object whose caption you want to modify.

2. Open the Properties window by pressing F4 or by selecting Properties from the View menu.

3. Click the Font property and click the ellipsis (...) that appears in the settings box. Visual Basic displays a dialog box like the one you saw in Figure 4-6.

4. Click the font style you want to use and click OK. Visual Basic immediately changes the caption's appearance.

Changing the background and foreground colors of captions

Captions normally appear in boring black, white, and shades of gray. To make your captions stand out more colorfully, you can change the background and foreground colors. The BackColor property of an object represents its background color, and the ForeColor property represents its foreground color, as shown in Figure 4-8.

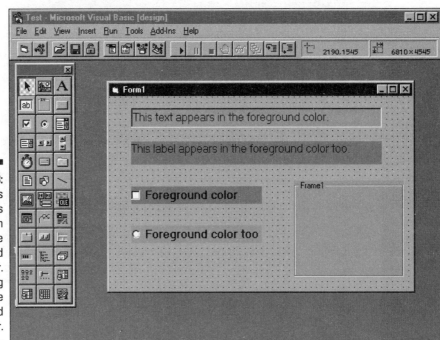

Figure 4-8:
The letters themselves appear in the foreground color. Everything else is in the background color.

Unlike other types of objects, command buttons have only a BackColor property. The BackColor property simply changes the color that surrounds the caption when the command button is highlighted.

To change the color surrounding an object's caption, follow these steps:

1. Click the object whose background color you want to change.

2. Open the Properties window by pressing F4 or by selecting Properties from the <u>V</u>iew menu.

3. Click the BackColor property in the Properties window. Visual Basic displays the current color in a seemingly useless series of letters and numbers.

4. Click the downward-pointing arrow to the right of the current color value. Visual Basic displays a color palette.

5. Click the color you want. Visual Basic instantly obeys.

Moving objects on the screen

Objects can appear anywhere on the screen. Visual Basic provides two ways to define the position of an object on the screen:

- ✔ Using the mouse
- ✔ Changing the Left and Top properties in the Properties window

To change the position of an object using the mouse, follow these steps:

1. Click the object you want to move so that black handles appear around it. (To move a form, click anywhere on the form but do not click any objects on the form.)

2. Hold down the left mouse button and move the mouse to where you want the object to appear.

3. Release the mouse button.

In case you haven't figured it out by now, when you create and place an object for the first time, that position is where Visual Basic displays the object. Use the mouse whenever you want to move an object quickly without regard to exact placement on the screen.

For more-precise measurements when moving an object, use the Properties window to type in values for the Left and Top properties.

For forms, the Left property measures the distance from the left edge of the screen to the left edge of the form. The Top property measures the distance from the top of the screen to the top of the form.

For objects, the Left property measures the distance from the left edge of the form to the left edge of the object. The Top property measures the distance from the top of the form to the top of the object.

To change the position of an object using the Properties window, follow these steps:

1. Click anywhere on the form. (Do not click any objects on the form.)

2. Open the Properties window by pressing F4 or by selecting Properties from the View menu.

3. Click the Left property and type a new value.

4. Click the Top property and type a new value.

Deleting objects off the face of the earth

Sometimes you may draw an object and then decide that you don't need it after all.

To delete an object, follow these steps:

1. Click the object you want to delete.

2. Press Delete or choose Delete from the Edit menu.

Copying objects because you're too tired to draw new ones

After you've drawn an object that is the exact size you need, you may want to make a copy of the object rather than create a new one and go to the trouble of resizing it.

To copy an object, follow these steps:

1. Click the object you want to copy.

2. Press Ctrl+C or choose Copy from the Edit menu.

3. Press Ctrl+V or choose P̲aste from the E̲dit menu. Visual Basic displays a dialog box that asks whether you want to create a control array. If you know what a control array is and want to create it, click Y̲es; otherwise, click N̲o. Visual Basic displays a copy of your object in the upper left corner of the form.

4. Move this copy of the object anywhere on your screen.

Selecting more than one object to move, copy, or delete

Before you can move, copy, or delete any object, you have to select it by clicking it. However, if you want to move, copy, or delete *more than one* object at the same time, you have two choices:

✔ Use the mouse to select multiple objects.

✔ Click multiple objects while holding down Ctrl or Shift.

To use the mouse to select multiple objects, follow these steps:

1. Position the mouse at the upper left corner of the group of objects you want to select.

2. Hold down the left mouse button while you drag the mouse to the lower right corner of the group of objects you want to select (see Figure 4-9). Visual Basic displays a dotted line around all the objects you selected.

3. Release the mouse button. Visual Basic displays a gray rectangle around all the objects you selected.

To click multiple objects while holding down Ctrl or Shift, follow these steps:

1. Click the first object that you want to select. Visual Basic displays black handles around the object.

2. Point to the second object that you want to select.

3. Press Ctrl or Shift while clicking the second object. Visual Basic displays gray rectangles around this object and each of your previously selected objects.

4. Repeat steps 2 and 3 until you've selected all the objects you want.

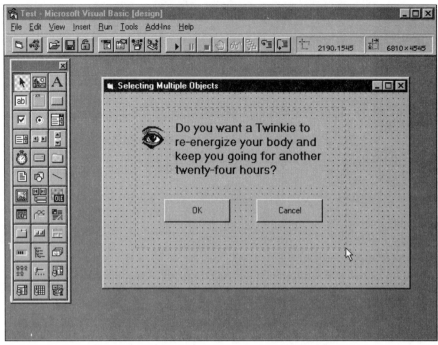

Figure 4-9:
The box that
appears
when you
drag the
mouse.

Changing the size of objects

After creating an object, the next step is to define its size, which is a topic most men tend to exaggerate. Visual Basic provides two ways to change the size of an object:

 ✔ Use the mouse.
 ✔ Change the Height and Width properties in the Properties window.

To change the size of an object using the mouse, follow these steps:

1. Click the object that you want to resize. Little black handles appear around the edges of the object.

2. Move the mouse to the edge of the object until the mouse pointer turns into a double arrow, as shown in Figure 4-10.

3. Hold down the mouse button and drag the mouse. When the object is in the shape you want, release the mouse button.

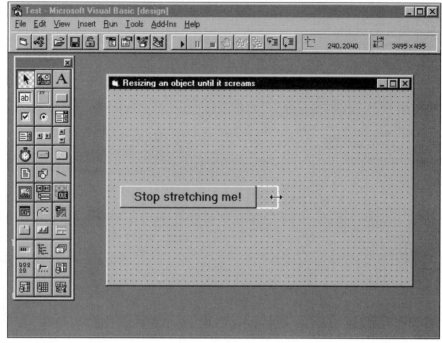

Figure 4-10:
The double-arrow mouse pointer stretching a command button.

To change the size of a form using the Properties window, follow these steps:

1. Click the object you want to resize.

2. Open the Properties window by pressing F4 or by selecting Properties from the View menu.

3. Click the Height property, type a new value, and press Enter.

4. Click the Width property, type a new value, and press Enter.

Use the mouse method when the exact size of your object isn't crucial. Change the Height and Width properties manually when you want absolute precision or when you feel like being picky about things that nobody else cares about.

The incredible shape-changing mouse

Whenever you move the mouse pointer over your objects, the mouse pointer appears as a white arrow on the screen. However, Visual Basic actually gives you fifteen shapes that you can use to display your mouse pointer, as shown in Figure 4-11.

▷	0 - Default mouse cursor	⌘	8 - Size NW SE
▷	1 - Arrow	⇔	9 - Size W E
+	2 - Cross	⇧	10 - Up Arrow
I	3 - I-Beam	⌛	11 - Hourglass
▣	4 - Icon	⊘	12 - No Drop
✥	5 - Size	▷⌛	13 - Arrow and Hourglass
▱	6 - Size NE SW	▷?	14 - Arrow and Question
⇕	7 - Size N S	✛	15 - Size All

Figure 4-11:
The many
different
mouse
shapes you
can choose
from.

Now you may be wondering, "Why would I want to change a perfectly good mouse pointer into an up arrow or an hourglass?" The answer is so that the user knows that something special is happening.

For example, whenever you save a file, most programs change the mouse pointer to an hourglass shape. This tells the user, "I'm busy even though nothing seems to be happening on the screen." When the program has finished (saving a file, calculating a result, wiping out your hard disk, and so on), it changes the mouse pointer back to a white arrow.

To have the appearance of the mouse pointer change when it appears over a specific form or object, follow these steps:

1. Click the object or form that will change the mouse pointer.

2. Open the Properties window by pressing F4 or by selecting Properties from the View menu.

3. Click the MousePointer property.

4. Click the arrow to display a list of all the mouse pointers you can choose from.

5. Select the mouse pointer that will appear when the mouse moves over that object or form.

Defining the TabIndex property of your objects

The TabIndex property determines the order in which Visual Basic highlights buttons when the user presses one of six keys: Tab, up arrow, down arrow, right arrow, left arrow, and Shift+Tab.

- ✔ The Tab, down-arrow, and right-arrow keys highlight the object with the next highest TabIndex value.
- ✔ The Shift+Tab, up-arrow, and left-arrow keys highlight the object with the next lowest TabIndex value.
- ✔ The spacebar or Enter key selects a highlighted object.

(Image buttons don't have a TabIndex property, so they can't be highlighted by pressing any keys.)

An object with a TabIndex property set to 0 appears highlighted as soon as your program runs. If the user presses Tab, the object with a TabIndex property of 1 is highlighted next, and so on.

The first object that you create has a TabIndex property of 0. The second object that you create has a TabIndex property of 1, and so on.

The only way to highlight an object stored inside a frame (see "Grouping Command Buttons" in Chapter 5) is to press Tab. After an object inside a frame is highlighted, pressing the up-, down-, left-, and right-arrow keys only highlights other command buttons or objects in that frame.

Although most users will probably use a mouse to highlight and select objects, some users may not have a mouse. For those rare instances, the keyboard is the only way these behind-the-times people can select your program's objects.

To change the TabIndex property of an object, follow these steps:

1. Click the object that you want to modify.

2. Open the Properties window by pressing F4 or by selecting Properties from the View menu.

3. Click the TabIndex property and type a number (such as 1 or 4).

Whenever you change the TabIndex property of a button, Visual Basic automatically renumbers the TabIndex of your other buttons. Thus, it's impossible for two buttons to have identical TabIndex values.

If you have created lots of objects, you can set the TabIndex properties for them quickly and easily by following these steps:

1. Click the object that you want highlighted last (the object that will have the highest TabIndex property value).

2. Open the Properties window by pressing F4 or by selecting Properties from the View menu.

3. Click the TabIndex property and type **0**.

4. Click the object that you want highlighted second to last.

5. Repeat steps 2 through 4 until you've set the TabIndex properties for all your objects to 0.

If you follow these steps, the last object you clicked will have a TabIndex of 0, the second-to-last object you clicked will have a TabIndex of 1, and so on.

Dimming objects

If you don't want the user to press a particular object (such as a command button, a check box, or an image box), you can dim it, as shown in Figure 4-12. A dimmed object tells the user, "Sometimes you can click this object but not right now. So there."

To dim an object, follow these steps:

1. Click the object that you want to dim.

2. Open the Properties window by pressing F4 or by selecting Properties from the View menu.

3. Click the Enabled property and set it to False.

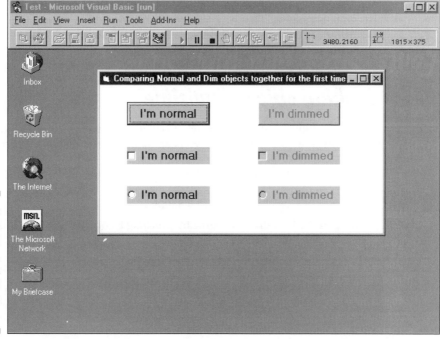

Figure 4-12:
Dimmed
command
buttons,
check
boxes, and
radio
buttons.

A dimmed object doesn't do anything, so you eventually have to undim it by using BASIC code if you want to undim it during run-time events.

To give you a sneak preview of the incredible power of BASIC code, here's how BASIC undims and dims a button.

To undim a button, set the button's Enabled property to True. The following example undims a command button named cmdExit:

```
cmdExit.Enabled = True
```

To dim a button using BASIC code, set the button's Enabled property to False. The following example dims a command button named cmdExit:

```
cmdExit.Enabled = False
```

You can only dim and undim buttons using BASIC code and only while your program is running. That way, you can dim and undim buttons in response to whatever the user is doing (typing, moving the mouse, pounding helplessly on the keyboard, and so on).

Making objects invisible

Rather than dimming an object (which essentially taunts the user that the object is there but unavailable), you can make objects disappear completely.

To make an object disappear, follow these steps:

1. Click the object you want to disappear.
2. Open the Properties window by pressing F4 or by selecting Properties from the View menu.
3. Click the Visible property and set it to False.

You can also make an object disappear using BASIC code. To do so, set the object's Visible property to False. The following example makes a command button named cmdNew disappear:

```
cmdNew.Visible = False
```

Like dimmed objects, invisible objects are useless unless you can make them visible once in awhile. To make an object appear again, you have to use BASIC code to set the object's Visible property to True. The following example makes a command button named cmdNew appear:

```
cmdNew.Visible = True
```

Try It Yourself

The following sample program lets you change the caption on the form by typing a new caption in a text box and by clicking the cmdCaption command button. Just create a user interface according to the following table and see for yourself the amazing power of Visual Basic.

Object	*Property*	*Setting*
Form	Caption	The Incredible Changing Caption
Label1	Caption	This caption can be changed by clicking the command button below
	Height	600
	Left	1000
	Name	lblHeadline
	Top	480
	Width	5200
Label2	Caption	Type a new caption here:
	Height	300
	Left	120
	Top	1680
	Width	2000
Text1	Left	2640
	Multiline	True
	Name	txtCaption
	Text	(Empty)
	Top	1680
	Width	1935
Command1	Caption	Change Caption
	Left	2640
	Name	cmdCaption
	Top	2860
	Width	2175

```
Private Sub cmdCaption_Click()
  lblHeadline.Caption = txtCaption.Text
End Sub
```

When you run this program, just type a new caption in the text box and click the command button labeled Change Caption. Visual Basic immediately displays your newly typed text in the top label.

Chapter 5

Forms and Buttons

● ●

In This Chapter

▶ Creating forms and drawing borders

▶ Choosing the order in which forms are displayed

▶ Creating buttons

▶ Making a Toolbar with image buttons

● ●

*T*he main part of a user interface is a window, which Visual Basic calls a *form*. Every Visual Basic program must have at least one form, but most programs use two or more forms.

For example, a typical program might use one form to display a list of command buttons to click. If the user clicks a command button, a second form appears displaying information such as names, addresses, and telephone numbers of people who owe you money.

Creating Forms

Each time you load Visual Basic or select New Project from the File menu, a blank form automatically appears on the screen, as shown in Figure 5-1. This is Visual Basic's way of saying, "Okay, I'm ready. Start drawing your user interface."

For simple programs, one form should be enough. But for larger programs, you may need two, three, or even a dozen forms. To create another form, Visual Basic gives you two choices:

✔ Select Form from the Insert menu

✔ Click the Form icon on the Visual Basic Toolbar

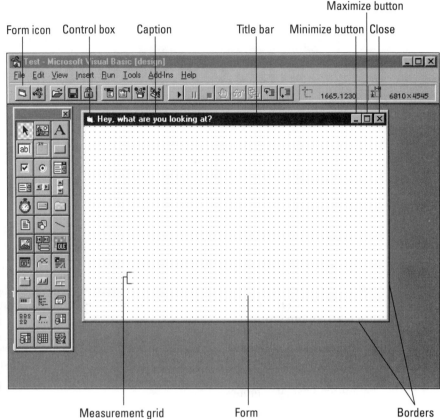

Form icon   Control box   Caption   Title bar   Minimize button   Close

Maximize button

Figure 5-1:
The parts of
a newly
created
form.

Measurement grid   Form   Borders

Saving forms

After you've created a form, you should save it (if not for religious purposes, at least for practical ones) so that you won't have to create it all over again later. To save a form, Visual Basic gives you two choices:

 ✔ Select Save File from the File menu
 ✔ Press Ctrl+S

If you have two or more forms displayed on the screen and you want to save changes to all the forms, select Save Project from the File menu or click the Save Project icon (see Figure 5-2). This command automatically saves every file (listed in the VBP project file) that makes up your entire Visual Basic program.

Save Project icon

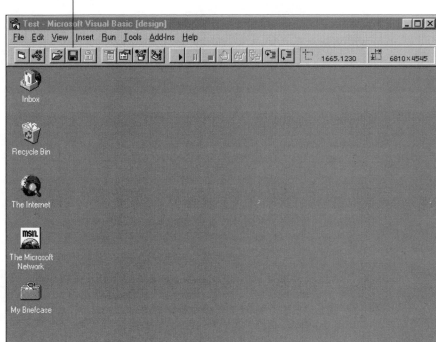

Get into the habit of periodically saving your forms. If your computer fails, the power goes out, or terrorists raid your home and riddle your computer with bullets, you'll lose only the changes you've made since you last saved the form.

If you haven't saved a form to disk at least once, the Project window displays the form name with the first letter capitalized and the rest of the name in lowercase. The moment you save a form for the first time, Visual Basic displays it with the FRM file extension in uppercase letters (see Figure 5-3). To display the Project window, press Ctrl+R or select Project from the View menu.

Drawing borders around forms

Borders make forms look pretty, and they also give nations something to argue about. By changing the BorderStyle property, forms can have one of six types of borders, as shown in Figure 5-4:

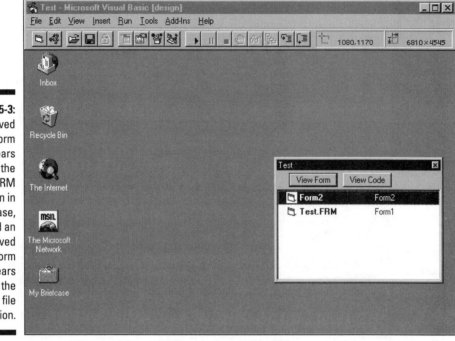

Figure 5-3:
A saved
form
appears
with the
FRM
extension in
uppercase,
and an
unsaved
form
appears
without the
file
extension.

✔ 0 – None

✔ 1 – Fixed Single

✔ 2 – Sizable

✔ 3 – Fixed Dialog

✔ 4 – Fixed ToolWindow

✔ 5 – Sizable ToolWindow

After you change the BorderStyle property of a form, the form still looks the same on the screen. However, when you run your program, your form magically appears with the BorderStyle property you selected.

In addition to making your forms look pretty, each border style also affects whether the user can move or resize the form.

The *0 – None* style makes your form invisible, but any objects your form contains can still be seen. A user cannot move, resize, or minimize this type of form (mainly because the user can't see it).

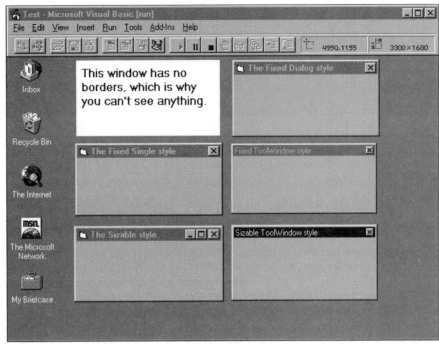

Figure 5-4:
Comparison
of all six
border
styles.

The *1 – Fixed Single* style displays a Control box, title bar, and Close box. Users can move this type of form but cannot resize it.

The *2 – Sizable* style is the default style. This style displays a Control box, a title bar, Minimize and Maximize buttons, and the Close box. Users can move, resize, and minimize or maximize this form.

The *3 – Fixed Dialog* style displays a Control box, a title bar, and a Close box. Users can move this form but cannot resize, minimize, or maximize it.

The *4 – Fixed ToolWindow* style displays a title bar and Close box. Users can move this form but cannot resize, minimize, or maximize it.

The *5 – Sizable ToolWindow* style displays a title bar and Close box. Users can move and resize this form.

To change the borders around your form using the Property window, follow these steps:

1. Click anywhere on the form. (Do not click any objects on the form.)

2. Open the Properties window by pressing F4 or by selecting Properties from the View menu.

3. Click the BorderStyle property.

4. Choose one of the following:

0 – None

1 – Fixed Single

2 – Sizable

3 – Fixed Dialog

4 – Fixed ToolWindow

5 – Sizable ToolWindow

Minimizing and maximizing forms

Forms can cover part of the screen or the entire screen. Any form that hogs the whole screen is considered *maximized*. On the other extreme, forms can be shrunken and displayed on the screen as icons. A shrunken form is considered *minimized*. Any form that just covers part of the screen is considered *normal*. Anyone who thinks computers invent too many definitions is also considered normal. Figure 5-5 shows all three sizes of forms.

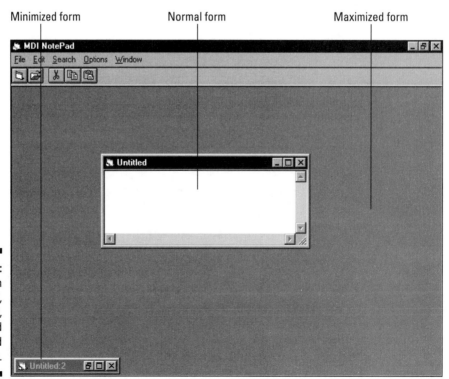

Figure 5-5:
Comparison of normal, minimized, and maximized forms.

To display a form as normal, minimized, or maximized while your program runs, follow these steps:

1. Click anywhere on the form. (Do not click any objects on the form.)

2. Open the Properties window by pressing F4 or by selecting Properties from the View menu.

3. Click the WindowState property in the Property window.

4. Choose one of the following:

    0 – Normal

    1 – Minimized

    2 – Maximized

You can also give the user the option of minimizing or maximizing a form. To do so, your form needs to display Minimize and Maximize buttons.

To display Minimize and Maximize buttons on a form, follow these steps:

1. Click anywhere on the form. (Do not click any objects on the form.)

2. Open the Properties window by pressing F4 or by selecting Properties from the View menu.

3. Click the MinButton (or the MaxButton) property in the Property window.

4. Choose True or False. (Depending on the border style you chose for your form, the default setting for the MinButton and MaxButton settings may be True or False.)

Displaying icons for minimized forms

Icons are special graphics symbols with the ICO file extension. Normally, Visual Basic displays a minimized form on the screen with a default icon that looks like a sail flapping in the wind. If you don't like this icon, you can customize it. Figure 5-6 shows a default icon and a customized icon.

To change an icon with the Property window, follow these steps:

1. Click anywhere on the form. (Do not click any objects on the form.)

2. Open the Properties window by pressing F4 or by selecting Properties from the View menu.

3. Click the Icon property in the Properties window.

4. Click the ellipsis (. . .) to the right of the current icon value. Visual Basic displays a Load Icon dialog box.

5. Choose the icon you want to use.

Default icon   Customized icon

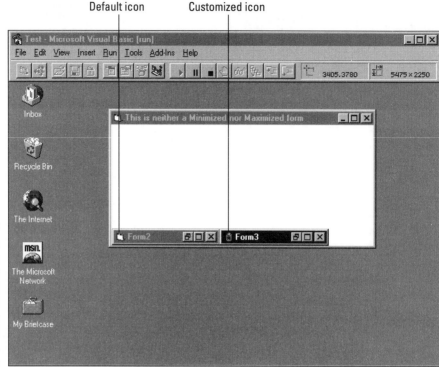

Figure 5-6:
Comparison
of default
and
customized
icons for a
minimized
form.

The Control Box

Users can move or resize a form by using the mouse. To minimize or maximize a form, simply click the Minimize or Maximize button. For those users who haven't caught up with current technology or refuse to use a mouse, each form provides a Control box as well.

To activate a Control box, press Alt+spacebar. A menu appears, which lets the user move, resize, minimize, or maximize a form.

The Control box appears on all forms. But if you think it looks really ugly and want to remove it, follow these steps:

1. Click anywhere on the form. (Do not click any objects on the form.)

2. Open the Properties window by pressing F4 or by selecting Properties from the View menu.

3. Click the ControlBox property in the Property window.

4. Choose True or False. (Depending on the border style you chose for your form, the default value may be True or False.)

Which Form Will Visual Basic Display First?

When your program runs, the first form it displays is generally the first form you created.

To make another form appear first, follow these steps:

1. From the Tools menu, select Options. Visual Basic displays an Options dialog box.

2. Click the Project tab. Visual Basic displays the Project dialog box (see Figure 5-7).

3. Click the Startup Form list box to display a list of all the forms of your project.

4. Choose the form you want to display first.

5. Click OK.

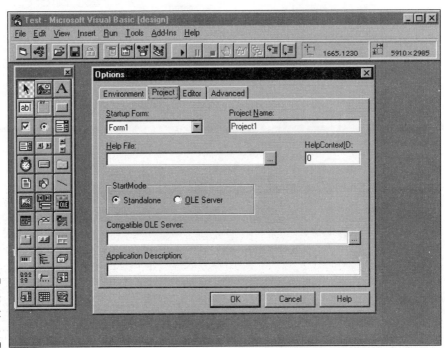

Figure 5-7:
The Project
dialog box.

Displaying forms within a form

Believe it or not, you can actually display multiple forms within a form. In computer geek language, this arrangement of windows within a window is called a *multiple-document interface,* or *MDI.* The container form is called the *MDI form,* and any forms inside the container form are called *child forms.* These forms are shown in Figure 5-8. You can have only one MDI form but any number of child forms. (These restrictions do not apply when you are in design mode.)

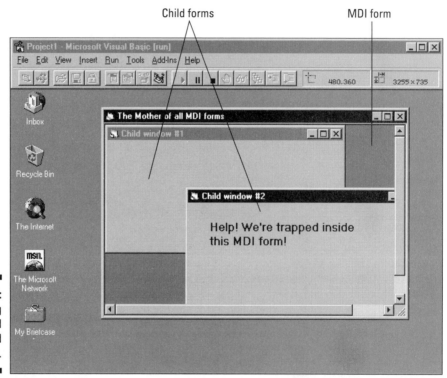

Figure 5-8:
The amazing
MDI and
child
windows.

You can minimize and maximize MDI forms just like any other forms. If you maximize a child form, however, it can only expand to the maximum size of the MDI form. When you minimize a child form, its icon appears within the MDI form. Although you can move an MDI form anywhere on the screen, you can move a child form only within the boundaries of the MDI form that contains it.

To create an MDI form and its child forms, follow these steps:

1. From the Insert menu, select MDI Form. Visual Basic displays a new form with the caption "MDIForm" in its title bar.

2. From the Insert menu, select Form, or click the Form icon in the Toolbar.

3. For each form created in step 2, open the Properties window (by pressing F4) and change its MDIChild property to True.

4. Repeat steps 2 and 3 until you create all the child forms you need or until you get bored and want to do something else.

Defining units of measurement on a form

The reason to have a form is so that you can place objects on it. You may notice, therefore, that every form always displays a grid to help you align objects.

By default, each form uses a unit of measurement called a *twip*, which sounds like something Elmer Fudd would say. ("I'm tying stwing acwoss this path so that wabbit will twip over it. Eh, eh, eh, eh.")

In case you actually care, 1440 twips equal one inch. If you don't like using twips as your preferred unit of measurement, Visual Basic offers seven options:

- ✔ Twips (1440 twips = one inch)
- ✔ Points (72 points = one inch)
- ✔ Pixels (The number of pixels that equals one inch depends on your monitor's resolution.)
- ✔ Characters (A character is $\frac{1}{6}$ inch high and $\frac{1}{12}$ inch wide.)
- ✔ Inches (1 inch = one inch — amazing, isn't it?)
- ✔ Millimeters (25.4 mm = one inch)
- ✔ Centimeters (2.54 cm = one inch)

Hard-core programmers will be happy to know that Visual Basic even lets you create your own customized coordinate system. If you're thinking about doing that, you probably should be reading a book like *Visual Basic For Hard-Core Programming Geniuses* instead of this book. For the rest of us, Visual Basic's seven available units of measurement are more than sufficient.

To change your form's grid scale, follow these steps:

1. Click anywhere on the form. (Do not click any objects on the form.)

2. Open the Properties window by pressing F4 or by selecting Properties from the View menu.

3. Click the ScaleMode property.

4. Click the arrow to display a list of all the different measurement units you can use. Figure 5-9 shows this list.

5. Select the unit of measurement you want your form to use.

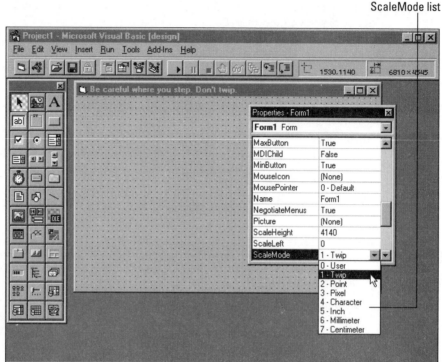

Figure 5-9:
The
ScaleMode
list dis-
played.

Pushing Buttons

Pushing a button is a simple thing that anyone can do. Even children can push buttons, which gives them the power to throw a hot dog in a microwave oven and shout with glee when it explodes before their eyes.

Everyone uses buttons. Your disk drive probably has a button that you press to eject a floppy disk. Your monitor has a button to turn it on and off. Even your mouse has a button (or two or three).

Because buttons are so familiar and easy to use, programs often display buttons on the screen that you can push with a mouse. Instead of forcing you to wade through various menus to find the right command, buttons conveniently display your options right before your eyes. All you have to do is figure out which button you want to press.

Buttons are a feature of nearly every program. Therefore, the rest of this chapter is all about making, modifying, and pushing your own buttons.

Types of Buttons

Essentially, a *button* is nothing more than an area on the screen that the user can click with the mouse. When pushed (clicked on), a command button rushes off and performs a command. (That's why they call them *command buttons.*) Visual Basic lets you create two types of buttons: command buttons and image buttons.

A *command button* displays a label. This label can be as unimaginative as OK, Cancel, or Quit. Or it can represent a particular command such as Erase File, Next Screen, or Lose Mr. Johnson's Airline Reservation.

Command buttons often appear in dialog boxes where the program displays a message, such as, "Do you really want to erase your IRS tax files to avoid criminal prosecution?" The available choices may be Yes and No.

An *image button* displays a picture on the screen. Image buttons often appear in groups located at the top of the screen. Visual Basic even uses groups of image buttons to make up its Toolbar.

The advantage of image buttons is that they can be smaller than command buttons. The disadvantage is that unless the user knows which command each image button represents, the user has no idea how to use your image buttons. Command buttons and image buttons are shown in Figure 5-10.

Because image buttons aren't as self-explanatory as command buttons, commands are rarely represented by an image button alone.

For example, if the only way to exit your program is to click an image button that shows an open door, people may not understand the connection and may wind up turning off their computer to exit your program instead. (And then they probably won't use your program again either.)

Creating Buttons

To create a command button, follow these steps:

1. Click the Command button icon in the Visual Basic Toolbox.

2. Move the mouse to the place on the form where you want to draw the command button.

3. Press and hold the left mouse button and drag the mouse to form a command button box.

4. Release the left mouse button to complete the operation. Visual Basic displays a boring label like Command1 in the command button.

Image buttons   Command buttons

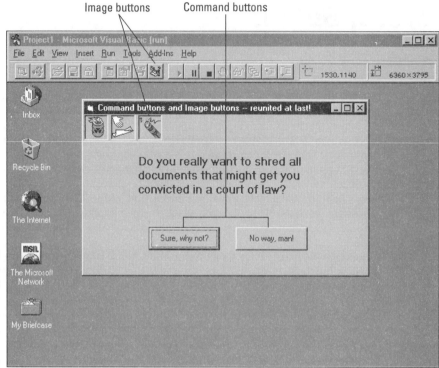

Figure 5-10:
Examples of
command
buttons and
image
buttons.

To create an image button, follow these steps:

1. Click the Image icon in the Visual Basic Toolbox.

2. Drag the mouse to the place on the form where you want to draw the image button.

3. Open the Properties window by pressing F4 or by selecting Properties from the View menu.

4. Click the Picture property and click the ellipsis (. . .) to the right of the list box. Visual Basic cheerfully displays a Load Picture dialog box.

5. Load any graphics file (bitmap, icon, or metafile). Visual Basic displays this icon as your image button.

Changing the size of an image button

Visual Basic lets you freely draw an image box any size you want; however, if your graphics image is too big for your image button, the graphics image appears cut off.

To make your graphics image change in size when you change the image button's size, you need to change the value of its Stretch property to True. (The default value of the Stretch property is False.)

For example, in Figure 5-11, the image box in the upper left corner has its Stretch property set to False, so it cuts the graphics image off if the image is too big. The other three image boxes have their Stretch properties set to True; therefore, the graphics image adjusts in size when you change the size of the image box.

Image button with Stretch property set to False

Image buttons with Stretch property set to True

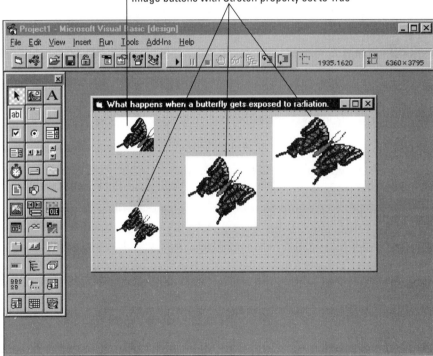

Figure 5-11: How the Stretch property affects the size of graphics images in image buttons.

Creating a default command button

The *default command button* is the one button that users can choose by pressing the Enter key right away. The purpose of a default button is to let the user push the most likely choice. If you want to suggest a command that a user should choose, you need to create a default button.

For example, if the user gives a command to launch nuclear missiles at another nation, a dialog box might pop up asking, "Wouldn't you rather play a nice game of chess?" If the default button were Yes, the user could mindlessly hit Enter and save the world from a nuclear holocaust.

Only command buttons can be default command buttons. Image buttons can never be default command buttons because Visual Basic says so.

There are two ways to create a default command button:

- ✔ Set the command button's TabIndex property to zero. This highlights the command button designated as the default button.
- ✔ Set the default command button's Default property to True. This works only if no other object has a TabIndex value of zero.

To create a default command button using the TabIndex property, follow these steps:

1. Click the command button that you want to be the default button.

2. Open the Properties window by pressing F4 or by selecting Properties from the View menu.

3. Click the TabIndex property and type **0**.

If no other command buttons on your form have a TabIndex property of zero, you can create a default button by setting the Default property of a command button to True.

To create a default command button using the Default property, follow these steps:

1. Click the command button that you want to be the default button.

2. Open the Properties window by pressing F4 or by selecting Properties from the View menu.

3. Click the Default property and set its value to True.

4. Make sure that no other objects on the form have a TabIndex of zero.

What happens if one command button has a TabIndex of zero but another command button has its Default property set to True? The default command button will be the one with the TabIndex of zero. So there.

Defining the Cancel button

When users bang on Esc, they usually want to cancel their last command or exit out of the program. Any button that lets the user do this should be designated the Cancel button. Only one command button can be defined as the Cancel button. (Another good name for the Cancel button is the Panic button, but that destroys the image that programming is a fine science rather than an incoherent art.)

To create a Cancel command button, follow these steps:

1. Click the command button that you want to be the Cancel button.

2. Open the Properties window by pressing F4 or by selecting Properties from the View menu.

3. Click the Cancel property and set it to True. Change the button's caption to "Cancel" or something similar.

Grouping Command Buttons

Occasionally, you may want to group related command buttons on the screen to give the illusion of organization, as shown in Figure 5-12.

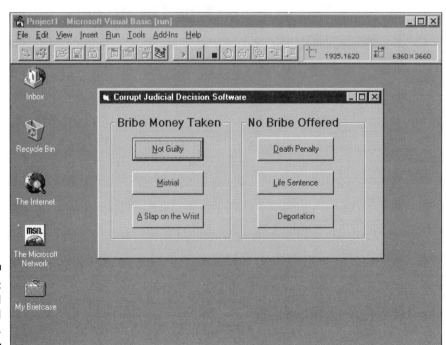

Figure 5-12:
Grouped
command
buttons.

To create a group of command buttons, follow these steps:

1. Click the Frame icon in the Visual Basic Toolbox.

2. Move the mouse to where you want to draw the frame.

3. Hold down the mouse button and move the mouse to draw a frame.

4. Click the Command button icon in the Visual Basic Toolbox.

5. Move the mouse inside the frame to where you want to draw a command button.

6. Hold down the mouse button and move the mouse to draw your command button inside the frame.

7. Repeat steps 4 through 6 until you've drawn all the command buttons you need or until you decide it's time to do something else.

After you've drawn a command button inside a frame, it remains forever trapped inside the frame. When you move the frame, all command buttons inside move along with it.

You cannot create a command button outside a frame and then try to move it inside a frame, so don't bother trying.

Test your newfound knowledge

1. Why do command buttons have names and captions?

    a. So you have twice as many chances to call it a four-letter word.

    b. The name is a bad word you can call the command button, and the caption is there so that you can write a funny punchline.

    c. The name identifies the command button, and the caption is what actually appears on the screen.

    d. Because Visual Basic says so, and any product sold by Bill Gates can't be wrong because he's a billionaire.

2. Why would you want to group buttons together in a frame?

    a. To keep them from escaping into the wild.

    b. So related commands are easy to find on the screen.

    c. To make it harder for anyone to understand what your program is supposed to do.

    d. No reason, except to cause more confusion to people trying to learn how to program a computer for the first time.

As a final modification for grouped command buttons, set the TabStop properties of all grouped buttons to False. Then set the TabStop property of the first command button to True. That way, if a lame user presses Tab, only the first command button in a group will be highlighted.

To turn off the TabStop properties for a group of buttons, follow these steps:

1. Click any command button within the frame, except for the first command button.

2. Open the Properties window by pressing F4 or by selecting Properties from the View menu.

3. Click the TabStop property and set it to False.

4. Repeat steps 1 through 3 until the TabStop property for all the command buttons (except the first command button) has been set to False.

5. Go to the kitchen and reward yourself with a Twinkie for your good deed.

Making a Toolbar with Image Buttons

Image buttons can be grouped to form a Toolbar, which nearly every Windows-based program provides these days. By clicking on these icons, users can quickly choose commands without digging through pull-down menus.

Toolbars normally appear at the top or bottom of the screen, but you can put them anywhere you want.

To create a Toolbar, follow these steps:

1. Click the Picture box icon in the Visual Basic Toolbox.

2. Move the mouse to where you want to draw the Toolbar.

3. Hold down the mouse button and move the mouse to draw a picture box.

4. Open the Properties window by pressing F4 or by selecting Properties from the View menu.

5. Click the Align property and choose one of the following:

   0 – None

   1 – Align Top

   2 – Align Bottom

   3 – Align Left

   4 – Align Right

6. Click the Image icon in the Visual Basic Toolbox.

7. Move the mouse inside the picture box to where you want to draw the image button.

8. Hold down the mouse button and move the mouse to draw your image button.

9. Open the Properties window by pressing F4 or by selecting Properties from the View menu.

10. Click the Picture property and click the ellipsis (. . .) to the right of the list box. Visual Basic cheerfully displays a Load Picture dialog box.

11. Load any graphics file (bitmap, icon, or metafile). Visual Basic displays this icon as your image button.

12. Repeat steps 6 through 11 until you've drawn all the image buttons you need.

Toolbars are best for displaying commonly used commands. The purpose of a toolbar is to give users a simple one-click process for choosing a command. No matter how easy a toolbar might seem, however, some users will never get used to clicking an icon, so make sure that an equivalent pull-down menu command is always available, too.

Chapter 6

Making Choices with Boxes and Buttons

. . . .

. . . .

*I*n school, multiple-choice tests were always easier than essay tests because you could substitute guessing for thinking and still get a decent grade. However, students aren't the only ones who don't want to think if they can help it. Most users are the same way — they want choices clearly laid out in front of their eyes. That way, they can make wild guesses and be on their merry way.

Visual Basic provides several ways to offer choices to users: *check boxes, radio buttons* (also called *option buttons*), *list boxes,* and *combo boxes*. Check boxes let users choose one or more options. Radio buttons let users choose only one option. List boxes and combo boxes offer users multiple choices.

Creating Check Boxes and Radio Buttons

Check boxes get their name from those silly questionnaires that ask, "Check all that apply," as in

Why do you want to work here? (Check all that apply.)

[ ] I need the money.

[ ] I want to participate in employee theft.

[ ] I like bossing people around.

[ ] Isn't this a government job? That means I won't have to work for my money after all.

Radio buttons get their name from those old AM car radios that let you push a button to change stations quickly. Just as you can listen to only one radio station at a time, radio buttons let you choose only one option at a time.

The following is an example of radio buttons:

What is your sex? (Choose only one.)

○ Male

○ Female

○ Ex-male (surgically a female)

○ Ex-female (surgically a male)

Aligning your boxes and buttons

Check boxes and radio buttons are usually left-aligned, which means they look like the following:

[ ] This is left-aligned.

For some odd reason known only to those few programmers who actually use it, you can also right-align check boxes and radio buttons.

This is right-aligned. [ ]

To left-align or right-align a check box or radio button, follow these steps:

1. Click the check box or radio button that you want to align.

2. Open the Properties window by pressing F4 or by selecting Properties from the View menu.

3. Click the Alignment property and set it to 0 – Left Justify or 1 – Right Justify.

Grouping check boxes

Check boxes rarely appear by themselves. More likely, you see two or more check boxes huddled together like frightened farm animals. The best way to isolate groups of check boxes is to use a *frame*. Frames visually separate different groups of check boxes.

To create a group of check boxes, follow these steps:

1. Click the Frame icon in the Visual Basic Toolbox (see Figure 6-1).

2. Move the mouse to where you want to draw the frame.

3. Hold down the left mouse button and move the mouse to draw a frame.

4. Click the Check box icon in the Visual Basic Toolbox.

5. Inside the frame, move the mouse to where you want to draw a radio button.

6. Hold down the left mouse button and move the mouse to draw your check box.

7. Repeat steps 4 through 6 until you've drawn all the check boxes you want inside your frame or until you decide it's time for a break.

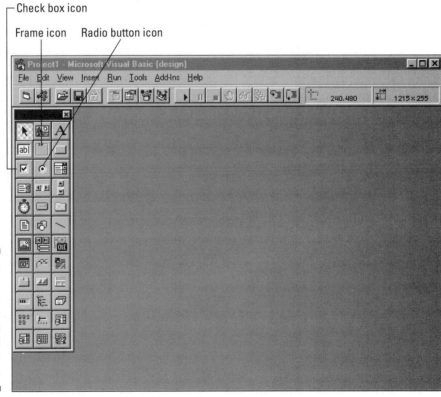

Check box icon

Frame icon   Radio button icon

Figure 6-1:
The Frame,
Check box,
and Radio
button icons
on the Visual
Basic
Toolbox.

As a final modification to a group of check boxes, set the TabStop properties of all grouped check boxes to False. Then set the TabStop property of the first check box to True. That way, when someone presses the Tab key, only the first check box in that frame will be highlighted.

To turn off the TabStop properties for a group of check boxes, follow these steps:

1. Click any check box within the frame, except the first check box.

2. Open the Properties window by pressing F4 or by selecting Properties from the View menu.

3. Click the TabStop property and set it to False.

4. Repeat steps 1 through 3 until the TabStop property has been set to False for all but one of the check boxes.

Grouping radio buttons

If the radio buttons on a form are not grouped, Visual Basic assumes that all radio buttons appearing on the same form belong to the same group. Thus, even if two radio buttons have nothing in common with each other but they appear on the same form, only one of the radio buttons can be chosen at any time. Figure 6-2 shows that only one radio button can be selected in each group of radio buttons.

If you need to display two or more groups of radio buttons, you have to group them within a frame. Otherwise, Visual Basic lumps all the radio buttons in a single group, which means that only one radio button can be chosen at any given time. To create a group of radio buttons in a frame, follow these steps:

1. Click the Frame icon in the Visual Basic Toolbox.

2. Move the mouse to where you want to draw the frame.

3. Hold down the left mouse button and move the mouse to draw a frame.

4. Click the Radio button icon in the Visual Basic Toolbox.

5. Inside the frame, move the mouse to where you want to draw a radio button.

6. Hold down the left mouse button and move the mouse to draw your radio button.

7. Repeat steps 4 through 6 until you've drawn all the radio buttons you want inside your frame or until you decide it's time for a break.

After you've drawn a radio button inside a frame, it remains trapped inside that frame forever. When you move the frame, all radio buttons inside move along with it.

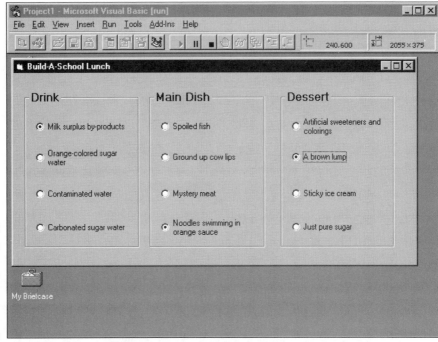

Figure 6-2:
How radio
buttons
affect each
other on a
form.

More Choices with List Boxes and Combo Boxes

When you have only a few choices, check boxes and radio buttons work nicely. If you have ten or more choices, however, bombarding the user with a screen full of check boxes or radio buttons can be intimidating and ugly. To present many choices to the user, Visual Basic provides two alternatives to check boxes and radio buttons: list boxes and combo boxes.

List boxes display long lists of options from which users can choose. If users want to choose something that isn't on the list, too bad. They can't.

Combo boxes also display long lists of options for the user to choose. The difference is that combo boxes also let the user type a choice if it's not found on the list. Figure 6-3 shows an example of a list box and a combo box. Notice that the combo box displays items only if you click the down arrow; the list box always displays items.

Combo box   List box

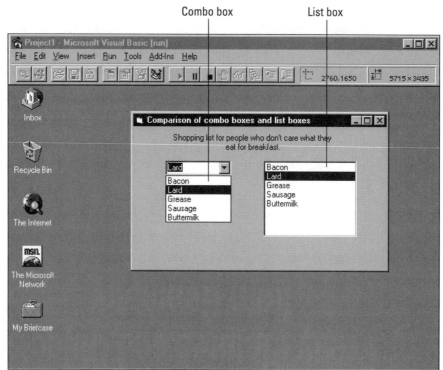

Figure 6-3:
Comparison
of a list box
to a combo
box.

Creating a List Box

List boxes are like fast food menus. You can only choose what's on the menu because the teenagers working there don't know how to handle special requests. Combo boxes are like fancy restaurants where you have a choice of ordering off the menu or saying, "I know this is a vegetarian restaurant, but I'd like the cook to grill me a steak anyway."

To create a list box, follow these steps:

1. Click the List box icon in the Visual Basic Toolbox.

2. Move the mouse to the place on the form where you want to draw the list box.

3. Hold the left mouse button and draw the list box. Visual Basic displays one list box with a dull caption such as List3.

4. Repeat steps 1 through 3 until you've drawn all the list boxes you need.

To create a combo box, follow these steps:

1. Click the Combo box icon in the Visual Basic Toolbox.

2. Move the mouse to the place on the form where you want to draw the combo box.

3. Hold the left mouse button and draw the combo box. Visual Basic displays one combo box with a dull caption such as `Combo1`.

4. Repeat steps 1 through 3 until you've drawn all the combo boxes you need.

Combo Box Styles

A combo box lets you type a choice or select one from the displayed list. For added variety, three styles of combo boxes are available (as shown in Figure 6-4):

- ✔ Drop-down combo box (Style 0 — the default)
- ✔ Simple combo box (Style 1)
- ✔ Drop-down list box (Style 2)

Test your newfound knowledge

1. What is the main difference between a check box and a radio button?

   a. You can choose one or more check boxes but only one radio button.

   b. Radio buttons tune in to your favorite radio station, but check boxes are places where you save canceled checks.

   c. I don't know. Aren't you supposed to be the teacher with all the answers?

   d. Everything is one, man. Like, it's all in your point of view.

2. What is the major difference between a list box and a combo box?

   a. A combo box gives you a choice of typing an item or choosing one from a displayed list. A list box forces you to choose an item from a displayed list.

   b. A list box is spelled L-I-S-T, but a combo box is spelled C-O-M-B-O.

   c. Combo boxes are cooler than list boxes because a combo box tends to be more confusing to the average user.

   d. No difference. In fact, two out of three French chefs think they both taste exactly like butter.

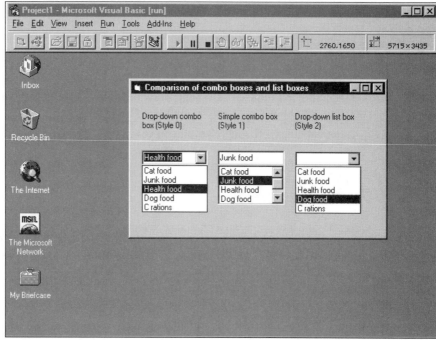

Figure 6-4:
Three
combo box
styles.

The *drop-down combo box* lets users type an item. If users have no idea what to type, they can click the arrow to the right of the combo box, and the combo box politely displays a list of possible choices. Visual Basic always creates this type of combo box unless you change its Style property.

The *simple combo box* always displays the list on the screen but also gives users the choice of typing an item.

The *drop-down list box* is actually a list box and always displays a range of choices, but you can't type anything of your own.

At this point, you may be asking, "Wait a minute. Why would I want to create a combo box and then turn it into a stupid list box?" Unlike ordinary list boxes, a drop-down list box doesn't display its list on the screen until the user clicks the arrow to the right of the box. This type of list box is useful when you need to conserve screen space.

To define the style for a combo box, follow these steps:

1. Click the combo box that you want to change. (This assumes that you've already created the box.)

2. Open the Properties window by pressing F4 or by selecting Properties from the View menu.

3. Click the Style property.

4. Click the arrow in the settings box to display your list of choices. (Hey, what do you know? This is an example of a drop-down combo box!)

5. Click the combo box style you want.

Adding Items to List Boxes and Combo Boxes

After you've created your list box or combo box, you have to fill it up with items. (Otherwise, there's no real point in creating a list box or combo box, now is there?) Alas, the only way you can add items to a list box or combo box is by using BASIC code.

The secret BASIC command to add an item to a list is AddItem. So if you want to add the item "Pick me" to a list box named lstCommands, here is the magic BASIC code that does it:

```
lstCommands.AddItem "Pick me"
```

You can add items to a list box or combo box any time your program is running, but the most common time is when the program first begins.

To add items to a list when your program begins, follow these steps:

1. Click the form of your program that Visual Basic will load and display first. (If you don't know which form this is, go back to Chapter 5 and read the section "Which Form Will Visual Basic Display First?")

2. Open the Code window by pressing F7 or by selecting Code from the View menu. Visual Basic politely displays the following procedure in the Code window:

```
Private Sub Form_Load()
End Sub
```

3. For each item you want to display in a list box or combo box, use the AddItem secret command. For example, if you had a list box named lstToDo and a combo box named cboHideIn, the Sub Form_Load() procedure might look like this:

```
Private Sub Form_Load()
  lstToDo.AddItem "Call stock broker"
  lstToDo.AddItem "Make airline reservations"
  lstToDo.AddItem "Act normally until noon"
  lstToDo.AddItem "Steal $250,000"
  lstToDo.AddItem "Fake headache"
  lstToDo.AddItem "Leave work early"
  lstToDo.AddItem "Go to airport"
  cboHideIn.AddItem "Acapulco"
  cboHideIn.AddItem "Rio de Janeiro"
  cboHideIn.AddItem "Paris"
  cboHideIn.AddItem "Tokyo"
  cboHideIn.AddItem "New York"
  cboHideIn.AddItem "Bangkok"
End Sub
```

This procedure adds these items to the lstToDo list box and to the
cboHideIn combo box whenever the first form of your program loads. See
Figure 6-4 for an example of the end product.

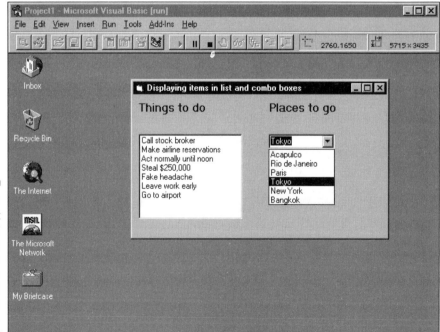

Figure 6-5:
What
lstToDo and
cboHideIn
look like
after the
Form_Load
procedure
runs.

Highlighting default items

The purpose of list boxes and combo boxes is to provide users with choices. To make choosing items even more mindless and thus more efficient from the user's point of view, combo boxes can display default items. (With list boxes, the first item is the default item.) A *default item* is the item that the computer assumes the user wants unless instructed otherwise. (It doesn't really make much sense for a default item to be the least likely choice.)

To create a default item for a combo box, follow these steps:

1. Click the combo box for which you want to assign a default item.

2. Open the Properties window by pressing F4 or by selecting Properties from the View menu.

3. Click the Text property.

4. Type the item that you want to appear as the default item in this combo box.

When a user clicks the combo box, the default item is highlighted, as shown in Figure 6-6. If you don't define a default item, Visual Basic uses the combo box's generic name (Combo1, Combo2, and so on). Because this looks very ugly and amateurish, you should always define a default item for your combo boxes.

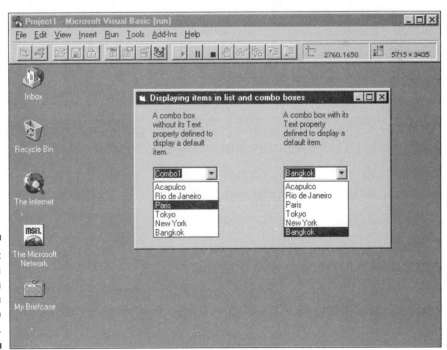

Figure 6-6: What a default item looks like in a combo box.

Sorting items in a list box or combo box

The order that you add items to a list box or combo box is the order that the items appear. For a little variety, Visual Basic lets you sort items in two ways:

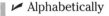

- ✔ Alphabetically
- ✔ Any way you want

When Visual Basic sorts a list alphabetically, it does so regardless of whether items are capitalized. For example, Visual Basic considers "Your Momma" and "YOUR MOMMA" to be identical.

To sort items in a list box or combo box alphabetically, follow these steps:

1. Click the list box or combo box in which you want to display items alphabetically.

2. Open the Properties window by pressing F4 or by selecting Properties from the View menu.

3. Click the Sorted property and set it to True.

Visual Basic always sorts items with the *A*'s on top and the *Z*'s at the bottom. There's no way to sort items in descending order, with the *Z*'s on top and the *A*'s at the bottom (unless, of course, you flip your monitor upside down).

If alphabetic sorting isn't what you want, you have to sort items one-by-one yourself. Visual Basic assigns an index number (which is just an ordinary number like 1 or 3) to each item in a list.

The first item in a list is assigned an index number of 0, the second item is assigned an index number of 1, the third item is assigned an index number of 2, and so on (see Figure 6-7). If you've ever been in a European elevator where the ground floor is labeled 1, the first floor is labeled 2, and the second floor is labeled 3, you'll recognize the confusing way that Visual Basic assigns index numbers.

To put an item at the top of a list, you still have to use the magic AddItem BASIC command in this way:

```
cboHideIn.AddItem "Harare", 0
```

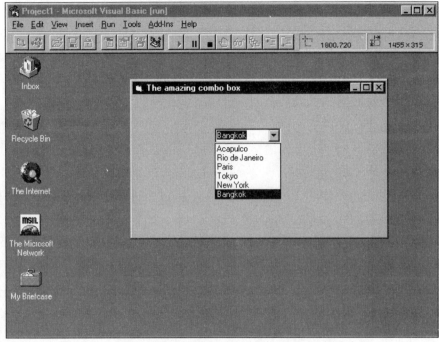

Figure 6-7:
Acapulco
has an index
number of 0,
Rio de
Janeiro has
an index
number of 1,
and so on up
to Bangkok,
which has
an index
number of 5.

If you omit the index number, Visual Basic adds items to a list in one of two ways:

  ✔ If the Sorted property of the list box or combo box is False, the item goes
    to the bottom of the list.

  ✔ If the Sorted property of the list box or combo box is True, the item goes in
    its correct alphabetic order.

Figure 6-8 shows how "Harare" is placed in alphabetical order in the sorted list
and is placed at the end in the unsorted list.

If you set the Sorted property of a list box or combo box to True *and* add items
using index numbers, Visual Basic adds the item according to the index number
and will not sort the newly added items alphabetically.

Sorted property is False

Sorted property is True

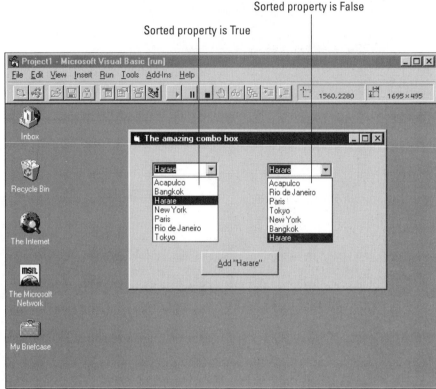

Figure 6-8:
Visual
Basic's
placement
of a new
item in a
sorted list
and an
unsorted
list.

Removing items from a list box or combo box

Adding items and sorting them may make your lists look nice, but sometimes it's more fun to wipe out an item to satisfy that destructive urge that everyone experiences once in a while.

Visual Basic gives you two ways to remove an item from a list:

   ✔ Use the RemoveItem BASIC command to remove items one at a time.

   ✔ Use the Clear BASIC command to wipe out an entire list at once.

To use the RemoveItem BASIC command, you have to know the index number of the item you want to remove. For example, to remove the item with an index number of 5 that's located in a list box named lstToDo, use the following BASIC command:

```
lstToDo.RemoveItem 5
```

To use the `Clear` BASIC command to wipe out an entire list in a single blow, you need the name of the list box or combo box that contains the list you want to kill. To wipe out the entire contents of a combo box named `cboHideIn`, use the following BASIC command:

```
cboHideIn.Clear
```

Before using the `Clear` BASIC command, make sure that you really want to wipe out an entire list.

Multiple Column List Boxes

For aesthetic purposes, or just because you're bored and want to goof around, you can display multiple columns in a list box.

Visual Basic provides three types of multiple columns:

- ✔ *Value 0* — A single column list with vertical scrolling (the default appearance of list boxes)
- ✔ *Value 1* — A single column list with horizontal scrolling (but no vertical scrolling)
- ✔ *Value any number greater than 1* — A multiple column list of two or more columns with horizontal scrolling (but no vertical scrolling)

These styles are illustrated in Figure 6-9.

To change the way a list box displays items in columns, follow these steps:

1. Click the list box that you want to modify.

2. Open the Properties window by pressing F4 or by selecting Properties from the <u>V</u>iew menu.

3. Click the Columns property and type **0**, **1**, or any number larger than 1.

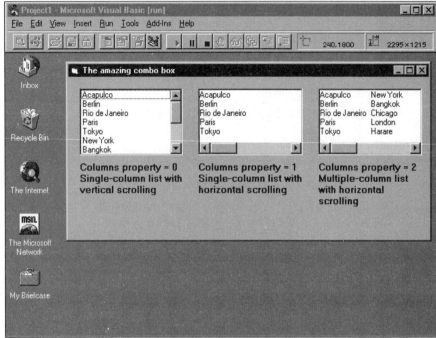

Figure 6-9:
Comparison
of three list
box styles.

Making Listed Items Look Pretty

To spice up your lists and make them look a little less like boring shopping lists, Visual Basic lets you change the font, type style, and size of your list's items.

Fonts are different ways to display text. Normally, Visual Basic uses the MS Sans Serif font, but you can use any font in your computer. (MS Sans Serif is similar to the Helvetica font, and the Visual Basic MS Serif font is similar to the Times Roman font.)

To change the font of items that appear in a list box or combo box, follow these steps:

1. Click the list box or combo box whose font you want to modify.

2. Open the Properties window by pressing F4 or by selecting Properties from the View menu.

3. Click the Font property and click the ellipsis (. . .) that appears in the settings box. Visual Basic displays a font dialog box.

4. Click the font you want and click OK. Visual Basic immediately changes the font in the list box or combo box.

Be careful when you use fonts. Novices often get carried away and use so many bizarre fonts that all semblance of normality is lost. Unless you have a really good reason to use different fonts, let Visual Basic use its default font of MS Sans Serif.

You can also change the size of your items, making them smaller or larger. However, the larger the type size is, the larger your list box or combo box must be to show the entire item at once.

For example, if you choose the MS Sans Serif font, Visual Basic gives you the following font sizes to choose from:

- ✔ 8
- ✔ 10
- ✔ 12
- ✔ 14
- ✔ 18
- ✔ 24

The larger the font size, the more the items in your list boxes and combo boxes stand out. It's usually best to use one size for all your list boxes or combo boxes to avoid confusing the user any more than you have to.

To define the font size, follow these steps:

1. Click the list box or combo box whose font size you want to modify.

2. Open the Properties window by pressing F4 or by selecting Properties from the View menu.

3. Click the Font property and click the ellipsis (. . .) that appears in the settings box. Visual Basic displays a font dialog box.

4. Click the font size you want and click OK. Visual Basic immediately changes the font size of the list box or combo box.

Changing the font and size of items can be fun, and Visual Basic also gives you options for changing the appearance of your captions. For example, if you use the MS Sans Serif font, you can choose to display fonts in the following font styles:

- ✔ Regular
- ✔ **Bold**
- ✔ *Italic*

> ✔ ***Bold Italic***
> ✔ ~~Strikeout~~
> ✔ <u>Underline</u>

To set any one or more of these font styles, follow these steps:

1. Click the list box or combo box whose fonts you want to modify.

2. Open the Properties window by pressing F4 or by selecting Properties from the <u>V</u>iew menu.

3. Click the Font property and click the ellipsis (. . .) that appears in the settings box. Visual Basic displays a font dialog box.

4. Click the font style you want and click OK. Visual Basic immediately changes the font style of the list box or combo box.

The more attractive you make your list boxes and combo boxes, the more likely the user will at least notice it (if not use it). Just remember that you should make your program easy to use, not a work of art. If you want to get creative, take up finger painting. If you want to create useful programs and make millions of dollars, make your programs easy, fun, and simple to use.

The 5th Wave   By Rich Tennant

"THERE! THERE! I TELL YOU IT JUST MOVED AGAIN!"

Chapter 7

Text Boxes for Typing and Showing Words

In This Chapter

▶ Creating text boxes

▶ Filling text boxes and hiding passwords

▶ Using different fonts, sizes, type styles, and colors

Despite the growing acceptance of icons and graphical user interfaces, not all choices can be offered through command buttons, radio buttons, or combo boxes. Sometimes your program may need to display a word, sentence, paragraph, or novel on the screen. And sometimes the user may want to type in a good word or two, as well.

What's the solution? Combo boxes work with words or short phrases, but if your program needs to display a chunk of text or if the user needs to type in a substantial amount of information, a *text box* can make your job a whole lot easier.

Text boxes have two purposes in life:

✔ To show text on the screen

✔ To let the user type text

Creating a Text Box

Text boxes are like miniature word processors but lack the fancy features that make WordPerfect and Microsoft Word so expensive, complicated, and easy to use. Text boxes display text with only one font, one size, and one type style. So even if you like lots of different fonts, you can't have them in your text box.

When a user types text in a text box, the following Windows keys and key combinations work:

- ✔ Delete erases the character to the right of the cursor.
- ✔ Backspace erases the character to the left of the cursor.
- ✔ Shift+arrow highlights a block of text.
- ✔ Ctrl+← moves the cursor one word to the left.
- ✔ Ctrl+→ moves the cursor one word to the right.
- ✔ Home moves the cursor to the beginning of the line.
- ✔ End moves the cursor to the end of the line.
- ✔ F11 and F12 don't do anything at all and are about as useful as wisdom teeth.

To create a text box, follow these steps:

1. Click the Text box icon in the Visual Basic Toolbox.
2. On the form, move the mouse to where you want to draw the text box.
3. Hold the left mouse button and draw the text box. Visual Basic displays your text box with a dull caption, such as Text3.
4. Repeat steps 1 through 3 until you've drawn all the text boxes you need or until you decide to take up another hobby besides programming.

Putting pretty borders around text boxes

Normally, Visual Basic displays a single line around a text box, defining the boundaries of the text box. If for some odd reason you like to keep your users guessing where a text box is, you can remove this border. Figure 7-1 gives examples of a text box with and without a border.

To change the borders around a text box, follow these steps:

1. Click the text box whose border you want to change.
2. Open the Properties window by pressing F4 or by selecting Properties from the View menu.
3. Click the BorderStyle property and choose one of the following:

   0 – None
   1 – Fixed Single

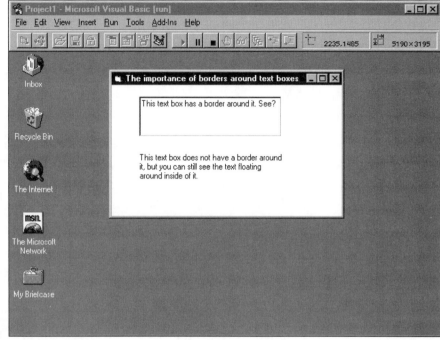

Figure 7-1:
Comparison
of a
bordered
text box and
an
unbordered
text box.

Displaying words in text boxes

After you've created your text box, it's only natural to put some text in it. By default, Visual Basic displays the text box's name in the text box, just to have something to display.

Changing the text in a text box does not affect the Name property of the box, so if you want your text box to display something more exciting than, say, Text3, you have to change the Text property (see Figure 7-2).

The Text property can contain anything from a blank line (in which case your text box appears empty on the screen), to ordinary text, to a mass of incomprehensible garbage that resembles a typical computer manual.

To change the Text property of a text box, follow these steps:

1. Click the text box whose Text property you want to modify.

2. Open the Properties window by pressing F4 or by selecting Properties from the View menu.

3. Click the Text property.

4. Type whatever text you want displayed initially in the text box.

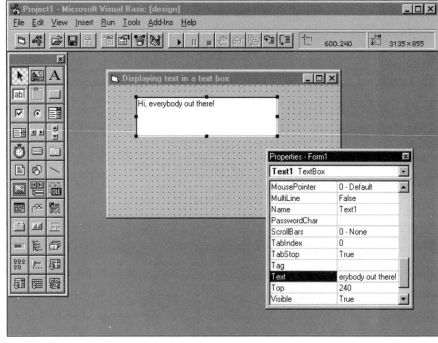

Displaying text in a text box

Hi, everybody out there!

Properties - Form1

Text1 TextBox

MousePointer	0 - Default
MultiLine	False
Name	Text1
PasswordChar	
ScrollBars	0 - None
TabIndex	0
TabStop	True
Tag	
Text	erybody out there!
Top	240
Visible	True

Figure 7-2:
How the contents of the Text property appear inside a text box.

Aligning text in a text box

To make a text box look nice and organized, Visual Basic can align the text as left-justified, right-justified, or centered, as shown in Figure 7-3.

To align text in a text box, follow these steps:

1. Click the text box whose text you want to align.

2. Open the Properties window by pressing F4 or by selecting Properties from the View menu.

3. Click the MultiLine property and set its value to True. (If the MultiLine property is set to False, Visual Basic will ignore any changes you make to the Alignment property.)

4. Click the Alignment property.

5. Choose one of the following:

   0 – Left Justify
   1 – Right Justify
   2 – Center

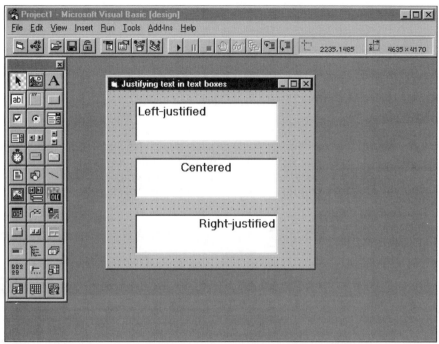

Figure 7-3:
Comparison
of left, right,
and center
justification.

Word-wrapping text boxes

Most people don't know that computer programmers invented *word wrapping* for word processors. Word processors essentially made it easy for nonwriters to write and call it "literature." Word wrapping made it easy for nontypists to type without thinking.

As word processors became more prevalent, musicians later invented word *rapping* for use in music. Rap music essentially made it easy for nonmusicians to make noise and call it "music." Word rapping made it easy for nonsingers to sing without thinking.

In the world of Visual Basic, word wrapping is used in text boxes. Besides just displaying text, text boxes also have the magical capability to let users type in words. These words can be as simple as a four-letter word or as complicated as a string of four-letter words arranged in a grammatically correct sentence and directed at an English teacher.

By default, a text box is pretty stupid at handling text. When someone types text, the text box cheerfully displays the text as one huge line that goes scrolling out of sight. To make a text box wrap words like a real word processor, you have to set the text box's MultiLine property to True.

To set the MultiLine property to True for a text box, follow these steps:

1. Click the text box in which you want to wrap words.

2. Open the Properties window by pressing F4 or by selecting Properties from the View menu.

3. Click the MultiLine property and set it to True.

When a text box has its MultiLine property set to True, the text box happily word-wraps text within the boundaries of the box (see Figure 7-4). If you change the width of a text box in the middle of your program, the text box automatically word-wraps the text within the new size. (Wow! This is utterly amazing. Quick! Somebody call *Ripley's Believe It or Not!*)

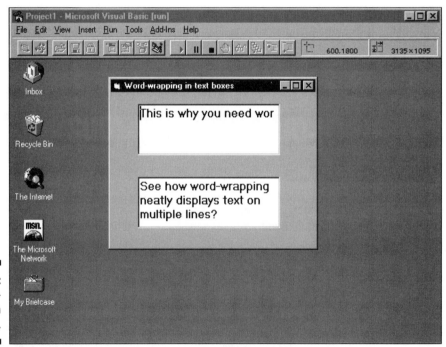

Figure 7-4: Word-wrapping in text boxes.

Adding horizontal and vertical scroll bars in text boxes

Word wrapping is a fine way to spend a lazy summer afternoon. However, if a text box isn't tall enough, word wrapping cheerfully buries the text out of sight. For chunks of text too big to fit inside a text box, Visual Basic offers *horizontal scroll bars* and *vertical scroll bars* (see Figure 7-5).

Horizontal scroll bar   Vertical scroll bar

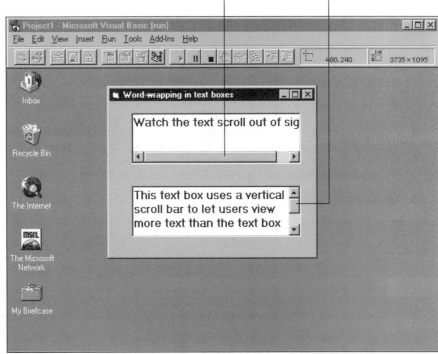

Figure 7-5:
Horizontal
and vertical
scroll bars
in text
boxes.

Be careful! Adding a horizontal scroll bar will turn off word wrapping. When a text box uses horizontal scroll bars, the only way the user can type on the next line is to press Enter.

Adding a vertical scroll bar lets users type and display more text than the text box can display. Users can also press PgUp and PgDn to display text in a text box that uses vertical scroll bars.

To add scroll bars to a text box, follow these steps:

1. Click the text box in which you want to use scroll bars.

2. Open the Properties window by pressing F4 or by selecting Properties from the View menu.

3. Click the ScrollBars property and choose one of the following:

   0 – None
   1 – Horizontal
   2 – Vertical
   3 – Both

Vertical and horizontal scroll bars work only if you've set the text box's MultiLine property to True. (There's really no point in having scroll bars if you can't have more than one line.)

Making a Password Text Box

In case you work for the CIA, FBI, NSA, DIA, or any other organization with lots of money, a penchant for secrecy, and a three-letter acronym, Visual Basic lets you create special *password text boxes*. Instead of displaying the character you're typing, password text boxes display another character, such as an asterisk (*), to mask your text. Figure 7-6 shows how the password "Secret" appears as only asterisks in the "How to break into the Pentagon" text box.

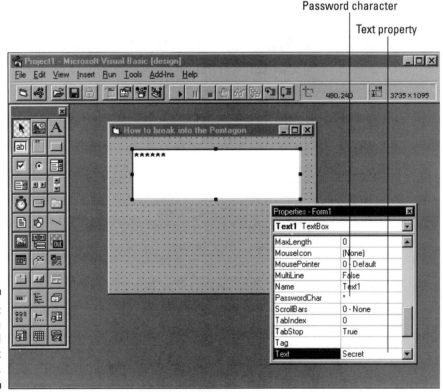

Password character

Text property

Figure 7-6:
How a password text box works.

Always set the MultiLine property of a password text box to False. Otherwise, the password text box won't mask typed characters. This is Visual Basic's way of saying that passwords shouldn't be so long that they require two or more lines to write. Obviously, the longer the password, the more likely it is that a user won't be able to remember it.

To define the character that a text box will display to mask the actual text, follow these steps:

1. Click the text box that you want to be your password text box.

2. Open the Properties window by pressing F4 or by selecting Properties from the View menu.

3. Click the MultiLine property and set it to False.

4. Click the PasswordChar property and type the masking character, such as an asterisk. The masking character can be only one character.

Limiting the Length of Text

To prevent people from getting too wordy, you can set the maximum length of text for a text box. This prevents people from typing useless rambling discourses, such as essays on what they did last summer.

To define the maximum number of characters that a text box will accept from the user, change the MaxLength property. If the user tries to type any characters beyond the MaxLength limit, Visual Basic will beep and accept no more.

(Alas, Visual Basic doesn't have a minimum length property. For ordinary text boxes, this won't be a problem; but if you're trying to create a secure password text box, at least one bozo user is bound to choose a one-letter password that some hacker will easily guess.)

To define the maximum length of characters that a text box will accept, follow these steps:

1. Click the text box whose maximum character length you want to define.

2. Open the Properties window by pressing F4 or by selecting Properties from the View menu.

3. Click the MaxLength property.

4. Type any number greater than zero. A value of zero means that the only text limit is the amount of memory your computer has.

Test your newfound knowledge

1. Give two uses for text boxes.

   a. To store letters from your Scrabble game and to contain words that might win you a million dollars on Wheel of Fortune.

   b. To display text on-screen and to let users type text into a program.

   c. To store all the computer books you buy but never read and to make cardboard forts that your children can hide in.

   d. To use as a litter box and to give your cat something to read.

2. If a text box had its PasswordChar property set to * (asterisk) and its MaxLength property set to 10, what would happen?

   a. I'd have to flip back through the pages of this book to find the answer that I should already know.

   b. I'm not sure, but it must be important or else this question wouldn't be listed here.

   c. This would define the secret password to break into the Pentagon's computers.

   d. The text box would accept a maximum of 10 characters and display an asterisk (*) in place of an actual typed character.

Fonts, Sizes, and Type Styles

Visual Basic displays a persistent lack of imagination by showing text in the same boring font. For variety, and to keep users from falling asleep in front of their computers, you can spice up your text with fonts.

Unfortunately, text boxes can display only one type of font. When choosing a font for your text box, choose one that's easy on the eyes, or your user's head may explode from severe eye strain. Visual Basic normally uses the MS Sans Serif font, but you can use any font in your computer. (MS Sans Serif is similar to the Helvetica font, and the Visual Basic MS Serif font is similar to the Times Roman font.)

To change the font that appears in a text box, follow these steps:

1. Click the text box whose font you want to modify.

2. Open the Properties window by pressing F4 or by selecting Properties from the View menu.

3. Click the Font property and click the ellipsis (. . .) that appears in the settings box. Visual Basic displays a font dialog box.

4. Click the font you want and click OK. Visual Basic immediately changes the font in the list box or combo box.

Be careful when using fonts. Beginners often get carried away and choose bizarre fonts that confuse more than they clarify. Unless you have a really good reason to use a different font, let Visual Basic use its default font, MS Sans Serif.

You can also change the size of your text, making it smaller or larger. However, the larger the type size, the larger your text box must be to show the entire text.

For example, if you chose the MS Sans Serif font, Visual Basic lets you choose from the following font sizes:

- 8
- 10
- 12
- 14
- 18
- 24

The larger the font size, the less text your text box can display. It's usually best to use one size for all your text boxes to avoid confusing the user any more than you have to.

To define the font size, follow these steps:

1. Click the text box whose font size you want to modify.

2. Open the Properties window by pressing F4 or by selecting Properties from the View menu.

3. Click the Font property and click the ellipsis (. . .) that appears in the settings box. Visual Basic displays a font dialog box.

4. Click the font size you want, then click OK. Visual Basic immediately changes the font size of the text displayed in the text box.

Changing the font and size of items can be fun, and Visual Basic also gives you options for changing the appearance of your captions. For example, if you use the MS Sans Serif font, you can choose to display fonts in the following ways:

- Regular
- **Bold**
- *Italic*
- ***Bold Italic***
- ~~Strikeout~~
- <u>Underline</u>

To set one or more of these font styles, follow these steps:

1. Click the text box whose font you want to modify.

2. Open the Properties window by pressing F4 or by selecting Properties from the View menu.

3. Click the Font property and click the ellipsis (. . .) that appears in the settings box. Visual Basic displays a font dialog box.

4. Click the font style you want and click OK. Visual Basic immediately changes the font style of the list box or combo box.

Coloring Text Boxes

If you loved writing in different colors with crayons when you were a kid, you'll love this aspect of Visual Basic.

Normally, Visual Basic harks back to the days of the fifties by displaying text in black and white. For more creativity, you can change the *foreground* and *background* colors of your text (see Figure 7-7).

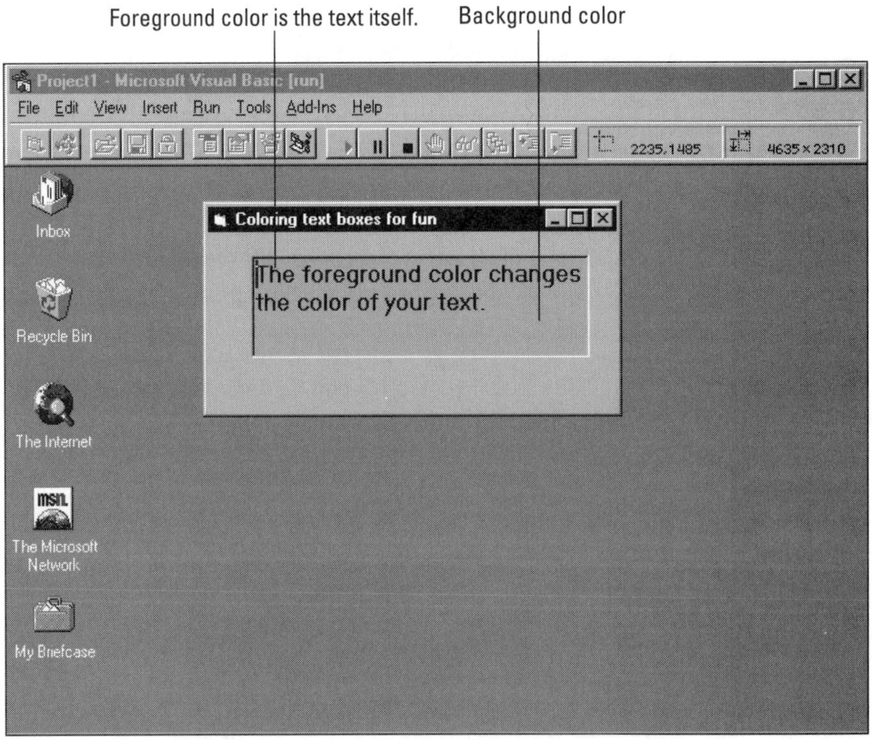

Foreground color is the text itself.   Background color

Figure 7-7:
Background
and
foreground
colors of a
text box.

The color inside the text box (background color) is defined by the BackColor property. The color of the text itself (foreground color) is defined by the ForeColor property.

To change the background or foreground color of a text box, follow these steps:

1. Click the text box whose background or foreground color you want to change.

2. Open the Properties window by pressing F4 or by selecting Properties from the View menu.

3. Click the BackColor or ForeColor property in the Property window. Visual Basic displays the current color in a useless series of letters and numbers.

4. Click the ellipsis (. . .) to the right of the current color value. Visual Basic displays a color palette.

5. Click the color you want. Visual Basic instantly obeys.

Text boxes give you the most flexibility because you can display instructions in a text box and the user can type a reply using ordinary words. Perhaps if you use enough text boxes in your program, you can help increase literacy among our young children today.

Chapter 8

Scroll Bars and Labels

· ·

· ·

*N*ot all choices in life can be divided into neat categories like check boxes, radio buttons, or list boxes. Sometimes users may need to make choices that require a wide range of gradual adjustments.

Think of adjusting the volume on a stereo. If the only three choices you had were soft, medium, and loud, you wouldn't be able to adjust the volume to your taste. That's why most stereos let you turn a knob or press a button that gradually adjusts the volume higher or lower.

For minute measurements, or for moving through long lists of information, use *scroll bars*. Although text boxes, forms, and list boxes have built-in scroll bars, you can create separate scroll bars on your own. The parts of a scroll bar are labeled in Figure 8-1.

Creating Scroll Bars

Visual Basic lets you create two types of scroll bars: horizontal scroll bars and vertical scroll bars. *Horizontal scroll bars* point left and right, just like the fast forward and rewind buttons on your VCR or tape player. *Vertical scroll bars* point up and down, just like the volume control on some stereos.

Scroll box   Scroll bar shaft

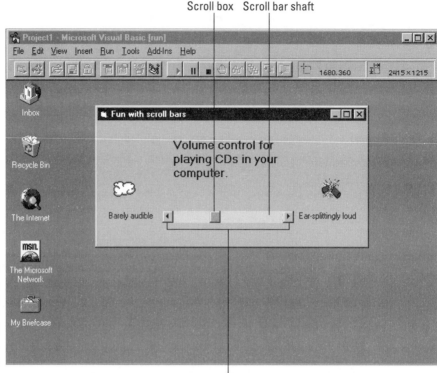

Figure 8-1:
The parts of
a scroll bar
in a real
program.

Scroll arrows

To create a scroll bar, follow these steps:

1. Click the Horizontal or Vertical scroll bar icon in the Visual Basic Toolbox.

2. Move the mouse cursor on the form to where you want to draw the scroll bar.

3. Hold down the left mouse button and move it to draw the scroll bar. Release the left mouse button.

4. Repeat steps 1 through 3 until you've drawn all the scroll bars you feel like making.

Scroll bar maximum and minimum values

Scroll bars are actually graphical representations of numeric values. The value of a scroll bar can range from –32,768 to 32,767. These numerical values can represent anything you want, such as measurements or quantities.

By default, Visual Basic sets the maximum value to 32,767 and the minimum value to 0.

On horizontal scroll bars, the maximum value is represented when the scroll box is at the rightmost position on the scroll bar. The minimum value is represented when the scroll box is at the leftmost position on the scroll bar.

On vertical scroll bars, the maximum value is represented when the scroll box is at the bottommost position on the scroll bar. The minimum value is represented when the scroll box is at the topmost position on the scroll bar.

Obviously, the default values of 32,767 and 0 may be too extreme for most programs. (How many programs do you know that offer users 32,767 choices?) To define a smaller range of values, you have to change the scroll bar's Max and Min settings.

To change the Max and Min settings for a scroll bar, follow these steps:

1. Click the scroll bar whose Max and Min values you want to change.

2. Open the Properties window by pressing F4 or by selecting Properties from the View menu.

3. Click the Max property and type a new value.

4. Click the Min property and type a new value.

If the Min value is larger than the Max value, the scroll bar acts topsy-turvy. In this case, the scroll bar represents the maximum value at the leftmost or topmost position and the minimum value at the rightmost or bottommost position.

Where does the scroll box appear in my scroll bars?

By default, Visual Basic assigns scroll bars a value of 0. This means that if your Max and Min values are positive, the scroll box always appears in the topmost position in a vertical scroll bar and the leftmost position in a horizontal scroll bar (see Figure 8-2).

Normally, having the scroll box represent the minimum value of the scroll bar won't cause any problems. However, if you want your scroll bars to display a default value of something other than the minimum value, you have to change the scroll bar's value.

Minimum value   (default position)

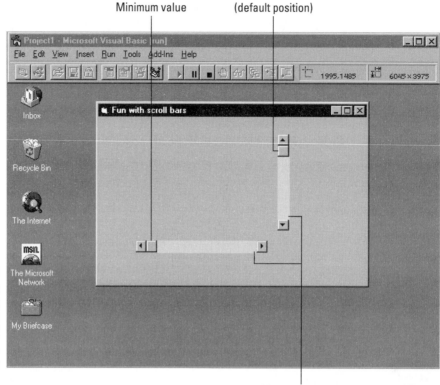

Figure 8-2:
Default
position of
the scroll
boxes.

Maximum value

To change the scroll bar's value, follow these steps:

1. Click the scroll bar whose value you want to change.

2. Open the Properties window by pressing F4 or by selecting Properties from the View menu.

3. Click the Value property and type a new value. Visual Basic dutifully changes the scroll bar's value while you watch.

Moving the scroll box

The scroll box represents the current value of the scroll bar. To move the scroll box, users can do any of the following:

🖉 Drag the scroll box within the scroll bar

🖉 Click the scroll arrows at each end of the scroll bar

🖉 Click in the area between the scroll box and each scroll arrow

Each time the user clicks the scroll arrows, the scroll box moves a certain distance. By default, this distance is 1. Therefore, if your Min value is 0 and your Max value is 12, you have to click the scroll arrow 12 times to move the scroll box from one end of the scroll bar to the other.

To modify the distance the scroll box moves when the user clicks a scroll arrow, follow these steps:

1. Click the scroll bar that you want to modify.

2. Open the Properties window by pressing F4 or by selecting Properties from the View menu.

3. Click the SmallChange property and type a new value.

Likewise, each time the user clicks the scroll bar shaft (in the area between the scroll box and the scroll area), the scroll box moves a certain distance. By default, this distance is 1, which means that if the Min value is 0 and the Max value is 5, you have to click five times to move the scroll box from one end of the scroll bar to the other.

To modify the distance the scroll box moves when the user clicks in the scroll shaft, follow these steps:

1. Click the scroll bar that you want to modify.

2. Open the Properties window by pressing F4 or by selecting Properties from the View menu.

3. Click the LargeChange property and type a new value.

The values for LargeChange and SmallChange can vary between 1 and 32,767. The smaller the value, the smaller the distance the scroll box moves. The larger the value, the larger the distance the scroll box moves.

Here's some information you might never use. You can set LargeChange or SmallChange to values greater than the Max value. This just means that when the user clicks your scroll bar, the scroll box immediately jumps to one end of the scroll bar.

Test your newfound knowledge

1. When would you use a scroll bar?

   a. When you want to give the illusion of complexity.

   b. When the user needs to choose a range of values.

   c. When you need to rewrap toilet paper that your cat unrolled onto the floor.

   d. When nothing else seems to work, and you've run out of ideas on how to make your program easier to use.

2. What are the three ways to move the scroll box within a scroll bar?

   a. Press the arrow keys, flip the mouse upside down, or hit the computer with a hammer.

   b. Telekinesis, verbal threats, or pushing the scroll box with your finger.

   c. It never moves. This is a trick question, right?

   d. Drag the scroll box with the mouse, click the scroll arrows, or click the scroll bar shaft inside the scroll bar.

Creating Labels

For pure decoration, you can sprinkle labels on any of your Visual Basic forms. Labels simply identify the objects on your form.

In real life, you see labels all the time, such as the label MEN or WOMEN on a restroom door, FIRE EXTINGUISHER over a fire extinguisher in a public building, or POWER next to your monitor's on and off button. The labels simply call your attention to something you may otherwise overlook.

Both text boxes (see Chapter 7) and labels can display text on-screen. The main difference is that a user can modify the text inside a text box but can't modify the text in a label.

(*Psst*, although users can't modify the text in a label, BASIC code can modify a label's text. In this way, your labels can display changing messages to the user, such as "Sorry, that option isn't available at this time. Now printing page 2 of 9" or "What are you, stupid or something?" Some everyday examples are shown in Figure 8-3.)

A picture   A label

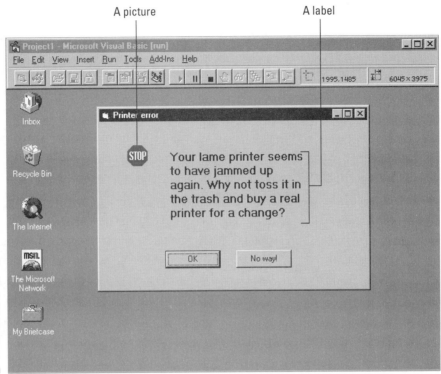

Figure 8-3:
Real-life
examples of
labels and
pictures in
programs.

To create a label, follow these steps:

1. Click the Label icon in the Visual Basic Toolbox (see Figure 8-4).

2. Move the mouse on the form to where you want to draw the label.

3. Hold the left mouse button and draw the label. Visual Basic displays a label with a dull caption such as Label3.

4. Repeat steps 1 through 3 until you've drawn all the labels you need or until you feel like going to get a snack in the kitchen.

Label icon

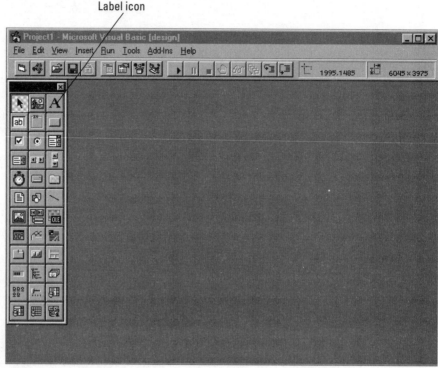

Figure 8-4:
The Label
icon on the
Visual Basic
toolbox.

Putting pretty borders around labels

Normally, labels don't have boundaries. But if you want to see an outline
around your label, you can. Visual Basic gives you two choices: a fixed single
line or nothing at all (see Figure 8-5). If this seems like a choice to you, a two-
party political system probably seems like a democracy, too.

To change the borders around a label, follow these steps:

1. Click the label whose border you want to change.

2. Open the Properties window by pressing F4 or by selecting Properties
   from the View menu.

3. Click the BorderStyle property and choose one of the following:

   0 – None
   1 – Fixed Single

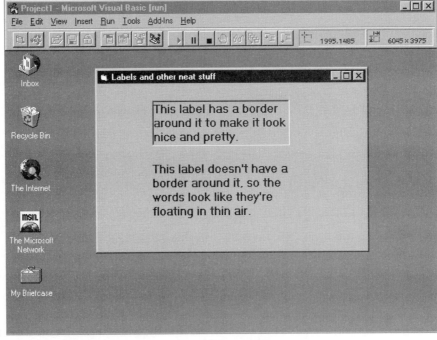

Figure 8-5:
Comparison
of a
bordered
label and an
unbordered
label.

Changing the size of labels

The size of a label on the screen determines the length of the caption it can display. If a label is too small, part of the caption will be cut off.

Note that the label caption (the text displayed on the screen) doesn't change in size when you change the size of a label. To change the size of the displayed text, you have to change the Font property.

Because you may not know how much room your captions need, it can be a real pain in the neck to keep adjusting the size of your labels. Because you're using a computer, why not let the computer take care of mundane details like this?

For your convenience, Visual Basic can automatically adjust the size of a label to fit any caption you stick inside it. Such automatic adjusting labels are perfect for displaying messages whose length may vary. Nonautomatic adjusting labels, on the other hand, display their captions within their fixed boundaries. Both types of labels are shown in Figure 8-6.

An automatic adjusting label grows or shrinks horizontally to match the length of the label's caption. So if you have a really long caption, the label cheerfully expands in size and disappears off the right side of the screen. To make an automatic adjusting label word-wrap text, you have to set the label's WordWrap property to True.

This label adjusts automatically.   This label doesn't.

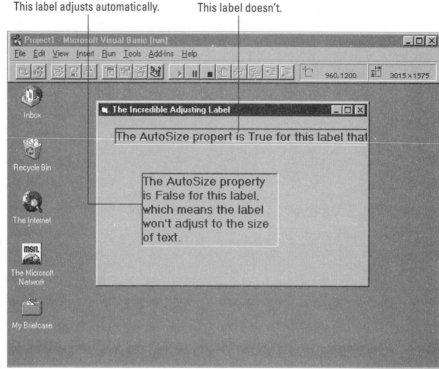

Figure 8-6:
Comparing
automatic
and
nonautomatic
adjusting
labels.

To create an automatic adjusting label, follow these steps:

1. Click the label that you want to automatically adjust to the size of its caption.

2. Open the Properties window by pressing F4 or by selecting Properties from the View menu.

3. Click the AutoSize property and set its value to True.

The advantage of automatic adjusting labels is that you can use BASIC code to give the labels captions of various sizes without ever worrying that a particular caption won't fit. The disadvantage is that you don't have control over the label's maximum size. If you're not careful, a label can get too big, grow in size, and cover other parts of your user interface.

Aligning text within a label

To make your label captions look nice and organized, Visual Basic offers three options for aligning captions, as shown in Figure 8-7:

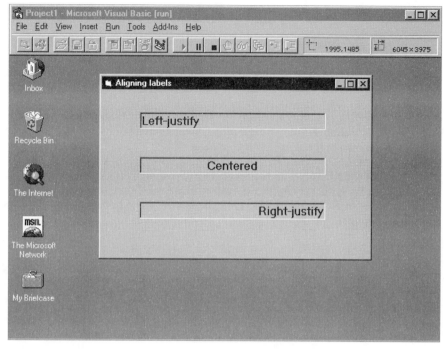

Figure 8-7:
Comparison
of left,
center, and
right
justification.

✔ Left-justify

✔ Right-justify

✔ Center

To align a caption, follow these steps:

1. Click the label whose caption you want to align.

2. Open the Properties window by pressing F4 or by selecting Properties from the View menu.

3. Click the Alignment property.

4. Choose one of the following:

   0 – Left Justify
   1 – Right Justify
   2 – Center

Word-wrapping labels

If you set a label's AutoSize property to True, it will expand horizontally as long as you keep stuffing it with text. However, if you want a label to expand vertically instead, you have to set both its AutoSize property and WordWrap property to True.

Setting both the AutoSize property and WordWrap property to False means that long captions may be cut off at the bottom if your label isn't tall enough, as shown in the first example in Figure 8-8.

Setting AutoSize to False and WordWrap to True has the same effect as setting both AutoSize and WordWrap to False, as shown in the second example in Figure 8-8. Long captions may be cut off at the bottom if your label isn't tall enough.

Setting AutoSize to True and WordWrap to False means that the label will expand horizontally to fit an entire caption. However, the label will show only one line of the caption, as shown in the third example in Figure 8-8.

Setting both the AutoSize property and WordWrap property to True means that a label will grow or shrink vertically (as shown in the last example in Figure 8-8).

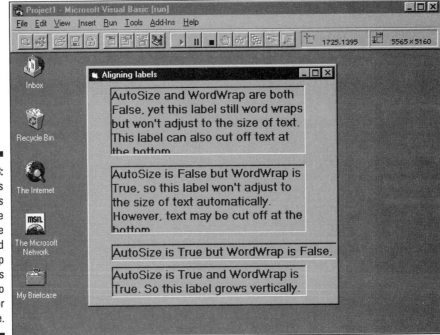

Figure 8-8: Four views of labels when the AutoSize and WordWrap properties are set to True or False.

To set the WordWrap property for a label to True, follow these steps:

1. Click the label in which you want to use word wrapping.

2. Open the Properties window by pressing F4 or by selecting Properties from the View menu.

3. Click the WordWrap property and set it to True.

When creating labels that adjust to the size of text, be careful that your labels don't accidentally "grow" over and cover up other parts of your user interface. Otherwise, you will really confuse someone trying to use your program for the first time.

Chapter 9

Pretty Pictures and Objects from Geometry

• •

In This Chapter

▶ Creating picture boxes and image boxes

▶ Making the picture boxes and image boxes fit their contents

▶ Creating geometric shapes

▶ Altering the appearance of lines, circles, and other shapes

• •

*Y*ou can sprinkle labels and pictures on any of your Visual Basic forms. Although pictures can make your forms look nice, they can also be an actual part of your program.

For example, a picture on the front of a road map showing a smiling gas station attendant with the label "Always Trust Your Car to the Man Who Wears the Star" is superfluous and decorative. However, a road map using pictures to show city highways and major side streets can be integral and necessary.

If you sprinkle plenty of labels and pictures in your user interface, your program will be easier to use and understand. After all, that's the purpose of creating a user interface in the first place.

Creating Pictures

Visual Basic provides two ways to display pictures on the screen:

✔ In a picture box

✔ In an image box

Use a *picture box* to display graphics or to group buttons together. Use an *image box* to display graphics or to create image buttons.

To create a picture box or image box, follow these steps:

1. Click the Picture box or Image box icon in the Visual Basic Toolbox.

2. Using the mouse, hold down the left mouse button on the form and drag to where you want to draw the picture box or image box.

3. Move the mouse to draw the box.

4. Repeat steps 1 through 3 until you've drawn all the picture boxes or image boxes you need.

Displaying pictures in picture boxes or image boxes

After you've created a picture box or an image box, it's only natural to put a picture in it. (Why else would you create the box?) Picture boxes and image boxes can display three types of graphics images:

✓ Bitmap files (which have BMP or DIB file extensions)

✓ Icon files (which have ICO file extensions)

✓ Metafiles (which have WMF file extensions)

Bitmap files consist of patterns of dots, or pixels. These types of files are created by paint programs such as Microsoft Paint. If you enlarge a bitmap image, the image tends to look grainy and ugly.

Icon files are special kinds of bitmap files with a maximum size of 32 pixels by 32 pixels.

Metafiles are images created by lines and geometric shapes that most people have forgotten about since high school geometry. These types of files are created by *draw* programs such as CorelDRAW.

To load a picture in a picture box or image box, follow these steps:

1. Click the picture box or image box into which you want to load a graphics file. (This assumes that you've already drawn the picture box or image box on a form.)

2. Open the Properties window by pressing F4 or by selecting Properties from the View menu.

3. Click the Picture property in the Property window.

4. Click the ellipsis (. . .) to the right of the settings box. Visual Basic displays the Load Picture dialog box, as shown in Figure 9-1.

5. Click the picture file you want. Visual Basic instantly loads the picture in the picture box or image box.

Besides loading pictures by using the Property window, you can also load and remove pictures while your program is running (during run time). To load a picture into a picture box or image box, use the LoadPicture command:

```
imgGreeting.Picture = LoadPicture("c:\graphics\martian.bmp")
```

The LoadPicture command specifies the exact drive, directory, and file to store in the Picture property of a picture box or an image box.

To remove a picture from a picture box or image box during run time, use the LoadPicture command as follows:

```
imgGreeting.Picture = LoadPicture("")
```

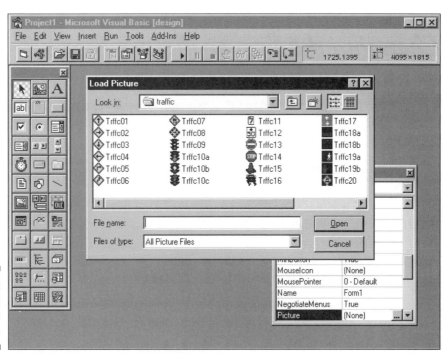

Figure 9-1:
The Load
Picture
dialog box.

This statement essentially loads a blank image into the Picture property of a picture box or image box.

Putting pretty borders around picture boxes and image boxes

To define the edge of your picture box or image box, Visual Basic can display a border. By default, neither type of box displays a border.

To change the border around a picture box or image box, follow these steps:

1. Click the picture box or image box whose border you want to change.

2. Open the Properties window by pressing F4 or by selecting Properties from the View menu.

3. Click the BorderStyle property and choose one of the following:

   0 – None
   1 – Fixed Single

Changing the Size of Picture Boxes or Image Boxes

Generally, the size of picture boxes or image boxes has no effect on the size of the graphics image that the picture box or image box displays. There are two exceptions to this:

- Metafile graphics always change size to fit within a picture box or an image box.
- If an image box's Stretch property is set to True, bitmap and icon graphics will change size to fit within the image box.

Changing the size of graphics images

Bitmap and icon graphics appear in their original size no matter what the size of the picture box or image box (unless the Stretch property is set to True). Therefore, if you create a huge picture box but load in a tiny bitmap graphics image, all you'll see is a tiny bitmap graphics image with lots of empty space around it.

Unlike bitmap or icon graphics, metafiles expand or shrink to fill an entire picture box or expand to their original size to fill an entire image box. To change the size of a metafile, just change the size of the picture box or image box holding it.

If you use a picture box, you can never (and I mean *never*) change the size of bitmap or icon graphics. If you use an image box, you can change the size of bitmap or icon graphics by changing the image box's Stretch property.

To change the size of bitmap or icon graphics in an image box, follow these steps:

1. Click the image box whose Stretch property you want to change.

2. Open the Properties window by pressing F4 or by selecting Properties from the View menu.

3. Click the Stretch property and set its value to True.

After an image box has its Stretch property set to True, you can adjust the size of bitmap or icon graphics just by changing the size of the image box. (Isn't it amazing what $2000 computers can do?)

Automatically changing the size of picture boxes

If you're too busy to bother creating and adjusting the size of your picture boxes, let Visual Basic do it automatically by setting the AutoSize property to True. Then the moment you load the bitmap or icon graphics image into a picture box, the picture box immediately shrinks or expands to fit tightly around the graphics image — just like shrink wrap around a box of floppy disks (see Figure 9-2).

To make a picture box automatically adjust its size around a graphics image, follow these steps:

1. Click the picture box whose AutoSize property you want to change.

2. Open the Properties window by pressing F4 or by selecting Properties from the View menu.

3. Click the AutoSize property and set its value to True.

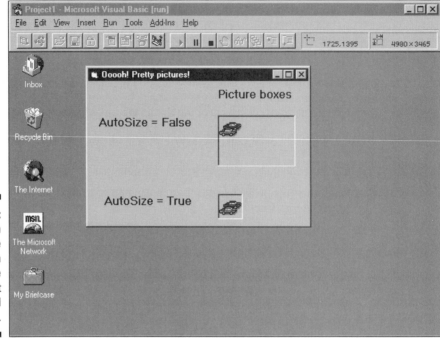

Figure 9-2:
Comparison
of picture
boxes with
the AutoSize
property set
to True and
False.

Coloring Picture Boxes

Visual Basic usually displays a plain gray background in picture boxes. If your graphics images fill up the entire picture box, the background color is irrelevant. But if the graphics image isn't big enough, the background color can be seen.

The background color is defined by the BackColor property. With a tasteful background color, you can highlight your graphics and make them more colorful.

To change the background color of a picture box, follow these steps:

1. Click the picture box whose background color you want to change.

2. Open the Properties window by pressing F4 or by selecting Properties from the View menu.

3. Click the BackColor property in the Property window. Visual Basic displays the current color in a useless series of letters and numbers.

4. Click the ellipsis (. . .) to the right of the current color value. Visual Basic displays a color palette.

5. Click the color you want. Visual Basic instantly obeys.

Test your newfound knowledge

1. Which lets you change the size of a bitmap or icon graphic: a picture box or an image box?

   a. Neither. Bitmaps and icon graphics are perfect just the way they are, and it would be blasphemous to believe that you can change anything for the better.

   b. A picture box because I don't have the slightest idea what the difference is but I'm taking a wild guess anyway.

   c. An image box, but only if you set its Stretch property to True.

   d. These questions are too hard. I need a nap.

2. What are the three types of graphics files you can load in a picture or image box?

   a. Bitmaps, icons, and metafiles.

   b. Bitmaps, graffiti, and forgeries of famous paintings.

   c. Bitmaps, centerfolds, and home videos.

   d. Bigfoot, UFOs, and grainy pictures of Elvis walking through downtown Manhattan.

Lines, Circles, and Other Nightmares from Geometry

What performs absolutely no useful function except a decorative one? If you answered, "The vice president of the United States," shame on you. The real answer is the parts of a user interface that make it look more attractive.

The prettier something looks, the friendlier people feel toward it. So if you make your user interface pretty, it's likely that more people will actually try to use it.

Visual Basic provides seven objects for adding visual makeup to your user interface, as shown in Figure 9-3. These objects are as follows:

- Lines
- Squares
- Rectangles
- Ovals
- Circles
- Rounded rectangles
- Rounded squares

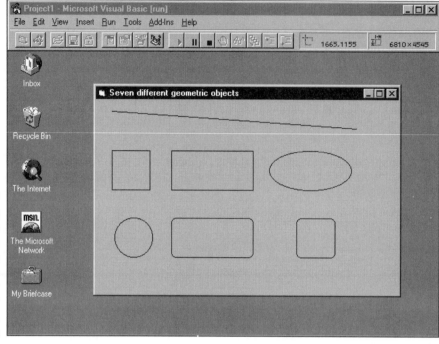

Figure 9-3:
The
geometric
objects
available to
add to your
user
interface.

Creating lines

Lines are useful for underlining or separating items on the screen.

To create a line, follow these steps:

1. Click the Line icon in the Visual Basic Toolbox.

2. On the form, move the mouse to where you want the line to start.

3. Hold down the mouse button and move the mouse to where you want the line to end.

4. Release the mouse button.

Creating circles and rectangles

Circles and rectangles can enclose and separate items on the screen. Or they can be an excuse for doodling on company time when the boss thinks you're really writing a program.

To create a circle or rectangle, follow these steps:

1. Click the Shape icon in the Visual Basic Toolbox.

2. On the form, move the mouse to where you want the top-left corner of the circle or rectangle to appear.

3. Hold down the left mouse button and move the mouse to where you want the bottom-right corner of the circle or rectangle to end.

4. Release the mouse button. At this point, Visual Basic displays a rectangle on the screen. If that's what you want, stop right here; otherwise, continue to step 5.

5. Open the Properties window by pressing F4 or by selecting Properties from the View menu.

6. Click the Shape property and click the arrow in the settings box. Visual Basic displays a list of shapes to choose from:

   0 – Rectangle
   1 – Square
   2 – Oval
   3 – Circle
   4 – Rounded Rectangle
   5 – Rounded Square

7. Click the shape you want to create.

Changing the color of lines and other shapes

Visual Basic usually draws lines, circles, and rectangles by using a solid black line. Although boring ol' black is okay for most purposes, sometimes a little color can spice up your user interface. The color of a line is defined by the BorderColor property.

To change the line color of a line or shape, follow these steps:

1. Click the line or shape whose line color you want to change.

2. Open the Properties window by pressing F4 or by selecting Properties from the View menu.

3. Click the BorderColor property in the Property window. Visual Basic displays the current color in a useless series of letters and numbers.

4. Click the downward-pointing arrow to the right of the current color value. Visual Basic displays a color palette.

5. Click the color you want. Visual Basic instantly obeys.

Changing the thickness of lines

Lines can be from 1 to 8,192 in thickness. (The numbers are relative and not related to an actual scale of measurement.) Any line thicker than 100, however, tends to look like a fat sausage on the screen.

To change the thickness of a line, follow these steps:

1. Click the line or shape whose line thickness you want to change.

2. Open the Properties window by pressing F4 or by selecting Properties from the View menu.

3. Click the BorderWidth property and type a new value. Visual Basic immediately changes the thickness of your line.

4. Marvel at the wonder of technology and how one day you'll be able to tell your children, "When I was going to school, we had to draw lines using an Etch-A-Sketch. You kids have it so easy with computers and everything."

Changing the appearance of lines, circles, and rectangles

Visual Basic usually draws lines, circles, and rectangles with a solid line. Although a solid line is easier to see, you may want to create special effects that look like perforations on a page or Morse code.

Visual Basic provides the following seven line styles, some of which are shown in Figure 9-4:

✔ Transparent

✔ Solid (the default)

✔ Dash

✔ Dot

✔ Dash-Dot

✔ Dash-Dot-Dot

✔ Inside Solid

If the thickness of a line is greater than 1, the only BorderStyle settings you can use are 1 (Solid) or 6 (Inside Solid). If you use a different BorderStyle setting, nothing will happen and you'll think Visual Basic is broken.

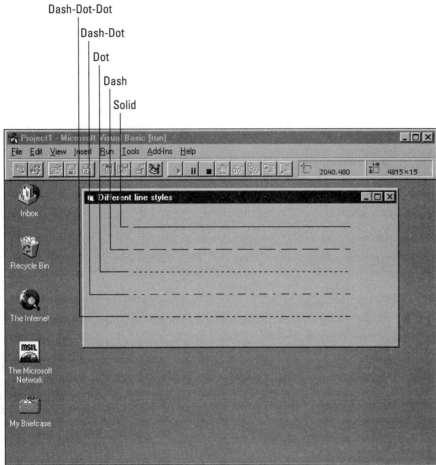

Dash-Dot-Dot

Dash-Dot

Dot

Dash

Solid

Figure 9-4:
Examples of
some of the
available
line styles.

To confuse matters even more, the appearance of a line is determined by its BorderStyle property. Normally, you think of a border as something surrounding an object. But in Visual Basic's world of twisted logic, the BorderStyle defines the appearance of a line.

To change the appearance of lines by themselves or lines that make up your circles or rectangles, follow these steps:

1. Click the line, circle, or rectangle whose appearance you want to change.

2. Open the Properties window by pressing F4 or by selecting Properties from the View menu.

3. Click the BorderStyle property and choose one of the following:

0 – Transparent
1 – Solid
2 – Dash
3 – Dot
4 – Dash-Dot
5 – Dash-Dot-Dot
6 – Inside Solid

4. If you chose any style from 2 to 5, set the BorderWidth property to 1.
Otherwise, Visual Basic will display the BorderStyle you selected as a
solid line.

Changing the size and position of lines

When you create a line, you should try to draw it as the exact size you need.
(What's the point of drawing a long line, knowing that you really need a
short one?)

Visual Basic provides two ways to change the size and position of a line:

- By using the mouse
- By changing the X1, X2, Y1, and Y2 properties in the Property window

The mouse is the quickest and sloppiest way to change the size and position of
a line. But if you insist on using it, follow these steps:

1. Click the line that you want to change. Visual Basic displays a black
rectangle at each end of the line. These rectangles are called *handles*.

   (Because clicking on a single line can be an exercise in frustration, you can
   also move the mouse above the line, hold down the mouse button, move
   the mouse below the line, and release the mouse button.)

2. Move the mouse over one of these handles until the mouse pointer turns
into a crosshair.

3. Hold down the mouse button and move the mouse. When the line is the
shape you want, release the mouse button.

If you prefer not to soil your hands by touching the mouse, you can use a
more refined method favored by kings and queens everywhere: Use the
Properties window.

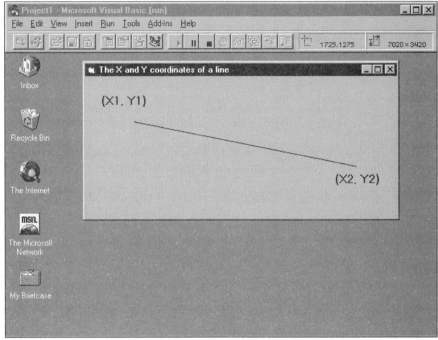

To change the size of a line using the Properties window, follow these steps:

1. Click the line you want to change.

2. Open the Properties window by pressing F4 or by selecting Properties from the View menu.

3. Click the X1 property and type a new value.

4. Click the Y1 property and type a new value.

5. Click the X2 property and type a new value.

6. Click the Y2 property and type a new value.

Figure 9-5 shows the x- and y-coordinates of a line.

Changing the size of circles, rectangles, and other shapes

Happily, changing the size of circles, rectangles, and other shapes is much easier than changing the size of a line. You can use the mouse or the Properties window to change the size of a shape.

To change the size of a shape using the mouse, follow these steps:

1. Click the shape you want to change. Visual Basic displays black handles around the shape.

2. Move the mouse over one of these handles until the mouse pointer turns into a double arrow.

3. Hold down the mouse button and move the mouse. When the object is the shape you want, release the mouse button.

For those who prefer using a keyboard at the expense of ease and convenience, you can change the size of a shape also by using the Properties window.

To change the size of a shape using the Properties window, follow these steps:

1. Click the shape you want to change.

2. Open the Properties window by pressing F4 or by selecting Properties from the View menu.

3. Click the Height property and type a new value.

4. Click the Width property and type a new value.

Filling Shapes with Colors and Pretty Patterns

The inside of a shape is usually empty, blank, and boring. For more excitement than most people's hearts can handle, you can change the color and pattern of the inside of a shape.

Visual Basic provides eight patterns that you can use to fill the inside of a shape. The *pattern* is defined by the FillStyle property. The *color* of the pattern is defined by FillColor property. Figure 9-6 shows the eight patterns that Visual Basic provides for filling the inside of a shape.

To define the fill pattern of a shape, follow these steps:

1. Click the shape whose inside pattern you want to change.

2. Open the Properties window by pressing F4 or by selecting Properties from the View menu.

3. Click the FillStyle property and choose one of the following:

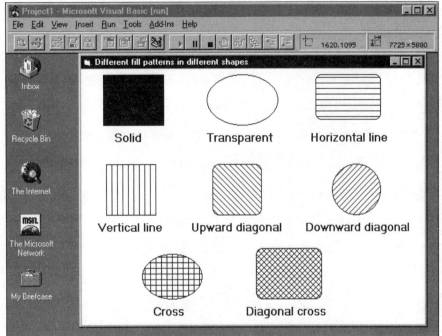

Figure 9-6:
The eight
patterns
available to
fill shapes.

0 – Solid
1 – Transparent
2 – Horizontal Line
3 – Vertical Line
4 – Upward Diagonal
5 – Downward Diagonal
6 – Cross
7 – Diagonal Cross

To change the color of a shape's fill pattern, follow these steps:

1. Click the shape whose pattern color you want to change.

2. Open the Properties window by pressing F4 or by selecting Properties from the View menu.

3. Click the FillColor property in the Property window. Visual Basic displays the current color in a useless series of letters and numbers.

4. Click the downward-pointing arrow to the right of the current color value. Visual Basic displays a color palette.

5. Click the color you want. Visual Basic obeys instantly.

Changing the Background Color of Shapes

Besides changing the color of the fill pattern inside a shape (FillColor) and the line color that makes up a shape (BorderColor), you can also change a shape's background color (BackColor). Confused? Take a look at Figure 9-7 for clarity.

Before you can change the background color of a shape, you must set its BackStyle property to Opaque. (The default is Transparent, which means that it's invisible. If it's invisible, changing its color won't do a thing.)

To change the background color of a shape, follow these steps:

1. Click the shape whose background color you want to change.

2. Open the Properties window by pressing F4 or by selecting Properties from the View menu.

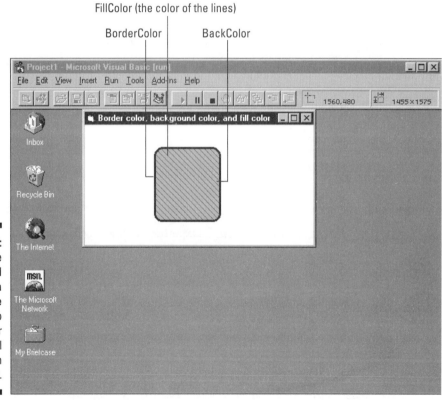

Figure 9-7:
The background color of a shape compared to its border color and fill pattern color.

3. Click the BackStyle property and set its value to Opaque.

4. Click the BackColor property in the Properties window. Visual Basic displays the current color in a useless series of letters and numbers.

5. Click the ellipsis (. . .) to the right of the current color value. Visual Basic displays a color palette.

6. Click the color you want. Visual Basic instantly obeys.

Try It Yourself

The following sample program lets you change a circle's thickness by using the horizontal scroll bar. To see for yourself, create three objects with the following property settings:

Object	Property	Setting
Form	Caption	The Shrinking/Growing Circle
Shape1	Height	1455
	Left	2640
	Name	shpCircle
	Shape	3 – Circle
	Top	1080
	Width	1695
HScroll1	Height	255
	Left	1800
	Max	20
	Min	1
	Name	hsbCircle
	Width	3255

Double-click the horizontal scroll bar and type the following in the Code window:

```
Private Sub hsbCircle_Change()
   shpCircle.BorderWidth = hsbCircle.Value
End Sub
```

Run the program by pressing F5. Then click the horizontal scroll bar and watch the circle grow before your eyes. Amazing! Astound your friends! Be the hit of your next cocktail party! Visual Basic reveals it all!

Part III
Menus to Make Your Program Look Less Ugly

Real Programmers don't use micros. If it weren't for mainframe delays, there wouldn't be time to go to the bathroom or talk to all the other Real Programmers.

In this part . . .

*U*ntil now, you've learned how to design a user interface so that people can tell your program what to do. Many programs use a generous sampling of command buttons, check boxes, and list boxes, but the main part of most user interfaces consists of pull-down menus at the top of the screen.

Although Visual Basic gives you the freedom to go wild and create pull-down menus that resemble nothing previously seen by humans, it's a good idea to follow the standards set by other programs.

Chapter 10

Creating Menus and Making Them Look Pretty

● ●

In This Chapter

▶ Creating menus and menu titles

▶ Adding separator bars

▶ Using shortcut keys and check marks

▶ Dimming or making menu commands disappear

● ●

*G*enerally, every menu bar contains the following menu titles: File, Edit, Window, and Help (see Figure 10-1). The File menu appears on the far left, the Edit menu appears next, the Window menu appears next to last, and the Help menu appears last. In between are menu titles unique to a particular program.

Every menu consists not only of *menu titles* but also *menu commands*, as shown in Figure 10-2. The menu titles appear at the top of the screen in a menu bar, and the menu commands appear in pull-down menus.

The Basic Elements of a Menu Bar

Before creating menus, decide how many menu titles your program needs and where each command belongs in your menu titles.

The *File* menu (refer again to Figure 10-2) should contain commands directly related to file operations, such as opening, closing, saving, and printing files, as well as quitting the program so that you can go to the kitchen and get something to eat.

The *Edit* menu, as shown in Figure 10-3, should contain commands related to editing (duh), such as Undo (and Redo), Cut, Copy, Paste, Clear, and Select All.

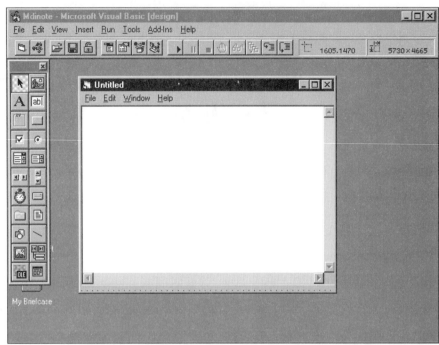

Figure 10-1:
A typical list
of pull-down
menus.

Menu commands   Menu titles

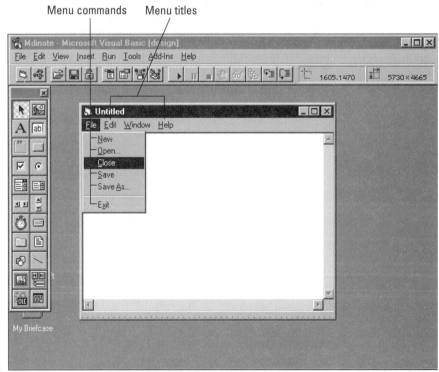

Figure 10-2:
Menu titles
and menu
commands.

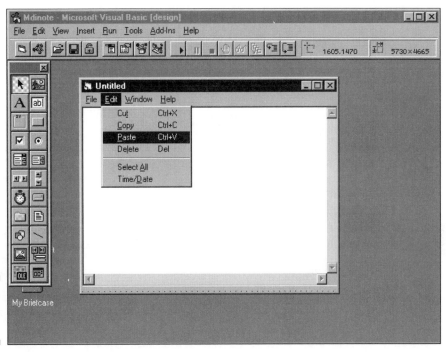

The *Window* menu, as shown in Figure 10-4, should contain commands related to opening, closing, arranging, and switching among different windows.

The *Help* menu (see Figure 10-5) should contain commands for getting help from the program. Typical help commands include a table of contents to the help system, an alphabetic index, propaganda about product support, and a useless About... command that displays information the programmers thought would look cute on the screen.

Any other menus you sandwich between the Edit and the Window menu titles should clearly organize the type of commands hidden underneath.

For example, many word processing programs have a Tools menu title that displays commands for grammar checking, hyphenation, macro creation, and other commands that ninety-nine percent of the working population of America will never use.

No matter how many menu titles you add to your program, make sure that they all fit on the menu bar. (Otherwise, what's the point of creating menu titles if nobody can see them?)

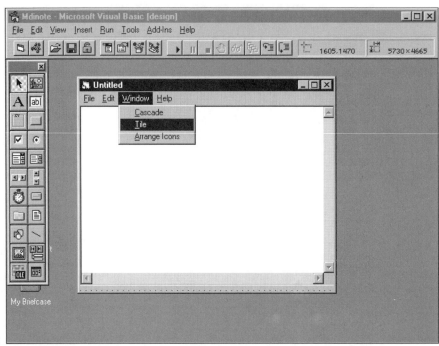

Figure 10-4:
A typical
Window
menu.

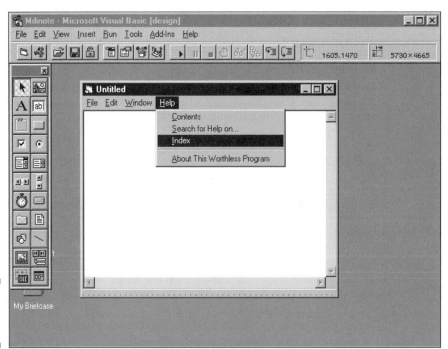

Figure 10-5:
A typical
Help menu.

Making Menus for Your User Interface

To create menus, you have to open the Menu Editor window, which is shown in Figure 10-6.

In the name of freedom and confusion, Visual Basic provides three ways to display the Menu Editor window:

- ✔ Press Ctrl+E.
- ✔ Select Menu Editor from the Tools menu.
- ✔ Click the Menu Editor icon in the Toolbar (refer again to Figure 10-6).

You can create one set of menus for each form. So if your program contains two forms, you can have a completely different menu for each form. Of course, this may confuse users, but if you're a typical programmer — who generally doesn't care what users think — this won't bother you a bit.

Menu design properties

Menu Editor icon   Shortcut key combo box

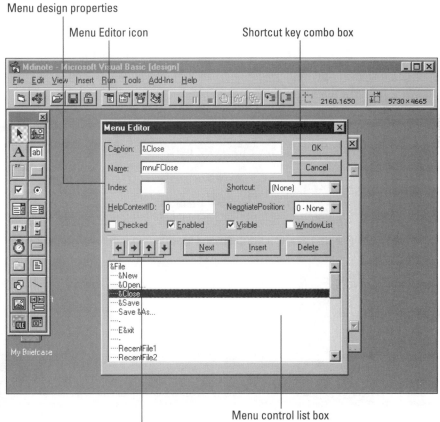

Figure 10-6:
Menu Editor window with its parts labeled.

Menu control list box

Arrow buttons for moving through menu items

The Menu Editor window is where you define everything to create your menus. The first two things you have to define for all your menu titles are their names and their captions.

Naming menus

Every menu title and menu command has a caption and a name. The *caption* is what appears on the screen. The *name* never appears on the screen; you use the name to identify which menu command the user chooses.

Captions can be up to 40 characters long, including numbers, spaces, punctuation, and the underscore character (_). Of course, the longer your caption is, the more space it's going to gobble up on the screen.

Because captions appear on the screen, you can use an ampersand (&) in your captions, such as &File or T&able. Why would you want to do such a silly thing? An ampersand in front of any letter makes that letter underlined in the caption, as you can see in Figure 10-7.

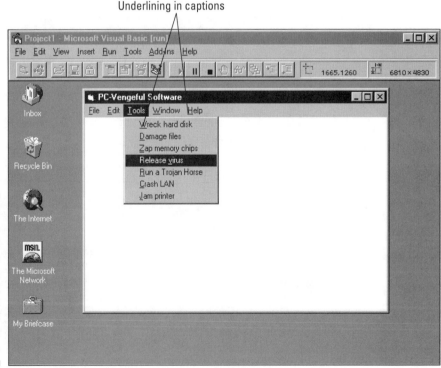

Underlining in captions

Figure 10-7:
The
ampersand
in the name
displays
underlining
in menu
items and
menu
commands.

When a letter is underlined in a menu title, users can pull down that menu by pressing and holding down the Alt key followed by whatever letter is underlined. If a menu caption is named &Window, it appears on the screen as Window, and users can pull it down by pressing Alt+W.

When the ampersand underlines a letter in a menu command caption, users can choose the caption simply by typing the underlined letter, without pressing Alt. So if a menu command caption is named &New, it appears on the screen as New, and users can choose it by first pulling down the menu and then typing **N**.

Names can be up to 40 characters long, including numbers and the underscore character. Because names never appear on the screen, you can make them as long as you want — until you reach the magic number of 40.

Unlike captions, names cannot include spaces, punctuation, or words that the editors at IDG Books deem offensive and, hence, may harm sales of this book.

For menu names, Visual Basic recommends that the name begins with *mnu*, as in the following examples:

```
mnuFile
mnuWindow
mnuFileOpen
```

Visual Basic couldn't care less whether you use uppercase and lowercase consistently. If you really wanted to, you could use the following names for menus:

```
MNufiLE
mNuwINDow
MNUfileOPEN
```

Not only is this hard to read, but it makes you look illiterate. So for consistency (and to protect your image), it's best to adopt your own style and stick with it whenever you use Visual Basic.

To identify menu commands that appear under certain menu titles, include the menu title as part of a menu command's name. (Huh?) For example, the menu title File might be named mnuFile. The Open, Save, and Exit commands that appear in the File menu would then have names like mnuFileOpen, mnuFileSave, and mnuFileExit.

Making menu titles

There are two steps to creating pull-down menus for your Visual Basic programs:

- First you create the menu titles that appear in the menu bar.
- Then you create the menu commands that appear under each menu title.

To create menu titles that appear in the menu bar at the top of a form, follow these steps:

1. Click the form to which you want to add menu titles.

2. Open the Menu Editor window by pressing Ctrl+E, by selecting Menu Editor from the Tools menu, or by clicking the Menu Editor icon in the Toolbar. Visual Basic cheerfully displays the Menu Editor window.

3. In the Caption text box, type the menu title that you want to appear on the screen, including any ampersands. As you type, Visual Basic displays your caption in the Menu control list box.

4. Press Tab to move the cursor to the Name text box.

5. Type your menu name, beginning with *mnu* followed by the menu caption itself, such as `mnuFile` or `mnuFilePrint`. (Remember, you can mix upper- and lowercase, but for consistency with Visual Basic programmers around the world, stick with the style `mnuFileExit`.)

6. Press Enter or click Next to create the next menu title.

7. Repeat steps 3 through 6 until you've created all the menu titles that will appear at the top of the screen in the menu bar.

8. Click OK. Visual Basic displays your menus at the top of the form.

Adding and deleting menu titles and commands

Creating menu titles is fairly straightforward. Unfortunately, nothing in life is permanent, and that includes your menu titles. At a later time, you may need to add or delete menu titles.

To add another menu title to a form, follow these steps:

1. Click the form to which you want to add another menu title.

2. Open the Menu Editor window by pressing Ctrl+E, by selecting Menu Editor from the Tools menu, or by clicking the Menu editor icon in the Toolbar. Visual Basic obediently displays the Menu Editor window.

3. Click the menu title that you want to appear to the right of your new menu title.

4. Click Insert. Visual Basic pushes the previously highlighted menu title down and highlights a blank line (see Figure 10-8).

5. Click the Caption text box.

6. Type your new menu title caption, such as &Tools or Forma&t.

7. Press Tab to move the cursor to the Name text box. Type your new menu name, such as mnuTools or mnuFormat, and press Enter.

8. Click OK.

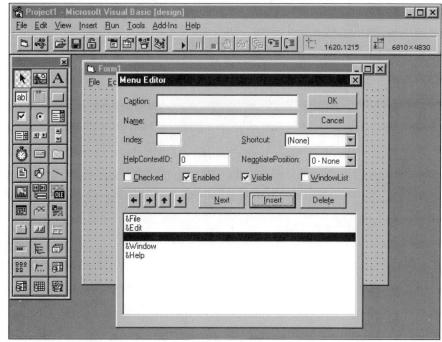

Figure 10-8: Inserting a new menu title in the Menu control list box affects the menu title positions in a menu bar.

To delete a menu title, follow these steps:

1. Click the form from which you want to delete a menu title.

2. Open the Menu Editor window by pressing Ctrl+E, by selecting Menu Editor from the Tools menu, or by clicking the Menu Editor icon in the Toolbar. Visual Basic obediently displays the Menu Editor window.

3. Click the menu title you want to delete.

4. Click Delete. Visual Basic deletes the highlighted menu title.

5. Click OK.

Creating Menu Commands under Menu Titles

After you've created the menu titles that appear in a menu bar at the top of a form, the next step is to create the commands that appear under each menu title.

In the Menu control list box, all flush left items are menu titles that appear in the menu bar. Indented items are menu commands that appear below a menu title.

To create menu commands, follow these steps:

1. Click the form to which you want to add menu commands.

2. Open the Menu Editor window by pressing Ctrl+E, by selecting Menu Editor from the Tools menu, or by clicking the Menu Editor icon in the Toolbar. Visual Basic happily displays the Menu Editor window.

3. Click the mouse under the menu title where you want to display the menu commands. For example, if you want to put commands under the File menu title, click the first menu title that appears below the File menu title.

4. Click Insert.

5. Click the Caption text box and type the menu command's caption, such as &Save or &Print.

6. Press Tab to move the cursor to the Name text box.

7. Type the menu command's name, such as mnuFileSave or mnuFilePrint.

8. Click the right-arrow button to indent the menu command. This indentation shows you that an item is a menu command and not a menu title, which appears in the menu bar. (How's that for enough similar but confusing terms?)

9. Click OK.

Moving Menu Titles and Commands

When you create your pull-down menus, you don't have to do it perfectly because you can move everything around.

Visual Basic gives you four ways to move menu titles and commands:

- ✔ Up
- ✔ Down
- ✔ Indent right
- ✔ Indent left

In the Menu Editor window, Visual Basic provides four arrow buttons that let you move items up, down, right, or left (refer back to Figure 10-6).

Moving an item up or down in the Menu control list box simply rearranges the item's position on the menu bar or in a pull-down menu.

To move an item up or down in the Menu control list box, follow these steps:

1. Click the form containing the menu titles or commands that you want to rearrange.

2. Open the Menu Editor window by pressing Ctrl+E, by selecting <u>M</u>enu Editor from the <u>T</u>ools menu, or by clicking the Menu Editor icon in the Toolbar.

3. Click the item that you want to move up or down.

4. Click the up-arrow button to move the item up or click the down-arrow button to move the item down.

5. Click OK when you've finished goofing around.

Moving an item up or down simply rearranges its position. Indenting an item to the right turns that item into a menu command (see Figure 10-9). Indenting an item to the left turns that item from a menu command into a menu title.

To indent an item left or right, follow these steps:

1. Click the form containing the menu whose titles or commands you want to rearrange.

2. Open the Menu Editor window by pressing Ctrl+E, by selecting <u>M</u>enu Editor from the <u>T</u>ools menu, or by clicking the Menu Editor icon in the Toolbar.

3. Click the item you want to move left or right.

4. Click the right-arrow button to indent the item to the right or click the left-arrow button to indent the item to the left.

5. Click OK when you're finished.

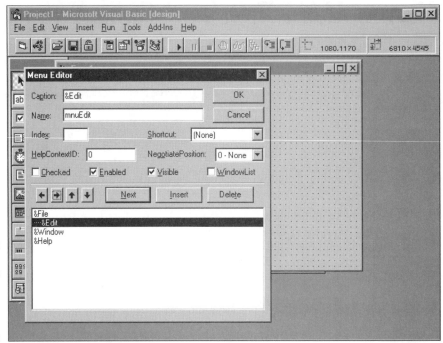

Figure 10-9:
The effect of
indenting an
item to the
left.

Making Menus Pretty

Pull-down menus conveniently list commands where users can find them. However, you need to make your pull-down menus pretty, or they'll be as appealing to use as a grease-splattered menu in a hole-in-the-wall restaurant.

Some ways to make your menus look better are to separate related commands with separator bars, display check marks next to currently used menu commands, add shortcut keys so that users don't have to use menus at all, and dim or remove items.

Putting separator bars in menus

Separator bars are lines in a menu that divide groups of items (see Figure 10-10). Generally, separator bars group three or more related items so that users can quickly find the command they want.

Separator bars

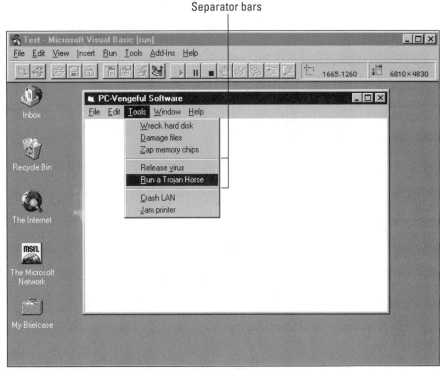

Figure 10-10:
Typical
separator
bars in
menus.

To create a separator bar, follow these steps:

1. Click the form containing the menus to which you want to add separator bars.

2. Open the Menu Editor window by pressing Ctrl+E, by selecting Menu Editor from the Tools menu, or by clicking the Menu Editor icon in the Toolbar.

3. Highlight the item you want to appear directly below the separator bar.

4. Click Insert so that Visual Basic displays an empty line. (If necessary, you may have to click the right- or left-arrow buttons to have the separator bar appear on the same level as the items it is dividing.)

5. Click the Caption text box, type a hyphen (-), and press Tab to move the cursor to the Name text box.

6. Type any name you want that helps you identify the separator bar. Ideally, the name should include the menu title and where it appears, such as `barFile1` or `sepEdit2`.

7. Click OK to close the Menu Editor window.

Test your newfound knowledge

1. Why are pull-down menus so useful?

   a. They hide commands so that users can never find them.

   b. They make programs easier to use because they follow standard guidelines that all Windows-based programs use.

   c. Because they make programmers think about food and getting something nutritious to eat, like Twinkies and Coke.

   d. If pull-down menus are so useful, how come people still need to buy 400-page books to teach them how to use Windows?

2. What's the only way to create pull-down menus in a Visual Basic program?

   a. Open the Menu Editor window by pressing Ctrl+E, by selecting Menu Editor from the Tools menu, or by clicking the Menu Editor icon in the Toolbar.

   b. By copying someone else's program and hope they won't notice.

   c. You can't, or Apple Computer will sue you for copyright infringement.

   d. Visual Basic can create pull-down menus?

Assigning shortcut keys

After a while, it can be a real pain in the neck to pull menus down every time you need to do something. For commonly used commands, it's a good idea to assign them *shortcut keys*, such as Ctrl+S to choose the Save command or Ctrl+X for the Cut command. Figure 10-11 shows some shortcut keys.

Shortcut keys appear on menus next to the commands they represent. In this way, users can quickly learn which shortcut keys your program offers and which commands the keys belong to.

To assign a shortcut key to a menu command, you have to use the Menu Editor window again.

Although it would sometimes be nice to make up your own shortcut keys, Visual Basic only lets you choose from a limited list of possible keys.

Visual Basic won't let you assign the same shortcut keys to different commands. If you try to, Visual Basic will scold you with an error dialog box.

To assign shortcut keys to menu commands, follow these steps:

1. Click the form containing the menus to which you want to add shortcut keys.

2. Open the Menu Editor window by pressing Ctrl+E, by selecting Menu Editor from the Tools menu, or by clicking the Menu Editor icon in the Toolbar.

3. Click the menu command for which you want to assign a shortcut key.

Shortcut keys

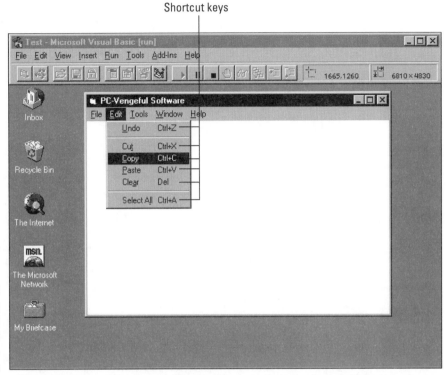

Figure 10-11:
Examples of
shortcut
keys.

4. Click the down-arrow button in the Shortcut list box. Visual Basic displays a list of possible keystroke combinations you can use.

5. Scroll through this list until you find the right keystroke combination. Ideally, you should choose keystroke combinations that are easy to remember, such as Ctrl+S for the Save command or Ctrl+X for the Cut command. Visual Basic displays your choice in the Menu control list box.

6. Click OK.

Now when you click your pull-down menus, shortcut keys appear next to some of the commands. Because you haven't written any BASIC code to tell these commands what to do, nothing happens if you press any of the shortcut keys.

Putting check marks next to menu commands

Check marks that appear next to items on a menu visually show that the items have already been selected (see Figure 10-12). These check marks are often useful in identifying which font, type style, or size is currently being used.

Why choose Ctrl+X and Ctrl+V for Cut and Paste?

To make programs consistent and intuitive (meaning that you can use them almost without thinking), most programs use similar shortcut keys. The logic behind this is to assign the first letter of each command to the Ctrl key. For example, the shortcut key for Save is Ctrl+S, the shortcut key for Print is Ctrl+P, and the shortcut key for Open is Ctrl+O.

Of course, you can't use the same letter twice. When a command such as Copy is assigned Ctrl+C, Cut can't be Ctrl+C because that shortcut key is already taken. Consequently, Cut is assigned the shortcut key Ctrl+X, which is reminis-

cent of making an X over text you want to cross out. Paste gets an even odder shortcut key, Ctrl+V, because the V symbolizes an editor's proof mark to insert something in a sentence.

The Undo command usually is assigned the Ctrl+Z shortcut. What does the Z stand for? It's one of those mysteries that everybody sees every day, but no one really has an answer for. Just think of the most illogical letter to represent the Undo command; then remember that any time you make a critical mistake, it would be illogical to suffer the consequences. That may help you remember to press Ctrl+Z to Undo your mistake.

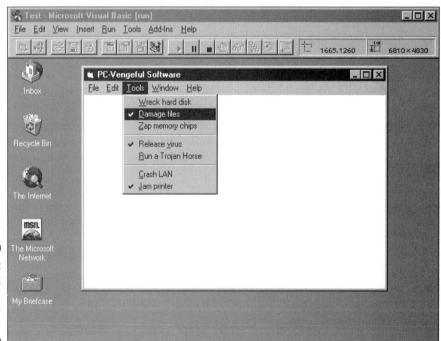

Figure 10-12:
Using check marks in a pull-down menu.

If you want to make any default choices in your pull-down menus, you can have check marks appear when your program runs.

Check marks can appear next to menu commands only and not menu titles. If you try to put a check mark next to a menu title, Visual Basic screams and displays the error message "Can't put check mark here."

To add check marks to menu commands, follow these steps:

1. Click the form containing the menus that you want to add check marks to.

2. Open the Menu Editor window by pressing Ctrl+E, by selecting Menu Editor from the Tools menu, or by clicking the Menu Editor icon in the Toolbar.

3. Click the menu command that you want a check mark to appear next to.

4. Click the Checked check box.

5. Click OK.

If you put check marks next to your menu commands, you'll have to remove the check marks eventually. To do that, you have to use (gasp!) BASIC code.

To remove a check mark that's next to a menu command, just set the command's Checked property to False. The following example removes a check mark from a menu command named `mnuFont12`:

```
mnuFont12.Checked = False
```

To add a check mark using BASIC code, just set the menu command's Checked property to True. The following example adds a check mark next to a menu command named `mnuFontHelvetica`:

```
mnuFontHelvetica.Checked = True
```

Dimming menu commands

Sometimes it won't make sense to use certain commands. For example, until you select a block of text, it's pointless to have the Cut or Copy commands as options. To prevent users from choosing menu commands that aren't available, you can dim the commands, as shown in Figure 10-13. That way, the commands still appear in the menus, but the user can't choose them.

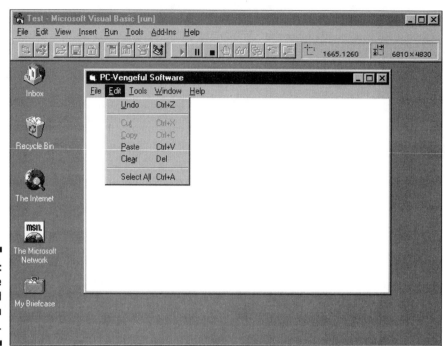

Figure 10-13:
An example
of dimmed
menu
commands.

To dim a menu item, follow these steps:

1. Click the form containing the menu commands that you want to dim.

2. Open the Menu Editor window by pressing Ctrl+E, by selecting Menu Editor from the Tools menu, or by clicking the Menu Editor icon in the Toolbar.

3. Highlight the menu item that you want to dim.

4. Click the Enabled check box to remove the X (see Figure 10-14).

5. Click OK.

If you dim a menu command, it makes sense that you'll eventually want to undim it. To do so, you have to use BASIC code. To undim a menu command, set its Enabled property to True. The following example undims a menu command named `mnuEditCut`:

```
mnuEditCut.Enabled = True
```

Enabled check box

Checked check box   Visible check box

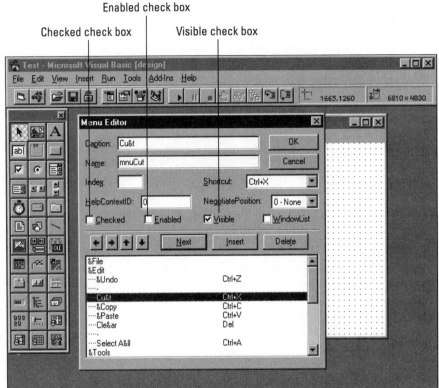

Figure 10-14:
The Enabled
check box in
the Menu
Editor
window.

To dim a menu command while your program is running, use BASIC code. Just set the menu command's property to False. The following example dims a menu command named `mnuEditCopy`:

```
mnuEditCopy.Enabled = False
```

Making menu commands disappear

Rather than dim a menu command, you can make it disappear. For example, some programs remove all menu titles except File and Help from the menu bar until the user opens or creates a file. (After all, it's pointless to display an Edit menu if there's nothing to edit.)

To remove a menu item, follow these steps:

1. Click the form containing the menu commands you want to make invisible.

2. Open the Menu Editor window by pressing Ctrl+E, by selecting <u>M</u>enu Editor from the <u>T</u>ools menu, or by clicking the Menu Editor icon in the Toolbar.

3. Highlight the menu item that you want to make invisible.

4. Click the Visible check box to remove the X (refer back to Figure 10-14).

5. Click OK.

After you make a menu command invisible, eventually you'll have to make it visible. To do so, you have to use BASIC code. To make a menu command visible, set its Visible property to True. The following example makes a menu title named mnuEdit visible:

```
mnuEdit.Visible = True
```

To make a menu command invisible while your program is running, use BASIC code and set the menu item's property to False. The following example makes a menu title named mnuTools disappear:

```
mnuTools.Visible = False
```

Just remember that all these fine points of beautifying your menus make your program easier to use and give it that professional look. As any professional programmer will tell you, if a program looks good, users assume that it must be their fault if anything goes wrong. And that's the real reason programmers spend so much time creating a user interface — so users won't blame them when the program fails catastrophically.

Chapter 11

Submenus, Growing Menus, and Pop-Up Menus

● ●

In This Chapter

▶ Creating submenus

▶ Dynamically growing menus

▶ Creating pop-up menus

● ●

A typical menu bar displays a list of menu titles at the top of the screen. Selecting one of the menu titles displays a pull-down menu.

Unfortunately, a menu bar can hold only a limited number of menu titles, and a pull-down menu can hold only as many commands as can appear on the screen simultaneously. So what happens if you write a killer application that requires more commands than can possibly appear on the menu bar or in multiple pull-down menus? The solution is to use submenus (or to redesign your program).

Creating Submenus

Submenus are often used to bury a command several layers deep within a series of pull-down menus. If organized properly, submenus clearly show the relationship between various topics. If organized improperly, your program won't look any different than the $495 commercial packages that millions of people are forced to use every day at work.

For example, many programs have a Text menu title. Under this Text menu may be commands such as TypeStyle, Font, and Size. Choosing Font often displays a submenu listing all the possible fonts available, as shown in Figure 11-1.

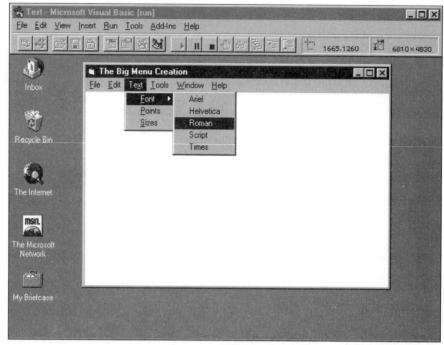

Figure 11-1:
A typical
Te**x**t pull-
down menu
offering a
Font
command
and a
submenu of
font types.

Visual Basic lets you create up to four levels of submenus, as shown in Figure 11-2. Although this number of submenus can be handy, most programs use only one level of submenus to avoid burying commands so deeply that no one can find them again. Rumor has it that the Watergate tapes, Jimmy Hoffa's body, and the location of the Holy Grail reside somewhere in a well-known program's submenus.

Whenever a menu item displays an arrowhead symbol, it means that a submenu exists for that item. When you create submenus, Visual Basic displays this arrowhead symbol automatically. Figure 11-3 shows an example of the arrow-head symbol.

The Menu Editor window is the only place where you can define submenus. Any item that appears flush left will appear as a menu title in the menu bar. Items indented once appear on the pull-down menus, items indented twice appear on the first submenu level, items indented three times appear on the second submenu level, items indented four times appear on the third submenu level, and items indented five times appear on the fourth and last submenu level.

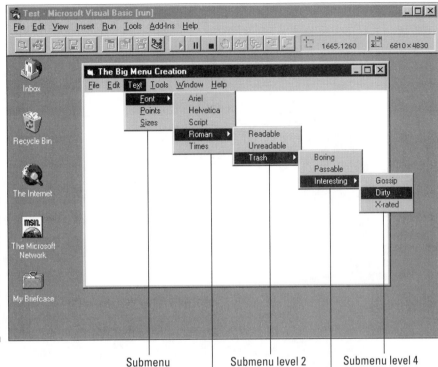

Figure 11-2:
Four levels
of
submenus:
when
enough is
really
enough.

Submenu   Submenu level 2   Submenu level 4

Submenu level 1   Submenu level 3

To create submenus, follow these steps:

1. Click the form on which you want to create submenus.

2. Open the Menu Editor window by pressing Ctrl+E, by selecting Menu Editor from the Tools menu, or by clicking the Menu Editor icon in the Toolbar.

3. In the Menu control list box, highlight the menu item that you want to make into a submenu.

4. Click the right-arrow button to indent the item.

5. Click OK.

Each level of indentation (*submenu level*) is represented by four dots (. . . .) in the Menu Control list box.

Submenu arrowheads

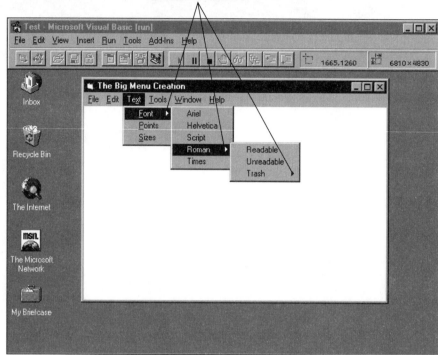

Figure 11-3:
The
arrowhead
symbol on a
menu
indicates
the
existence of
a submenu.

If you want to move submenus up a level, you can. Just follow these steps:

1. Click the form containing the submenus that you want to modify.

2. Open the Menu Editor window by pressing Ctrl+E, by selecting Menu Editor from the Tools menu, or by clicking the Menu Editor icon in the Toolbar.

3. In the Menu Control list, highlight the menu item box that you want to move up a level.

4. Click the left-arrow button to indent the item.

5. Click OK when you've finished playing around.

Rather than use multiple levels of submenus, most of the really cool programs use dialog boxes. A *dialog box* lets users make multiple choices all at once instead of making choices one at a time through many submenu levels.

Then again, what's the point of offering submenus if even Microsoft recommends against it? This is just one of the many ways that Microsoft gives you the freedom to write hard-to-use user interfaces so that your programs will never pose a real threat to theirs.

Changing Menu Captions While Your Program Is Running

In certain cases, it's necessary to change the caption of a menu command while the program is running. The most common menu command that changes is the Undo command in the Edit menu. After choosing the Undo command, most programs toggle Undo to display the Redo command.

To change a menu caption, you have to use BASIC code. Just find the name of the menu item that you want to change and set its Caption property to a new caption.

The following example changes the mnuEditUndo caption to Redo:

```
mnuEditUndo.Caption = "Redo"
```

The following example changes the mnuEditUndo caption back to Undo:

```
mnuEditUndo.Caption = "Undo"
```

When changing menu captions, you can use the ampersand (&) symbol to display a menu command hot key. For example, the following code changes the mnuEditUndo caption to Undo:

```
mnuEditUndo.Caption = "&Undo"
```

Dynamically Growing Menus

If you use many Windows-based programs such as Microsoft Word, you may notice an odd feature: Each time you load a program, the File menu displays a list of the last four or five files you worked on (see Figure 11-4). If you ever open two or more windows in the same program, you may notice that the Window menu also lists the names of the files currently open.

To create a dynamically growing menu, you have to create empty spaces in your menu. You do this by using the Menu Editor window and by creating BASIC code to add items to make the items visible.

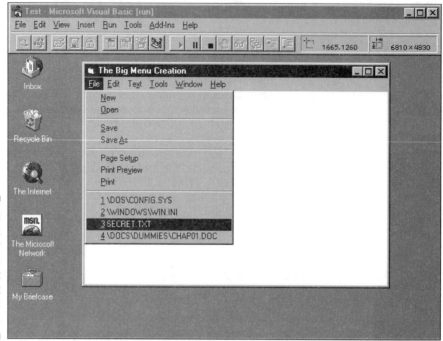

Figure 11-4:
A
dynamically
growing File
menu that
lists the last
four files
opened.

To create a dynamically growing menu, follow these steps:

1. Click on the form where you want to create a dynamically growing menu.

2. Open the Menu Editor window by pressing Ctrl+E, by selecting Menu Editor from the Tools menu, or by clicking the Menu Editor icon in the Toolbar.

3. Click below the last menu command under the menu title to which you want to add new items. For example, if you want to add new items under the File menu, click below the last menu command under the File menu title.

4. Click Insert to add the item.

5. Click the right-arrow button to indent the empty lines so that they appear as menu commands below the menu title.

6. Leave the Caption text box empty and press Tab.

7. In the Name text box, type the same name for each of these empty lines, such as `mnuFileArray`.

8. Type **0** in the Index text box for the first empty line. Each time you add another empty line, add 1 to the Index text box. The first empty line Index text box should contain 0, the second should contain 1, and so on.

9. Press Enter.

10. Repeat steps 3 through 9 until you have created four or five empty lines below the last menu title in the Menu Editor control list box. Make sure that each empty line has a different number in its Index text box.

11. Click OK.

The preceding steps create a dynamically growing menu, but to actually add items to this menu, you have to use BASIC code. The following example shows how to add an item to make a dynamically growing menu:

```
Private Sub Form_Load()
  mnuFileArray(0).Caption = "&1 " + "C:\VB\HELLO.VBP"
  mnuFileArray(0).Visible = True
End Sub
```

The first line sets the caption of the first empty line (named mnuFileArray) to 1 C:\VB\HELLO.VBP. The second line makes this item visible on the pull-down menu.

Creating Pop-Up Menus

Pop-up menus are often used to quickly display a list of commands on the screen. Any menu or submenu can appear as a pop-up menu. Pop-up menus are usually programmed to appear when the user presses the right mouse button. Figure 11-5 shows an example of a pop-up menu.

To create a pop-up menu, you have to use the BASIC command PopupMenu. The following example displays the mnuEdit menu as a pop-up menu when the user clicks the right mouse button:

```
Private Sub Form_MouseUp(Button As Integer, Shift As Integer,
          X As Single, Y As Single)
  If Button = 2 Then    ' Right mouse button pressed
    PopupMenu mnuEdit  ' Pops up the mnuEdit menu
  End If
End Sub
```

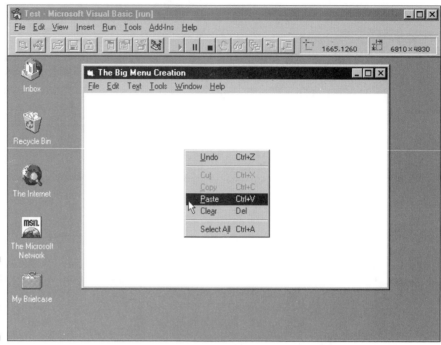

Figure 11-5:
An example
of a pop-up
menu.

To create a pop-up menu, follow these steps:

1. Click the form containing the menu that you want to turn into a pop-up menu.

2. Press F7 or choose <u>C</u>ode from the <u>V</u>iew menu. The Code Editor window appears.

3. Click in the Object list box and choose Form.

4. Click in the Proc list box and choose MouseUp. Visual Basic displays an empty `Private Form_MouseUp` procedure.

5. Type the following code below the `Private Sub Form_MouseUp` statement and above the `End Sub` statement:

```
If Button = 2 Then
  PopUpMenu (type the menu name here such as mnuEdit)
End If
```

Defining the location of pop-up menus

Normally, the pop-up menu appears wherever the mouse pointer happens to be. However, if you want pop-up menus to appear in a specific location on the screen, you can specify the exact coordinates, as shown in Figure 11-6.

For example, the following PopupMenu BASIC command displays a pop-up menu named mnuTools at x-coordinate 500 and y-coordinate 650:

```
PopupMenu mnuTools, 500, 650
```

For those people who are finicky about where the pop-up menu appears relative to the mouse pointer, you can specify whether it appears to the left, to the right, or dead center of the mouse. Use one of the following commands:

```
PopupMenu mnuEdit, 0    ' Left aligned
PopupMenu mnuEdit, 4    ' Center aligned
PopupMenu mnuEdit, 8    ' Right aligned
```

X- and y-coordinates measured from here

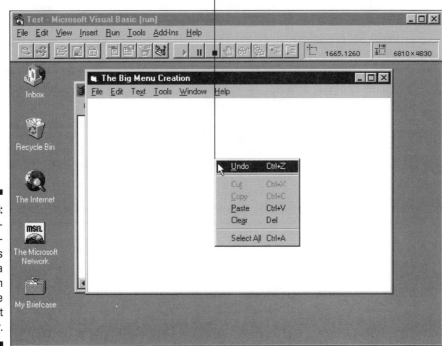

Figure 11-6:
How x-
and y-
coordinates
work on a
screen with
0,0 in the
upper-left
corner.

For convenience's sake, using numbers to specify right or left alignment can be confusing. To simplify matters, Visual Basic lets you assign these values to honest-to-goodness English phrases, such as the following:

```
Const POPUPMENU_LEFTALIGN = 0
Const POPUPMENU_CENTERALIGN = 4
Const POPUPMENU_RIGHTALIGN = 8
```

Essentially, these statements tell Visual Basic, "Hey stupid, whenever you see the words POPUPMENU_CENTERALIGN, substitute the number 4 instead."

Using the old method in a Visual Basic procedure would look like this:

```
Sub Form_MouseUp(Button As Integer, Shift As Integer, X As
            Single, Y As Single)
  If Button = 2 Then        ' Right mouse button pressed
    PopupMenu mnuEdit, 4  ' Old, confusing way
  End If
End Sub
```

Now here's what the modern, easy-to-read method using English looks like:

```
Sub Form_MouseUp(Button As Integer, Shift As Integer, X As
            Single, Y As Single)
Const POPUPMENU_CENTERALIGN = 4
  If Button = 2 Then        ' Right mouse button pressed
    PopupMenu mnuEdit, POPUPMENU_CENTERALIGN
  End If
End Sub
```

In case your mind is already racing ahead to new possibilities, you can left-, center-, or right-align a menu around a specific x-coordinate. For example, if you want to center-align the pop-up menu around a specific x-coordinate, here's how you do it:

```
PopupMenu mnuTools, 4, 500, 650
```

or

```
PopupMenu mnuTools, POPUPMENU_CENTERALIGN, 500, 650
```

This example displays the pop-up menu at the x- and y-coordinates of 500 twips and 650 twips, respectively.

If you change the units of measurement from twips to inches or centimeters, you may have to change the x- and y-coordinate values as well to correspond to your new scale.

Defining the right mouse button to work with pop-up menus

Normally, pop-up menus work like ordinary pull-down menus. To choose a command, you just click the command with the left mouse button. However, because the right mouse button is used about as often as you use your wisdom teeth, you may want to give users the capability to use either the left or right mouse button.

The following code example activates the right mouse button:

```
PopupMenu mnuEdit, 2
```

Once again, to replace numbers with English, you can substitute the following:

```
Const POPUPMENU_RIGHTBUTTON = 2
```

By default, Visual Basic assumes that you always want to use the left mouse button with any pop-up menu.

Trick question: How do you define both center alignment and right-button activation? The answer is to use the OR operator, as shown in the following:

```
PopupMenu mnuEdit, 2 Or 4
```

To use English instead of numbers, you can use the following:

```
Const POPUPMENU_CENTERALIGN = 4
Const POPUPMENU_RIGHTBUTTON = 2
PopupMenu mnuEdit, POPUPMENU_RIGHTBUTTON Or
            POPUPMENU_CENERALIGN
```

Most popular programs (such as WordPerfect, Excel, and Paradox) use submenus, dynamically growing menus, and pop-up menus. But for less-complicated programs, such as games, you probably won't need all these different menu features.

Test your newfound knowledge

1. Explain why you might want your menu captions to change while your program is running.

   a. To confuse your users so that they think they're doing something wrong.

   b. To move important commands every five minutes to keep users on their toes.

   c. To toggle menu captions like Undo and Redo.

   d. To boggle your mind with the amazing power of Visual Basic commands.

2. Explain what the following BASIC code does:

```
Sub Form_MouseUp(Button As Integer, Shift As Integer, X
          As Single, Y As Single)
   If Button = 2 Then   ' Right mouse button pressed
      PopupMenu mnuFont
   End If
End Sub
```

   a. When the user presses the right mouse button, the program displays the mnuFont menu as a pop-up menu.

   b. When the user presses the right mouse button, an image of a Pop-Tart appears.

   c. When the user presses any button, the mouse self-destructs with a loud Pop!

   d. A menu pops up on the screen, although I have no idea which menu it might be, what it might look like, or who really cares.

Fortunately, most users are already familiar with all these menu features, so it won't come as a shock to them when a pop-up menu or submenu appears on the screen. The secret is to use these features only if you have to. Remember, the more fancy features you add to your program, the more things you have to worry about. (Now aren't you glad you decided to learn how to program your computer?)

Chapter 12

Dialog Boxes

· ·

In This Chapter

▶ Creating dialog boxes

▶ Adding icons and buttons to dialog boxes

▶ Commonly used dialog boxes

· ·

*P*ull-down menus certainly make life easier for users (provided, of course, that the users know how to use the menus). In addition to pull-down menus, nearly every program also uses dialog boxes.

Dialog boxes are those tiny windows that pop up on the screen. Most of the time, the computer uses dialog boxes to let the user know what it's doing, such as, "Now printing page 4 of 67" or "Window application error."

However, dialog boxes also let the computer ask questions of users, such as "Cancel printing?" or "Do you really want to exit out of Windows?" A fancy dialog box might be crammed full of options so that the user can make multiple choices at once.

Just as most Windows-based programs use similar pull-down menus (File, Edit, Help), these programs also use similar dialog boxes.

Using Predefined Dialog Boxes

Out of the goodness of its heart, Microsoft included predefined dialog boxes for Visual Basic programmers to use. These dialog boxes are

🖌 An input box

🖌 An Open dialog box

🖌 A Save As dialog box

✔ A Color dialog box

✔ A Font dialog box

✔ A Print dialog box

Predefined dialog boxes require almost no modification by you to get them to work. The drawback is that if you don't like the way they look, you can't change them.

Creating an Input Box

An input box consists of three parts that you can modify:

✔ Title bar

✔ User prompt string

✔ Text input box

Input boxes also contain an OK and a Cancel command button that you cannot modify.

The *title bar* identifies the purpose of the dialog box, such as "File to Delete" or "Search for Text." The *user prompt string* tells the user what type of information the computer wants, such as the name of a file. The maximum length of this prompt string is 255 characters. The *text input box* is where the user types a response.

The following BASIC code displays the input box shown in Figure 12-1:

```
Private Sub Form_Load()
Candidate = InputBox("Enter your candidate choice:", "Write-
          in Vote")
End Sub
```

Any text the user types in the text input box gets stored in the variable `Candidate`. (Don't worry. You learn more about variables in Part IV.)

Normally, the text input box is blank. If you want to display a default value in the text input box, you can. Here's how to do it:

```
Private Sub Form_Load()
Candidate = InputBox("Enter your candidate choice:", "Write-
          in Vote", "George Washington")
End Sub
```

User prompt string   Title bar   Text input box

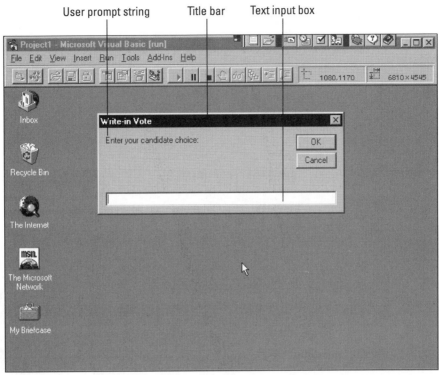

Figure 12-1:
Input box
created by
BASIC code.

Now when the input box appears, the name "George Washington" appears highlighted in the text box.

Normally, an input box appears centered on the screen, approximately one-third of the way down from the top of the screen. If you want an input box to appear in a specific location, you have to set the x- and y-coordinates, as in the following example:

```
Private Sub Form_Load()
Candidate = InputBox("Enter your candidate choice:", "Write-
         in Vote", "George Washington", 1500, 1650)
End Sub
```

This BASIC command displays the input box at x-coordinate 1500 and y-coordinate 1650.

Creating a Dialog Box

A *dialog box* displays a brief message on the screen along with one or more command buttons. Dialog boxes contain the following four parts that you can modify (as shown in Figure 12-2):

- A title bar
- A message
- An eye-catching icon
- One or more command buttons

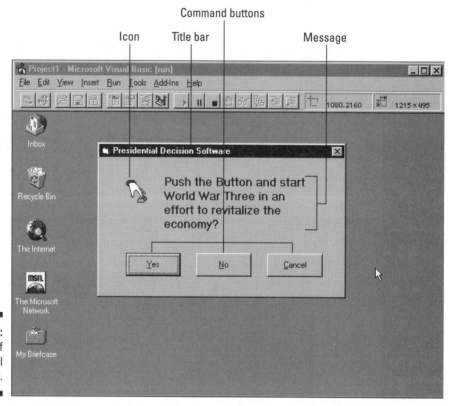

Figure 12-2:
The parts of
a typical
dialog box.

The *title bar* identifies the purpose of the dialog box, such as About This Program. The *message* contains text that appears in the dialog box, such as "Are you sure that you want to start World War III?" The *icon* provides visual information about the dialog box's importance. The number and type of *command buttons* can vary from one to three.

The simplest dialog box is one that displays a message on the screen and provides an OK command button so that the user can make the dialog box go away.

The following BASIC code creates the simple dialog box displayed in Figure 12-3:

```
Private Sub Form_Load()
  MsgBox "Wimpy Systems Software", , "About This Program"
End Sub
```

This simple dialog box does nothing more than appear on the screen and then disappear when the user clicks OK.

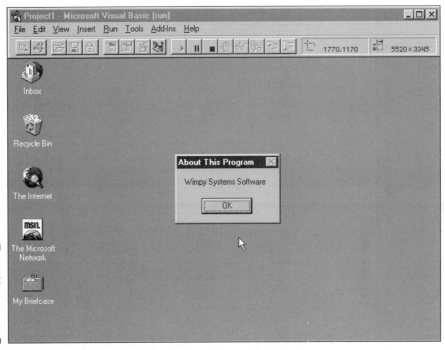

Figure 12-3:
The About
This
Program
dialog box.

Adding icons to a dialog box

Icons can help grab a user's attention to your dialog box. There are four icons in Visual Basic (see Figure 12-4):

- ✔ The Critical Message icon
- ✔ The Warning Query icon
- ✔ The Warning Message icon
- ✔ The Information Message icon

Icon	Name	Numeric Value
 ✖	Critical Message	16
 ?	Warning Query	32
 !	Warning Message	48
 i	Information Message	64

Figure 12-4: The four icons for dialog boxes and their numeric values.

The *Critical Message* icon alerts the user to an extremely important question, such as, "If you continue, you will erase all the files on your hard disk. Are you sure that you want to do this?"

The *Warning Query* icon (a question mark) highlights less-threatening questions, such as "Do you really want to exit from Microsoft Word?"

The *Warning Message* icon (an exclamation mark) emphasizes warnings that the user needs to know about, such as "Do you really want to replace all 79 pages of your document with a single sentence?"

The *Information Message* icon makes otherwise drab and boring messages look interesting, such as "Do you really want to exit Windows?"

To add an icon to a dialog box, just add the numeric value of the icon between the dialog box message and the title bar text, as follows:

```
Private Sub Form_Load()
MsgBox "Wimpy Systems Software", 64, "About This Program"
End Sub
```

This code creates the dialog box shown in Figure 12-5.

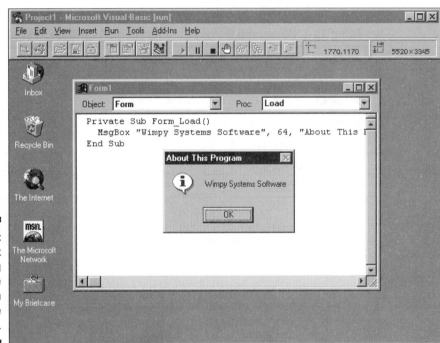

Figure 12-5:
A dialog box containing the Information Message icon.

Normally, Visual Basic lets you display only one of four possible icons in a dialog box. If this seems limiting and downright boring, you can fake a dialog box by creating a separate form, setting its BorderStyle property to Fixed Dialog, and drawing command buttons and an image box directly on this form. You can then draw an image box on the form and load any type of icon you want.

Just remember that creating a dialog box using a separate form requires you to draw the command buttons, label, and image box along with writing BASIC code to make the whole thing work. If you just want to create a dialog box quickly and easily, use the MsgBox command instead.

Defining the number and type of command buttons in a dialog box

Dialog boxes can contain from one to three command buttons. Each command button combination is represented by a numerical value. Table 12-1 lists the six command button combinations.

Table 12-1 Command Button Combinations Available in Visual Basic

Displays	*Value*
OK button	0
OK and Cancel buttons	1
Abort, Retry, and Ignore buttons	2
Yes, No, and Cancel buttons	3
Yes and No buttons	4
Retry and Cancel buttons	5

To define a command button combination, choose the combination you want and type its numerical value between the dialog box's message text and title bar text, such as:

```
Private Sub Form_Load()
  MsgBox "File not found", 2, "Error Message"
End Sub
```

Which command button did the user select in a dialog box?

Dialog boxes with two or more command buttons give users a choice. Of course, after the user has made a choice, your program must determine which choice the user has made.

The seven possible buttons a user can choose are represented by the numerical values in Table 12-2.

Table 12-2	Command Buttons a User Can Choose
Button Selected	*Numerical Value*
OK button	1
Cancel button	2
Abort button	3
Retry button	4
Ignore button	5
Yes button	6
No button	7

To make your program determine which command button a user chose, you have to set a variable equal to the MsgBox BASIC code, as shown in the following line:

```
Reply = MsgBox("File not found", 2, "Error Message")
```

This code displays a dialog box with the Abort, Retry, and Ignore command buttons. If the user clicks Abort, the value of Reply is 3. If the user clicks Retry, the value of Reply is 4. If the user clicks Ignore, the value of Reply is 5.

Whenever you assign a variable to represent the value chosen from a dialog box, you must use parentheses to enclose the dialog box parameters.

Commonly Used Dialog Boxes

Because Windows is becoming a standard for user interfaces, you may notice that most Windows-based programs use nearly identical dialog boxes for many commands, such as

✔ Open

✔ Save As

✔ Print

✔ Color

✔ Font

To ensure that your program has all the identity of a clone from *The Stepford Wives,* you too can add these commonly used dialog boxes in your Visual Basic programs. To give your program the capability to use one of these five dialog boxes, follow these steps:

1. Click the Common dialog box icon in the Visual Basic Toolbox, shown in Figure 12-6.

2. Move the mouse anywhere on the form. Then hold down the mouse button and move the mouse down and to the right. Let go. This draws the Common dialog box icon on the form, as shown in Figure 12-6.

Common dialog box icon

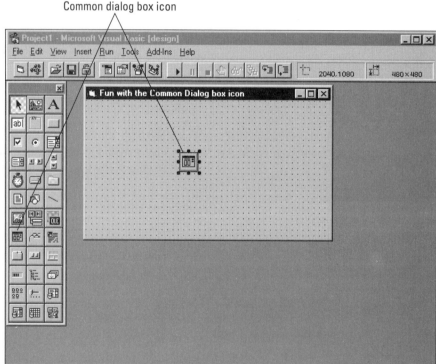

Figure 12-6:
The Common dialog box icon in the Toolbox and on a form.

Where you place the Common dialog box icon on a form is irrelevant because the icon is always invisible. Putting the Common dialog box icon on a form essentially tells Visual Basic, "Okay, this icon gives you the magical power to display the Open, Save As, Print, Color, or Font dialog box whenever I tell you to."

Because you need only one Common dialog box icon per form, don't bother changing the icon's name. Just use the default name that Visual Basic gives it, which is `CommonDialog1`.

Test your newfound knowledge

1. Why would you want to display an icon in a dialog box?

   a. In case an illiterate computer user wants to use your program.

   b. To catch the eye of the user and provide a visual cue. For example, a Critical Message icon can warn users that something terrible is about to happen if they don't do something immediately.

   c. To catch the eye of the user, verifying your mother's warnings that if you're not careful, you could poke your eye out.

   d. To see if the user is smart enough to realize that the dialog box has nothing important to say.

2. To use the predefined Open, Save As, Color, Font, or Print dialog box, what must you do first?

   a. Read the manual.

   b. Create a new form, draw three command buttons, two check boxes, one list box, and a partridge in a pear tree.

   c. Save your file and exit Visual Basic.

   d. Make that sure you have drawn the Common dialog box icon on your form.

Displaying the Open dialog box

The Open dialog box (see Figure 12-7) lets users choose a drive, directory, and file to open. The user also has the choice of displaying only specific file types, such as those matching the *.TXT or *.EXE criteria.

To display the Open dialog box, you need only one magic BASIC command that looks like this:

```
CommonDialog1.Action = 1
```

To define the list of files that the Open dialog box displays, you have to use something technical called a *filter*. A filter tells Visual Basic what types of files to display, such as all those with the TXT or BAT file extension.

A filter consists of two parts: the label that appears in the list box and the filter itself. Table 12-3 lists some examples of labels and filters. For added clarity, labels usually include the filter they use.

Text files, for example, usually have the file extension TXT, but sometimes they have the file extension ASC. So the label "Text Files (*.TXT)" lets you know that the dialog box shows only text files with the TXT file extension (and not text files with the ASC file extension).

Figure 12-7:
The Open
dialog box.

Table 12-3	Labels and Filters
Label	*Filter*
All Files (*.*)	*.*
Text Files (*.TXT)	*.TXT
Batch Files (*.BAT)	*.BAT
Executable Files (*.EXE)	*.EXE

To define your labels and filters, use BASIC code, as in the following example:

```
CommonDialog1.Filter = "All Files (*.*)|*.*|Text Files
        (*.TXT)|*.TXT|Batch Files(*.BAT)|*.BAT|Executable
        Files (*.EXE)|*.EXE"
```

After you have created your list of labels and filters, you have to define which
filter to use first. Again, you use BASIC code:

```
CommonDialog1.FilterIndex = 1
```

This code line displays "All Files (*.*)" in the List Files of Type list box. Or you can choose the following:

```
CommonDialog1.FilterIndex = 4
```

This line displays "Executable Files (*.EXE)" in the List Files of Type list box.

The order in which you define your filter (using the `CommonDialog1.Filter` command) determines the `FilterIndex` number. For example, if you change the filter to:

```
CommonDialog1.Filter = "Text Files (*.TXT)|*.TXT|All Files
          (*.*)|*.*"
```

the following code displays "Text Files (*.TXT)" in the List Files of Type list box:

```
CommonDialog1.FilterIndex = 1
```

How to create an Open dialog box

Obviously, if your program is going to store data in a file, it will have to open a file at some point. Because nearly every program needs to open files, make your life easy and use the Open dialog box.

To create an Open dialog box, follow these steps:

1. Click the Common dialog box icon in the Visual Basic Toolbox.

2. Move the mouse anywhere on the form, hold down the mouse button, and move the mouse down and to the right. Then let go. This draws the Common dialog box icon on the form.

3. Create a command button or menu command that will display the Open dialog box. Most likely this will be the Open command under the File menu (duh).

4. Click the command button and press F7 (or click the Open command under the File menu that you've created for your program). Visual Basic opens something mysterious called the Code window and displays something like this:

```
Private Sub Command1_Click()
End Sub
```

5. Type the following commands so the whole thing looks like the following:

```
Private Sub Command1_Click()
  CommonDialog1.Filter = "All Files (*.*)|*.*"
  CommonDialog1.FilterIndex = 1
  CommonDialog1.Action = 1
End Sub
```

If you created an Open command under the File menu, type the following instead:

```
Private Sub mnuFileOpen_Click()
  CommonDialog1.Filter = "All Files (*.*)|*.*"
  CommonDialog1.FilterIndex = 1
  CommonDialog1.Action = 1
End Sub
```

6. Test your Open dialog box by pressing F5 or by selecting <u>S</u>tart from the <u>R</u>un menu.

At this point, the Open dialog box looks nice and seems to work, but because you haven't written any BASIC code to tell the dialog box what to do, it won't do a thing.

Displaying a Save As dialog box

A Save As dialog box is nearly identical to the Open dialog box. However, the text of the title bar is not the same (the Open dialog box's title bar says "Open" and the Save As dialog box's title bar says "Save As"), and the Save As file list appears dimmed.

The only BASIC command you need to use to display a Save As dialog box is:

```
CommonDialog1.Action = 2
```

For example:

```
Private Sub mnuFileSaveAs_Click()
  CommonDialog1.Action = 2
End Sub
```

Displaying a Color dialog box

The Color dialog box lets users choose colors or make their own, as shown in Figure 12-8.

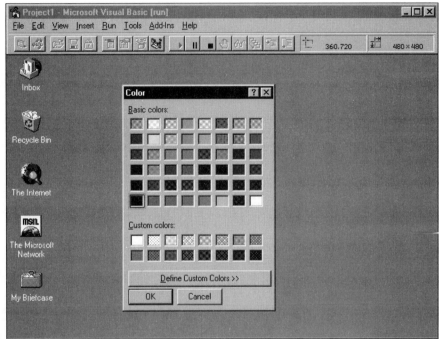

Figure 12-8:
The Color
dialog box.

To display a Color dialog box, you have to use two magic BASIC commands:

```
CommonDialog1.Flags = &H1&
CommonDialog1.Action = 3
```

For example:

```
Private Sub Command1_Click()
  CommonDialog1.Flags = &H1&
  CommonDialog1.Action = 3
End Sub
```

Displaying a Font dialog box

The Font dialog box, shown in Figure 12-9, lets users choose different fonts, font styles, and point sizes. Each time the user chooses an option, this dialog box displays a sample so that the user can see whether the font, font style, or point size looks okay.

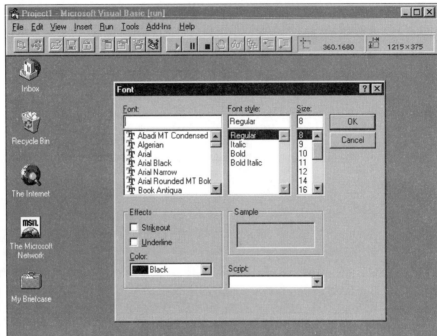

Figure 12-9:
The Font
dialog box.

To display a Font dialog box, you have to use two magic BASIC commands:

```
CommonDialog1.Flags = &H3& Or &H100&
CommonDialog1.Action = 4
```

For example:

```
Private Sub Command1_Click()
  CommonDialog1.Flags = &H3& Or &H100&
  CommonDialog1.Action = 4
End Sub
```

Displaying a Print dialog box

A Print dialog box (see Figure 12-10) lets users choose the printer, the print range, and the print quantity.

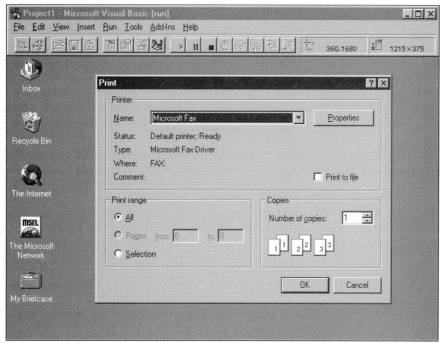

Figure 12-10:
The Print
dialog box.

To display a Print dialog box, use the following BASIC command:

```
CommonDialog1.Action = 5
```

For example:

```
Private Sub Command1_Click()
  CommonDialog1.Action = 5
End Sub
```

To set the default value for the number of copies to print, you have to use the following BASIC commands:

```
CommonDialog1.Copies = 1
CommonDialog1.ShowPrinter
```

For example:

```
Private Sub Command1_Click()
   CommonDialog1.Copies = 1
   CommonDialog1.ShowPrinter
   CommonDialog1.Action = 5
End Sub
```

Like the Open, Save As, Color, and Font dialog boxes, the Print dialog box looks like it works but really doesn't do anything until you write BASIC code that tells it how to work.

Still, using these common dialog boxes can give your programs that all-important professional look and feel that people have come to expect from software. As any professional programmer can tell you, the more your program looks like it will work, the more likely it is that people will believe that it does work. Computer programmers aren't necessarily engineers or mathematicians. They're more like magicians or con artists with the reputations of engineers or mathematicians.

Part IV
The Basics of Writing Code

"YES, WE STILL HAVE A FEW BUGS IN THE WORD PROCESSING SOFTWARE. BY THE WAY, HERE'S A MEMO FROM MARKETING."

In this part . . .

Hurray! Here's the first chapter where you actually start writing BASIC code to make your computer do something worthwhile. Until now, you've only drawn the parts that make up a user interface (with an occasional BASIC command thrown in). But everyone knows that looks aren't everything (except for rich old men dating extremely young Playboy bunnies). What matters is not only that your user interface looks good, but that it also responds to the user.

Although the thought of writing BASIC code may seem intimidating, relax. BASIC code is nothing more than step-by-step instructions telling the computer exactly what to do. All the BASIC code that you write in this part is simple and easy to understand. So get ready to start coding. You'll find that programming really can be fun, easy, and almost as addicting as drawing your user interface.

Chapter 13

Event Procedures

*W*henever the user takes any action, such as clicking the mouse, pressing a key, passing out on the keyboard, or putting a bullet through the monitor, it's called an *event*. The moment an event occurs, Visual Basic looks for BASIC code to tell the program what to do. The BASIC code that responds to a specific event is called an *event procedure*.

Visual Basic programs can have up to 5,200 event procedures. If you have that many, however, you have a tremendously complicated program or you're an incredibly incompetent programmer.

With so many possible events and so many possible event procedures in a single program, how does Visual Basic know which event procedure to use?

The answer is easy. When an event occurs, it's usually directed at some part of your program's user interface. For example, most users click the mouse button only when the mouse is pointing at an object, such as a command button, check box, or menu command on the screen.

Every object can have one or more event procedures, and each event procedure responds to a different event, such as clicking the mouse or pressing a key.

Types of Events

The most common types of events can be classified into three categories:

- ✔ Keyboard events
- ✔ Mouse events
- ✔ Program events

Keyboard events occur when the user presses a certain key, such as Tab, or a certain keystroke combination, such as Ctrl+P.

Mouse events occur when the user moves the mouse, clicks or double-clicks the mouse button, or drags the mouse across the screen.

Program events occur when a Visual Basic program loads, opens, or closes a form. Whereas keyboard and mouse events occur when the user does something, program events occur when BASIC code does something.

Although Visual Basic can respond to a multitude of events, you generally want your user interface to respond to one or two events, such as clicking the mouse or pressing a certain key.

As soon as Visual Basic detects an event, it immediately looks to see what part of the user interface should respond.

When the user clicks the mouse, for example, Visual Basic first identifies the event. ("Okay, it was a mouse click.") Next, Visual Basic looks to see where the user clicked the mouse. ("The user clicked the mouse on the OK command button.")

Visual Basic then finds that particular command button's event procedure, which gives instructions telling what to do when the user clicks the mouse button.

Creating event procedures

One object can respond to one or more events. For example, a command button can respond to the user clicking the mouse button or pressing Enter.

Two or more objects can respond to the same event. For example, both a command button and a check box can respond to a mouse click, but they may have different instructions that tell Visual Basic what to do next.

To write an event procedure, you have to perform the following tasks:

✔ Identify the part of your user interface that will respond.

✔ Open the code window.

✔ Identify the event to respond to.

✔ Write BASIC code to process the event.

Make sure that all the objects of your user interface have names before creating any event procedures. If you create an event procedure for an object and later change that object's name, you will have to rewrite your event procedures.

The following three parts of a user interface can respond to events:

✔ Forms

✔ Objects (command buttons, check boxes, and so on)

✔ Pull-down menus

To create an event procedure for a form, follow these steps:

1. Click anywhere on the form. (Make sure you do not click on any objects on the form.)

2. Open the Code window by pressing F7 or by selecting Code from the View menu. Visual Basic displays the Code window on the screen along with an empty event procedure (see Figure 13-1).

To create an event procedure for an object, such as a command button or check box, follow these steps:

1. Click the object so that little black rectangles (*handles*) appear around it.

2. Open the Code window by pressing F7 or by selecting Code from the View menu. Visual Basic displays the Code window on the screen along with an empty event procedure.

To create an event procedure for a pull-down menu, follow these steps:

1. Click the pull-down menu title containing the menu command you want.

2. Highlight the menu command you want.

3. Open the Code window by pressing Enter or by clicking the highlighted menu command once. Visual Basic displays the Code window on the screen along with an empty event procedure.

Split bar

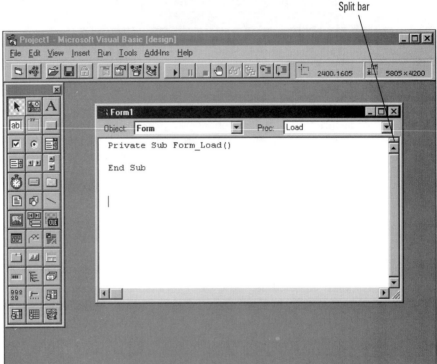

Figure 13-1:
Code
window with
an empty
event
procedure.

The parts of event procedures

Every time you create an event procedure for the first time, Visual Basic displays an empty event procedure in the code window. All empty event procedures consist of two lines, such as

```
Private Sub cmdExit_Click()
End Sub
```

The first line of any event procedure contains five parts:

- ✔ `Private Sub` — identifies the procedure as a subprogram
- ✔ The object's name — in this example, the object is named `cmdExit`
- ✔ An underscore
- ✔ The event name — in this example, the event is a mouse click
- ✔ A pair of parentheses, containing any data that the subprogram may need to work — in this example, the parentheses are empty

The preceding event procedure says to the computer, "Here are the instructions to follow whenever the user clicks the mouse on the command button named cmdExit. Now leave me alone."

Because this example contains no instructions to follow, this event procedure does absolutely nothing.

Any time you change the name of an object, make sure that you change the name of all event procedures connected to it as well. Otherwise, Visual Basic won't know which event procedures belong to which objects on your user interface.

Splitting the code window in half

Normally, the Code window displays only one event procedure at a time. If you want to view two event procedures, you can split the Code window in half horizontally. You can divide the Code window only in half (not in quarters, thirds, and so on).

To split the Code window in half, follow these steps:

1. Move the mouse pointer to the Split bar. The Split bar appears at the top of the vertical scroll bar. As soon as the mouse pointer appears over the Split bar, it turns into two horizontal parallel lines with arrows pointing up and down.

2. Hold down the left mouse button and drag the mouse down. When the Split bar has divided the Code window the way you want, let go of the mouse button (see Figure 13-2).

To display the Code window as a single window again, follow these steps:

1. Move the mouse pointer over the bar dividing the Code window in half. The mouse pointer turns into two horizontal parallel lines with arrows pointing up and down.

2. Hold down the left mouse button and drag the mouse up to the top of the Code window, then let go of the mouse button.

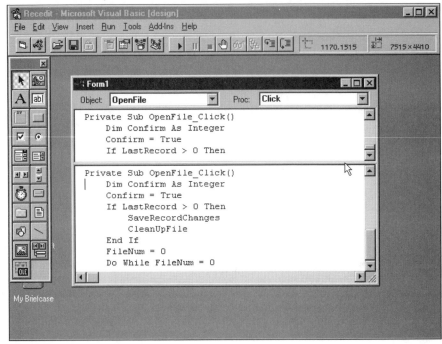

Figure 13-2:
The Code
window
displaying
multiple
event
procedures.

Viewing different event procedures

You can use any of the following methods to view an event procedure for each object that makes up your user interface (such as a command button, check box, radio button, or list box):

✔ Choose an object from the Object list box.

✔ Press Ctrl+↑ or Ctrl+↓.

✔ Click the View menu and then click Object Browser, or press F2 to display the Object Browser dialog box.

The Object Browser dialog box, shown in Figure 13-3, displays all the forms and modules in your program and all the procedures that belong to each form and module. Each time you click on a form or module in the Classes/Modules list box, the Methods/Properties list box displays only those procedures stored on the chosen form.

The Methods/Properties list box contains the names of all the objects on the currently displayed form. By clicking on an event procedure displayed in the Methods/Properties list box, you can quickly view each object's event procedure.

Classes/Modules list box   Methods/Properties list box

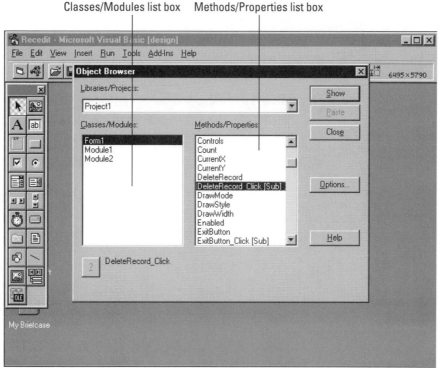

Figure 13-3:
The Object
Browser
dialog box.

The Object Browser dialog box is great for viewing different event procedures stored in different forms, but it's fairly complicated to use for viewing different event procedures stored in the same form.

To quickly view different event procedures stored in the same form, open the Code window (by pressing F7) and use the Object and Proc list boxes, shown in Figure 13-4.

The Object list box contains all the objects currently displayed on a form. By clicking the Object list box, you can find the object containing the event procedure that you want to see.

The Proc list box contains all the events that an object can respond to. Each time you select a different event, Visual Basic displays a different event procedure in the Code window.

Object list box   Proc list box

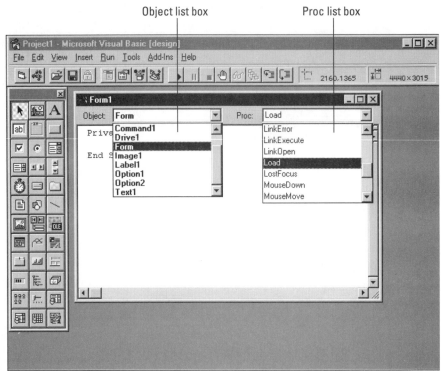

Figure 13-4:
The Code
window.

Table 13-1 lists the most common events to which objects can respond.

Table 13-1	Common Events
Event	*Occurs When. . .*
Activate	A form becomes the active window
Change	The contents of a combo box, directory list box, drive list box, scroll bar, label, picture box, or text box change
Click	The user clicks the mouse button once on the object
DblClick	The user clicks the mouse button twice in rapid succession on an object
Deactivate	A form changes from being an active window to an inactive window
DragDrop	The user holds down the mouse button on an object, moves the mouse, and releases the mouse button

Event	Occurs When...
DragOver	The user holds down the mouse button on an object and moves the mouse
DropDown	The list portion of a combo box drops down to display a list of choices
GotFocus	An object is highlighted when the user presses Tab or clicks an object
KeyDown	The user presses a key
KeyPress	The user presses and releases an ANSI key, such as a keyboard character, Ctrl key combination, Enter, or backspace key. (Basically, an ANSI key can be any letter, number, or oddball keystroke combination that you press.)
KeyUp	The user releases a key
LostFocus	An object is no longer highlighted because the user pressed Tab or clicked another object
MouseDown	The user presses a mouse button
MouseMove	The user moves the mouse
MouseUp	The user releases a mouse button

The combination of the object name and the event name defines the name for an event procedure. Because object names must always be unique, no two event procedures on the same form can have the same name.

Although no two event procedures on the same form can share the same name, event procedures on different forms *can* have the same name. For example, you could have the following event procedure on two different forms:

```
Private Sub cmdExit_Click()
End Sub
```

Two or more objects can share the same name if you make them into a *control array*. No need to memorize this term right now. Just make a note of it and move on.

Test your newfound knowledge

1. What is an event, and what are the three types of events?

    a. An event is something that you must get tickets for, such as a concert, a sports event, and the circus.

    b. Events are things that happen to your computer, such as having a drink spilled on the keyboard, having all your files erased by mistake, and having the dog eat a floppy disk.

    c. Events occur when the user presses a key or mouse button or when the program changes its appearance. The three types are keyboard, mouse, and program events.

    d. An event is a holiday or celebration that lets you take the day off from work. The three types of events are legal holidays, reunions, and weddings.

2. What do the Object list box and Proc list box do in the Code window?

    a. They list all the possible reasons why you should be writing your program in C++ or Pascal rather than in Visual Basic.

    b. The Object list box lets you choose an object to write an event procedure for. The Proc list box lets you choose all the possible events that an object can respond to.

    c. The Object list box contains a list of all the blunt objects you can use to hit your computer. The Proc list box lists all the events that you could be attending instead of staring at your computer screen.

    d. Neither list box does anything worth remembering, so don't bother answering this question again.

Editing in the Code Window

The Code window works like a simple word processor. Table 13-2 lists the different keystroke commands you can use to edit your event procedures.

Table 13-2	Common Editing Keys
Keystroke	*What Happens*
Delete	Deletes the character to the right of the cursor
Backspace	Deletes the character to the left of the cursor
Ctrl+Y	Deletes the line that the cursor is on
Home	Moves the cursor to the front of the line that the cursor is on
End	Moves the cursor to the end of the line that the cursor is on
Ctrl+Home	Moves the cursor to the first event procedure
Ctrl+End	Moves the cursor to the last event procedure

Keystroke	What Happens
Insert	Toggles the Insert mode on or off
Ctrl+X	Cuts a selected block of text
Ctrl+C	Copies a selected block of text
Ctrl+V	Pastes a previously Cut or Copied block of text
Ctrl+Z	Undoes the last thing you did (typed a letter, erased a sentence, and so on)
Ctrl+F	Finds a word that you specify
F1	Displays the Visual Basic help system
F3	Finds the next word that you specified previously using the Ctrl+F command
F4	Displays the Property window for the currently active form
Shift+F3	Finds the last occurrence of the word that you specified previously using the Ctrl+F command
Ctrl+H	Searches for a word and replaces it with something else
Ctrl+M	Indents an existing line by four spaces
Ctrl+→	Moves the cursor right one word
Ctrl+←	Moves the cursor left one word
Ctrl+↑	Moves the cursor to the preceding event procedure
Ctrl+↓	Moves the cursor to the next event procedure
Ctrl+P	Displays the Print dialog box

To help you write BASIC code, the Code window also automatically highlights in color BASIC reserved keywords. This enables you to see which commands are BASIC reserved keywords and which are commands you've created on your own.

To delete an entire event procedure, highlight the procedure using the mouse or the cursor keys and press Delete.

The Event Procedure That Every Program Needs

The simplest and most important event procedure that every program needs is one that stops your program. The following event procedure tells Visual Basic to stop running your program the moment the user clicks a command button named cmdExit:

```
Private Sub cmdExit_Click()
    End
End Sub
```

If you don't include an event procedure to stop your program, the only way a user can stop your program is by rebooting the computer or turning the whole thing off. Because this isn't the best way to exit a program, always make sure that your program contains at least one (or more) ways for the user to exit your program at any given time.

Chapter 14

Using Variables

● ●

In This Chapter

▶ Using variables

▶ Assigning numbers and strings to variables

▶ Declaring data types

● ●

*O*nce you know what you want your program to do, it's time to start writing BASIC code. The first code you need to write is inside your event procedures.

At the simplest level, an event procedure tells the computer what to do. An event procedure for exiting a program, for example, gives the computer a single End instruction:

```
Private Sub cmdExit_Click()
   End
End Sub
```

This event procedure requires absolutely no information from the user beyond the simple event of the user clicking the cmdExit command button.

What happens, however, when a user types a name, an address, or a telephone number into a program? Obviously, the program must read this information from the user interface and then do something with it.

Reading Data

Any information that a program gets from outside the computer is called *data,* like the name of the android in "Star Trek: The Next Generation."

Nearly all but the simplest programs receive data, do something to it, and spit it out again.

A word processor receives its data as words, which the word processor formats to look pretty and then prints neatly on paper. A database receives its data as names, addresses, and phone numbers. The database stores this information someplace and then displays it in a way that you think is useful. A nuclear missile guidance system receives its data as target coordinates. The missile system uses this data to guide a warhead to a target and wipe entire cities off the planet in the name of peace.

Every useful program in the world follows these three basic steps:

1. Get data.
2. Do something to the data.
3. Spit the data back out again.

Every useless program in the world has these four characteristics:

- Is too hard to learn and use
- Costs a great deal of money
- Claims to be user-friendly
- Doesn't work

The whole purpose of a program is to turn computers into electronic sausage grinders. Stick information in one end and out it comes on the other end. No matter what kind of program it is — word processor, spreadsheet, database, or game — all programs manipulate the following:

- Numbers
- Strings

Numbers can be positive or negative, whole numbers or fractions, or just about any other type of number you can think of (including telephone numbers to hot dates, numbers that form a combination to a safe containing wads of money, and imaginary numbers that no one except mathematicians truly understand).

Strings are characters strung together. A *character* is anything you can type from the keyboard, including letters, punctuation marks, and (don't get confused now) numbers.

Depending on how the program decides to treat them, numbers can be considered as numbers or as a string. For example, most programs treat your telephone number or street address as a string but treat your age or weight as a number.

A single letter is considered a string. An entire sentence is also a string. Even the first chapter of *War and Peace* can be considered a string. Strings can be any collection of letters, spaces, and numbers grouped together.

Values and Variables

When you type a number or a string into a program, how does the computer keep track of that number or string? After all, you may know that 555-1234 represents a phone number, but to the computer, it's just another number or string.

To store data, programs use *variables*, a time-tested concept from algebra. When you write a program, you have to tell it, "Okay, when someone types 555-1234, give this number a name, such as PhoneNumber, and store it someplace where you can find it again."

When your program needs to retrieve or manipulate this data, it says, "Okay, where did I put this information? Oh, that's right, it's stored in a place (variable) called PhoneNumber." The computer obediently rushes to the `PhoneNumber` variable and yanks out whatever number or word the computer stored there.

Variables can hold a wide variety of data (which is why they're called *variables;* it's also a more scientific-sounding name than *flaky, wishy-washy,* or *schizo-phrenic*). The information stored in a variable is called a *value* because it represents either a string or a number.

Using variables

There are two types of variables:

- Those you make up
- Those already defined as the properties of every object on a form

Every time you draw an object to make your user interface, Visual Basic automatically creates a whole bunch of variables (called *properties*) set with default values. To look at the values of an object's properties, you have to use the Properties window (press F4 or select Properties from the View menu).

Property values can represent numbers (such as defining the width and height of an object), True or False values (such as defining whether an object is visible), or strings (such as captions on a command button). Properties simply define the appearance of an object on the screen.

Just remember that variables are names that can represent any type of value, and properties are special names for variables that affect the appearance of an object.

To create a variable on your own, just give it a name. After you type a name for a variable, the variable magically springs into existence. There are two ways to create a variable:

- ✔ Declare it using the Dim statement.
- ✔ Just name it and assign a value to it.

The only place where you can type (and create) a variable name is in the Code window. The only place in the Code window where you can type a variable name is sandwiched between the first and last lines of a procedure.

Declaring variables

Creating a variable is as simple as typing its name and assigning a value to it, as shown in the following example:

```
Private Sub Form1_Load()
   PetName = "Bo the cat"
   Age = 2
End Sub
```

The preceding event procedure says the following:

1. When a form named Form1 loads, these are the instructions to follow.
2. First, create a variable called PetName and set its value to the string "Bo the cat".
3. Second, create a variable called Age and set its value to the number two.

Although it's perfectly acceptable to create a variable out of thin air in the middle of a procedure, it's not considered good programming practice. Unless you examine an event procedure line by line, you have no idea how many variables the procedure may be using.

A better programming practice is to declare your variables at the beginning of each event procedure. To declare a variable, use the Dim command, as shown in the following example:

```
Dim VariableName1, VariableName2
```

Type as many variable names as you want in the preceding command.

Rewriting the preceding event procedure causes it to look like the following:

```
Private Sub Form1_Load()
Dim PetName, Age
  PetName = "Bo the cat"
  Age = 2
End Sub
```

You can also declare variables explicitly, as in the following:

```
Dim PetName as String, Age as Integer
```

This technique is explained in detail later in the "Data Types" section.

Although declaring a variable can add an extra line or two to an event procedure, see how easy it is to find the names of all the variables used? Instead of examining an event procedure line by line, you can just glance at the first few lines and see a list of all the variable names used.

Using the Dim statement simply helps you, the programmer, understand what the procedure does. As far as the computer is concerned, it doesn't care whether you use the Dim statement or not. Examples of these ways to create variables are shown in Figure 14-1.

Naming variables

You can name your variables anything you want, and you can store anything you want in them.

However, it's pretty foolish to name a variable PhoneNumber and then stuff somebody's ZIP code in it.

To make your life easier, give your variables names that represent the data you're going to store in them. For example, naming a variable PhoneNumber makes sense if you're going to store phone numbers in it. Likewise, a variable named BusinessName should hold only the words that make up business names.

When naming your variables, here are some unbreakable rules that you must follow; otherwise, Visual Basic will throw a tantrum. All variables must:

- ✔ Begin with a letter
- ✔ Be a maximum of 255 characters in length (with an obvious minimum of one character in length)
- ✔ Contain only letters, numbers, and the underscore character (_) — spaces and punctuation marks are not allowed
- ✔ Be any word except a Visual Basic reserved word, such as End or Sub

Creating a variable without Dim   Assigning a value to a variable

Creating a variable with Dim

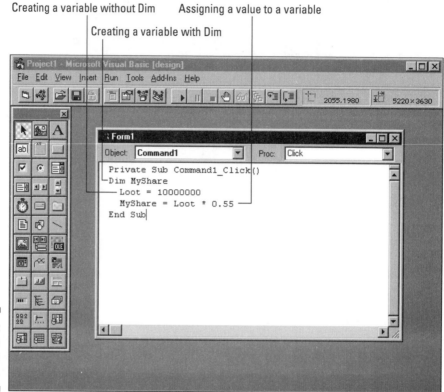

If your variable names meet these criteria, all will be well. (Of course, that doesn't mean your program will work, but at least Visual Basic will be happy.) The following are examples of Visual Basic-approved variable names:

```
Phone
Here_is_Your_Name
Route66
```

The following are some no-no's for variable names, which Visual Basic will refuse to use:

123Surprise	(This name begins with a number)
Just Work	(This name contains a space)
Sub	(This name is a Visual Basic reserved keyword)

Test your newfound knowledge

1. What do the following BASIC commands do?

```
txtMessage.Text = "Now erasing
your hard drive."

cmdChange.Caption = "Ha, ha,
ha!"

Gotcha = 1
```

a. Stuffs the string "Now erasing your hard drive" into the Text property of a text box called txtMessage, stuffs the string "Ha, ha, ha!" into the Caption property of a command button called cmdChange, and sets a variable called Gotcha to 1.

b. Erases your hard drive once, displays the message "Ha, ha, ha!", and inflicts severe psychological damage on the user.

c. Stuffs the string "1" into a variable called Gotcha and then erases your hard disk in retaliation for choosing this answer, which is obviously wrong.

d. These BASIC commands don't do anything if you don't turn on your computer and load Visual Basic. So there.

2. What is the purpose for declaring variables?

a. So programmers from the South can feel right at home talking to the computer. "Why, I declare! That looks just like a little ol' integer to me!"

b. So you can hide the fact that you really don't know what you're doing.

c. To provide a convenient list of all the variables used and to define them as particular data types.

d. To flush them out of hiding and into the open, where they can be tagged, tracked, and destroyed.

Assigning numbers to variables

Now that you know how to create variables by naming them, how do you assign a value to a variable and get the value back out again? Easy — you use something mysterious called an equal sign (=).

To assign a value to a variable, you have to write a BASIC command, as in the following example:

```
VariableName = Value
```

Rather than telling the computer, "Hey, stupid. Assign the number 36 to a variable named Age," you can just write:

```
Age = 36
```

Variables can hold only one value at a time. If a variable already holds a value and you assign another one to it, the variable cheerfully tosses out the old value and accepts the new one. You could give two commands, as in the following example:

```
Age = 36
Age = 49
```

Visual Basic would first say, "Okay, let my variable named Age hold the number 36." Then Visual Basic would look at the second line and say, "Okay, let my variable named Age hold the number 49, and we'll completely forget that the number 36 ever existed."

Because the properties of an object are variables, you can assign values to an object's property in the same way. For example, suppose that you wanted to change the Height property of a text box named txtPassword to 1200. Here's how you would do it:

```
txtPassword.Height = 1200
```

This tells Visual Basic, "Find the object named txtPassword and change its Height property to 1200."

If you want to be more specific, you can even do this:

```
frmSecret!txtPassword.Height = 1200
```

This tells Visual Basic, "On the form named frmSecret, find the object named txtPassword and change its Height property to 1200."

If you don't include the form's name, Visual Basic assumes that the object you want is located on the form containing your BASIC code.

Assigning strings to variables

Assigning strings to variables is similar to assigning numbers to variables. The only difference is that you have to surround a string with quotation marks so that Visual Basic knows where the string begins and ends.

For example, you could assign a variable with a single-word string:

```
Name = "John"
```

Or you can assign a variable with a string consisting of two or more words:

```
Name = "John Doe"
```

or

```
Name = "John Smith Doe the Third and proud of it"
```

Not all strings consist of letters. Sometimes you may want to assign a variable with a phone number or Social Security number, as follows:

```
PhoneNumber = "555-1234"
SocialSecurity = "123-45-6789"
```

What would happen if you didn't include the quotation marks and just typed the following?

```
PhoneNumber = 555-1234
SocialSecurity = 123-45-6789
```

Without the quotation marks, Visual Basic thinks the hyphen is a subtraction symbol and that you want the program to calculate a new result. Instead of storing 555-1234 in the `PhoneNumber` variable, Visual Basic would store the number –679. Instead of storing 123-45-6789 in the `SocialSecurity` variable, Visual Basic would store –6711.

The golden rule of assigning variables is this: When you assign a variable with letters or numbers that you want treated as a string, put quotation marks around the letters or numbers.

Modifying properties

Assigning a variable with numbers or strings isn't some dry, academic exercise that has little relation to anything in real life. For example, if you want to display a message on the screen, you'll need to modify the properties of a label or text box. If you want to create animation, you'll need to constantly change the Left and Top properties that define an object's position on the screen. Because the properties of an object are variables, you can modify an object by assigning new values to its properties.

Suppose that the two command buttons and the text boxes shown in Figures 14-2 and 14-3 have the following properties:

Object	Property	Setting
Text box	Name	txtMessage
	Text	(Empty)
Top command button	Name	cmdHello
	Caption	Hello
Bottom command button	Name	cmdBye
	Caption	Good-bye

Now suppose that the first command button had the following event procedures:

```
Private Sub cmdHello_Click()
  txtMessage.Text = "Hello, world!"
End Sub
```

And the second command button had the following event procedure:

```
Private Sub cmdBye_Click()
  txtMessage.Text = "Good-bye, cruel world!"
End Sub
```

When you click the Hello command button, this is what happens:

1. Visual Basic detects the Click event and notices that the mouse is pointing to a command button named cmdHello.

2. Visual Basic quickly finds the event procedure named cmdHello_Click() and looks for further instructions.

3. The cmdHello_Click() event procedure tells Visual Basic, "Find a text box named txtMessage and replace its Text property with the string Hello, world!"

4. The string "Hello, world!" pops up inside the text box named txtMessage (see Figure 14-2).

When you click the Good-bye command button, this is what happens:

1. Visual Basic detects the Click event and notices that the mouse is pointing to a command button named cmdBye.

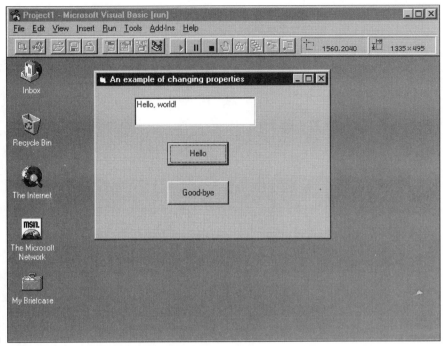

Figure 14-2:
Clicking the
Hello button.

2. Visual Basic quickly finds the event procedure named `Bye_Click()` and looks for further instructions.

3. The `cmdBye_Click()` event procedure tells Visual Basic, "Find a text box named txtMessage and replace its Text property with the string Good-bye, cruel world!"

4. The string `"Good-bye, cruel world!"` pops up inside the text box named `txtMessage` (see Figure 14-3).

You can use BASIC code to modify the properties of any object that appears on a form. By modifying the properties of other objects, you can display messages and information to the user.

The only property that BASIC code cannot change is the Name property of any object. The only way to change the Name property of an object is through the Property window.

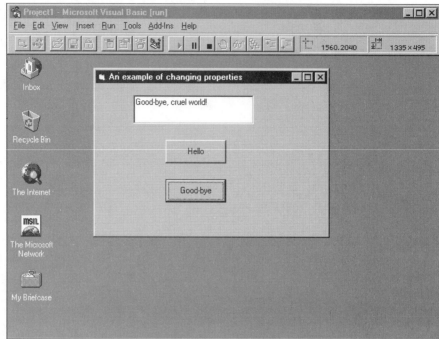

Figure 14-3:
Clicking the
Good-bye
button.

Assigning variables to other variables

Besides assigning numbers or strings to a variable, you can also assign the value of one variable to another variable. To do this, you have to write a BASIC command like the following:

```
FirstVariableName = SecondVariableName
```

For example, consider adding a second text box with the following properties (see Figure 14-4):

Object	Property	Setting
Second text box	Name	txtCopyCat
	Text	(Empty)

Consider the following modifications to the cmdHello_Click event procedure:

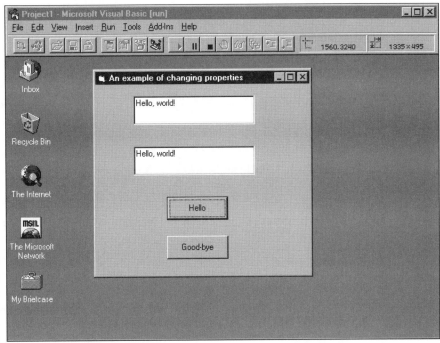

Figure 14-4:
Adding a
second text
box.

```
Private Sub cmdHello_Click()
   txtMessage.Text = "Hello, world!"
   txtCopyCat.Text = txtMessage.Text
End Sub
```

And to the `cmdBye_Click` event procedure:

```
Private Sub cmdBye_Click()
   txtMessage.Text = "Good-bye, cruel world!"
   txtCopyCat.Text = txtMessage.Text
End Sub
```

Now when you click the Hello command button, this is what happens:

1. Visual Basic detects the Click event and notices that the mouse is pointing to a command button named `cmdHello`.

2. Visual Basic quickly finds the event procedure named `cmdHello_Click()` and looks for further instructions.

3. The `cmdHello_Click()` event procedure tells Visual Basic, "Find a text box named txtMessage and replace its Text property with the string Hello, world!"

4. Visual Basic sees the second instruction that says, "Find a text box named txtCopyCat and replace its Text property with whatever is stored in the txtMessage.Text property."

5. The string `"Hello, world!"` pops up inside the text box named `txtMessage` and the text box named `txtCopyCat`.

And when you click the Good-bye command button, this is what happens:

1. Visual Basic detects the Click event and notices that the mouse is pointing to a command button named `cmdBye`.

2. Visual Basic quickly finds the event procedure named `cmdBye_Click()` and looks for further instructions.

3. The `cmdBye_Click()` event procedure tells Visual Basic, "Find a text box named txtMessage and replace its Text property with the string Good-bye, cruel world!"

4. Visual Basic sees the second instruction that says, "Find a text box named txtCopyCat and replace its Text property with whatever is stored in the txtMessage.Text property."

5. The string `"Good-bye, cruel world!"` pops up inside the text box named `txtMessage` and the text box named `txtCopyCat`.

Assigning Values to Objects Stored in Other Forms

To assign a value into an object's property, use this simple command:

```
ObjectName.PropertyName = Value
```

ObjectName is the name of the object. *PropertyName* is the property you want to change. *Value* is the number or string you want to assign to the property that will affect the object named *ObjectName*.

For example, to change the Text property of the `txtMessage` text box, you have to type the following:

```
txtMessage.Text = "Hello, world!"
```

So how can you change the property of an object stored on another form? The solution is easy. You just have to specify the name of the form on which the object is stored.

Figure 14-5, for example, shows two forms. Form #1 contains two text boxes, named `txtMessage` and `txtCopyCat`, and two command buttons, named `cmdHello` and `cmdBye`. Form #2 contains one text box with the following properties:

Object	*Property*	*Setting*
Form	Name	Form2
Text box	Name	txtNewBox
	Text	(Empty)

So how did the event procedure stored in Form #1 modify the Text property of an object stored on another form? You can simply use the following command:

```
FormName!ObjectName.PropertyName = Value
```

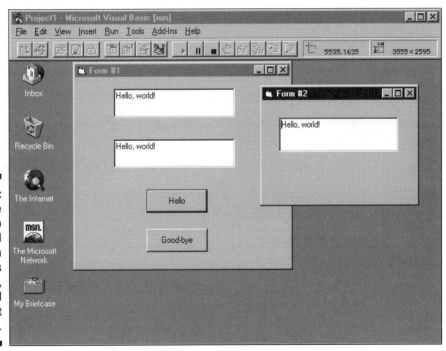

Figure 14-5:
Clicking the
Hello
command
button
displays
"Hello,
world!" in all
three text
boxes.

FormName specifies the name of the form that contains the object you want to modify. *ObjectName* is the name of the object. *PropertyName* is the property you want to change. *Value* is the number or string you want to assign to the property.

If you want the text box named `txtNewBox` to display the same message that the text boxes `txtMessage` and `txtCopyCat` display, you add the following command to the `cmdHello_Click` and the `cmdBye_Click` event procedures:

```
Form2!txtNewBox.Text = txtMessage.Text
```

The `cmdHello_Click` event procedure now looks like this:

```
Private Sub cmdHello_Click()
  txtMessage.Text = "Hello, world!"
  txtCopyCat.Text = txtMessage.Text
  Form2.Show
  Form2!txtNewBox.Text = txtMessage.Text
End Sub
```

And the `cmdBye_Click` event procedure now looks like this:

```
Private Sub cmdBye_Click()
  txtMessage.Text = "Good-bye, cruel world!"
  txtCopyCat.Text = txtMessage.Text
  Form2.Show
  Form2!txtNewBox.Text = txtMessage.Text
End Sub
```

The following explains what happens when you click the Hello command button:

1. Visual Basic detects the Click event and notices that the mouse is pointing to a command button named `cmdHello`.

2. Visual Basic quickly finds the event procedure named `cmdHello_Click()` and looks for further instructions.

3. The `cmdHello_Click()` event procedure tells Visual Basic, "Find a text box named txtMessage and replace its Text property with the string Hello, world!"

4. Visual Basic sees the second instruction that says, "Find a text box named txtCopyCat and replace its Text property with whatever is stored in the txtMessage.Text property."

5. The `Form2.Show` command tells Visual Basic, "Find a form named Form2 and display it on the screen."

6. The `Form2!txtNewBox.Text = txtMessage.Text` command tells Visual Basic, "On the form named Form2, look for a text box named txtNewBox and stuff its Text property with the value stored in the text box named txtMessage."

7. The string `"Hello, world!"` pops up inside all three text boxes, named `txtMessage`, `txtCopyCat`, and `txtNewBox`.

When you click the mouse on the Good-bye command button, the following happens:

1. Visual Basic detects the Click event and notices that the mouse is pointing to a command button named `cmdBye`.

2. Visual Basic quickly finds the event procedure named `cmdBye_Click()` and looks for further instructions.

3. The `cmdBye_Click()` event procedure tells Visual Basic, "Find a text box named txtMessage and replace its Text property with the string Good-bye, cruel world!"

4. Visual Basic sees the second instruction that says, "Find a text box named txtCopyCat and replace its Text property with whatever is stored in the txtMessage.Text property."

5. The `Form2.Show` command tells Visual Basic, "Find a form named Form2 and display it on the screen."

6. The `Form2!txtNewBox.Text = txtMessage.Text` command tells Visual Basic, "On the form named Form2, look for a text box named txtNewBox and stuff its Text property with the value stored in the text box named txtMessage."

7. The string `"Good-bye, cruel world!"` pops up inside all three text boxes, named `txtMessage`, `txtCopyCat`, and `txtNewBox`.

Data types

Variables can hold numbers and strings. However, you may want a variable called `FirstName` to contain nothing but strings. If a variable called `FirstName` wound up holding the number 56, it could cause an error if the computer expects a string but gets a number instead. To restrict the type of information a variable can hold, you can declare a variable to hold a specific data type. Data types tell Visual Basic, "See this variable? It can hold only strings or certain types of numbers, so there!"

If you write a BASIC command that attempts to assign a string into a data type that accepts only numbers, Visual Basic will squawk and display an error message. This helps you catch possible errors in your program long before you finish it and distribute it to others.

Visual Basic provides the seven data types shown in Table 14-1.

Table 14-1	Visual Basic's Data Types
Data Type	*Accepts Numbers That Range From. . .*
Integer	−32,768 to 32,767
Long	−2,147,483,648 to 2,147,483,647
Single	−3.402823E38 to −1.401298E-45 and 1.401298E-45 to 3.402823E38
Double	−1.79769313486232E308 to −4.94065645841247E-324 and 4.94065645841247E-324 to 1.79769313486232E308
Currency	−922337203685477.5808 to 922337203685477.5807
String	0 to 65,500 characters
Variant	Dates between January 1, 0000 to December 31, 9999
Numbers	Same range as Double
Strings	Same range as String

Declaring objects as data types

To store whole numbers, use the Integer data type. If you need to store really small or really large numbers, use the Long data type.

To store numbers with decimal points, use the Single data type. If you need to store really small or really large numbers with decimal points, use the Double or Numbers data type.

To store numbers representing currency (that's *money*, in nontechnical terms), use the Currency data type.

To store words and letters, use the String data type.

To store dates, use the Variant data type. You can also use the Variant data type to store numbers or strings.

By default, Visual Basic assigns all variables as a Variant data type unless you specifically tell Visual Basic otherwise. The only reason to specifically declare a variable as a Variant data type is for clarity in reading your "code." As far as Visual Basic is concerned, declaring a variable as a Variant data type is redundant, such as telling people that you drive a Ford Mustang automobile.

To declare a variable as a particular data type, use this command:

```
Dim VariableName As DataType
```

For example, to declare a variable named `MyName` as a string data type, you would use the following command:

```
Dim MyName As String
```

When Visual Basic sees this statement, it thinks, "Okay, this is a variable named MyName, and the programmer defined it as a String data type so that it can hold only strings."

When Visual Basic sees the statement

```
Dim MyName As Variant
```

it thinks, "Okay, this is a variable named MyName, and the programmer defined it as a Variant data type so that it can hold numbers or strings."

And when Visual Basic sees the statement

```
Dim MyName
```

it thinks, "Okay, this is a variable named MyName; because the programmer is too lame to define its data type, I'll automatically assume that it's a Variant data type."

An everyday event procedure

To study an actual, honest-to-goodness event procedure that declares variables as specific data types, consider the following:

```
Private Sub Form1_Load()
Dim PetName As String, Age As Integer
  PetName = "Bo the cat"
  Age = 2
End Sub
```

The variable declaration statement `Dim PetName As String, Age As Integer` tells Visual Basic, "Okay, create a variable named PetName and make sure that you use it to hold only strings."

Visual Basic continues. "Then create a variable named Age and make sure that it holds only numbers greater than or equal to –32,768 but less than or equal to 32,767."

The next command tells Visual Basic, "Assign the string "Bo the cat" to the variable PetName." Faster than a speeding bullet, Visual Basic checks to make sure that the `PetName` variable really can hold string values. Thankfully, the statement `Dim PetName As String` defined `PetName` to hold only string values, so everything is A-OK.

Finally, Visual Basic says, "Assign the number two to the variable Age." Quickly, Visual Basic checks that the variable Age really can hold a number as massive as 2. Because 2 falls within the declared range of an integer (between –32,768 and 32,767), Visual Basic cheerfully allows this statement to pass as valid.

Always use the smallest data type possible. For example, if you know the variable Age is never going to hold a number larger than 32,767, declare Age as an Integer. If you need larger or smaller numbers, choose the Long data type.

Here are the two primary reasons you use data types:

✔ So that you can easily see the type of data each variable can hold

✔ To prevent variables from accidentally storing the wrong type of data and causing an error

String data types

In case you want to restrict the length of the strings a variable can hold, you can define the maximum length by using the following command:

```
Dim VariableName As String * Size
```

The value of *Size* can vary from 1 to 65,500. So if you want to keep a variable from storing more than ten characters, you would use the following command to specify the Size as 10:

```
Dim VariableName As String * 10
```

For example, suppose that you declared the following:

```
Dim FirstName As String * 5
```

The following would be valid strings you could assign to the FirstName variable:

```
"12345"
"Bo"
"Jacob"
"Will"
```

If you try to assign to the FirstName variable a string that is longer than five characters, however, this is what happens:

String Assignment	What Really Happens
FirstName = "Marilyn"	FirstName = "Maril"
FirstName = "Bobcat"	FirstName = "Bobca"
FirstName = "King Edwards"	FirstName = "King "

If a string is too long for the declared string length of a variable, Visual Basic ruthlessly chops off the string. If you don't define a maximum string length, or if you define the variable as a Variant data type, the variable can hold up to 65,500 characters.

Scope of variables

The *scope* of a variable determines the accessibility of a variable within a Visual Basic program. Visual Basic lets you declare the scope of variables in three ways:

- ✔ Local
- ✔ Module
- ✔ Public

A *local* variable exists only within the procedure in which it is created, and it can be used only within the procedure in which it is declared. The purpose of a local variable is to isolate a specific variable in the single procedure in which it is being used. That way, if a variable is screwing up and storing the wrong value, it's easy to isolate the problem and fix it.

To declare a local variable, declare the variable within an event procedure, as follows:

```
Private Sub Command1_Click()
Dim FullName As String
End Sub
```

A local variable can be used only in the one event procedure in which it is declared. But what if you want to create a variable that two or more event procedures can share? In that case, you have to create a module variable.

Module variables can be used only by other procedures stored in the same file.

To declare a module variable, follow these steps:

1. Open the Code window by selecting Code from the View menu or by pressing F7.

2. Click the Object list box in the Code window and choose (General).

3. Click the Proc list box and choose (declarations).

4. Type your variable declaration using the Dim command, as shown in Figure 14-6.

Figure 14-6:
Module variables are always declared in the (General) object list and the (declarations) procedure box.

Module variables are useful for sharing a variable among procedures stored in the same file. If you want to use a variable that can be used by any event procedure, no matter what file it may be stored in, you need to create a public variable.

Public variables can be the most convenient to use, because every event procedure in your Visual Basic program can access them. But be careful! Most programmers avoid using public variables because if your program stores the wrong value in a public variable, you have to search your entire program to find the part that is messing up.

By comparison, if your program messes up a module variable, you can isolate the problem in the file in which you declared the module variable. Likewise, if your program messes up a local variable, the only possible place the problem could occur is in the procedure in which you declared the local variable.

To declare a public variable, follow these steps:

1. Select <u>M</u>odule from the <u>I</u>nsert menu or click the Module icon. This displays the Code window for a BAS module file.

2. Click the Object list box in the Code window and choose (General).

3. Click the Proc list box and choose (declarations).

4. Declare your public variable using the `Public` command, for example:

```
Public FullName As String
```

Figure 14-7 shows where to declare a public variable. Notice that the BAS module file is created by selecting <u>M</u>odule from the <u>I</u>nsert menu.

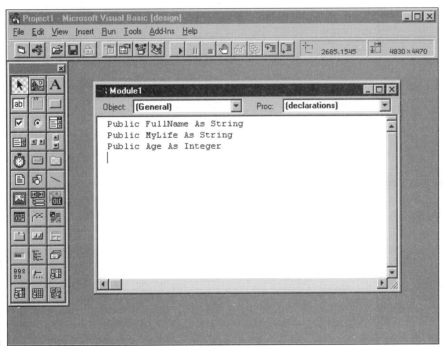

Figure 14-7:
Declaring a public variable.

To make sure that programs are easy to understand and modify later, languages such as C++ and Pascal force you to declare your variables as local, module, or public. BASIC gives you the choice of creating local, module, or public variables — or to throw caution aside and create variables as you need them in the middle of your programs.

If you plan to write large programs, always declare your variables. Like eating your vegetables, this is something that may seem distasteful at first but can actually be useful later on.

Chapter 15

Responding to the User

● ●

In This Chapter

▶ Getting data from text boxes

▶ Determining which radio button and check box the user chose

▶ Retrieving data from list boxes and scroll bars

● ●

A user interface makes your program look nice and pretty. Unfortunately, a nice and pretty user interface can be as empty-headed as the occasional date that nearly everyone has had the misfortune to meet at some point. If you want your program to have more substance than a good-looking color poster, you have to make sure that your program can respond to the user.

To make your user interface responsive, your program must

✔ Get information from the user interface

✔ Calculate a result

✔ Display that result back on the user interface

For example, when the user chooses an item from a list box, the program has no idea which item the user chose. If you look at the screen, you might be tempted to say, "Hey, stupid computer. If I can see which item the user has chosen, why can't you?"

But what you see on the user interface isn't what the computer sees. From the computer's point of view, it still has no idea which item the user selected from the list box.

To tell the computer what action a user took, you have to write BASIC code. This BASIC code grabs information off the user interface so that your program can then do something with the information.

Getting Data from the User Interface

A user interface is a simple way for users to give information to your program. A user interface shouldn't force users to type commands, such as the following:

```
FileName = "autoexec.bat"
```

Instead, a user interface should display a file list box on the screen so that users can click the file they want to use.

When a user presses a particular key or clicks a command button, file list box, and so on, Visual Basic stores this information in that object's property. From this point on, the program can use the information.

Figure 15-1 shows different ways a user can give your program information by clicking an object or by typing information.

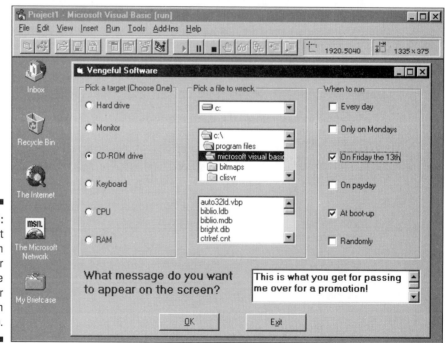

Figure 15-1: Different ways in which a user can give your program information.

The nine basic types of objects that can get data from the user interface are as follows:

- ✔ Check boxes
- ✔ Radio buttons
- ✔ Combo boxes
- ✔ List boxes
- ✔ Drive list boxes
- ✔ Directory list boxes
- ✔ File list boxes
- ✔ Horizontal and vertical scroll bars
- ✔ Text boxes

Finding Information in an Object

To find the information stored in an object, you need to know:

- ✔ The name of the object
- ✔ The object's property that contains the information
- ✔ The name of the form on which the object is located

An object's *property* is where Visual Basic stores the actual value. Different objects store information from the user in different properties. For example, a text box stores information in its Text property, but a check box stores information in its Value property.

Knowing which property you want isn't enough. You also need the name of the object that holds the property you want. And because objects on different forms can have the same names, you also need to know the form's name.

The combination of form name, object name, and property defines the specific location of the information from the user. Think of objects as mail boxes. To retrieve a letter, you have to know the state (form name), the city (object name), and the address (property).

So if you want to retrieve information from an object, you have to use the following combination:

```
FormName!ObjectName.Property
```

For example, you might want to retrieve information from a form named `frmAttack`, containing a text box named `txtWarning`, which stores data in the Text property, such as

```
frmAttack!txtWarning.Text
```

Whenever Visual Basic sees this code, it automatically says to itself, "Okay, let me find the form named frmAttack, look for the object named txtWarning, and find the value stored in the Text setting. Ah, here it is."

If you omit the form's name, Visual Basic looks for objects that appear only on the current form. If that's where you want to look, you can shorten this combination to the following:

```
ObjectName.Property
```

Getting data from text boxes

When a user types something in a text box, Visual Basic stores the information in its Text property. Typing in a text box is equivalent to assigning a value in the text box's Text property (see Figure 15-2).

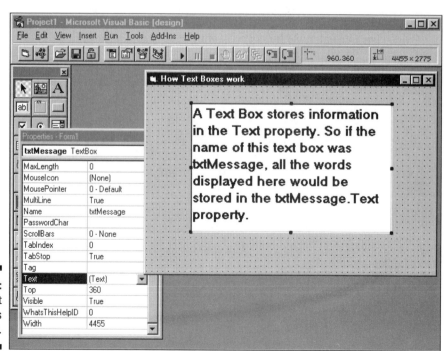

Figure 15-2:
Where a text box stores text.

If the user typed, "Greetings from Mars!" in a text box named `txtSecret`, it would be equivalent to the following BASIC code:

```
txtSecret.Text = "Greetings from Mars!"
```

Determining which radio button the user chose

A radio button can have one of two possible values stored in its Value property:

- True (selected)
- False (unselected)

An unselected radio button has its Value property set to False. Clicking an unselected radio button changes its Value property to True.

A selected radio button has its Value property set to True. Clicking a selected radio button changes its Value property to False.

To determine which radio button the user chose, you have to check the Value properties of all your radio buttons.

For example, if the user chose an unselected radio button named `optStation`, choosing the button is equivalent to the following BASIC code:

```
optStation.Value = True
```

If the user deselects a radio button, it is equivalent to the following BASIC code:

```
optStation.Value = False
```

Determining which check box the user chose

A check box can have one of three possible values stored in its Value property:

- 0 (unchecked)
- 1 (checked)
- 2 (grayed)

Figure 15-3 illustrates the possible values of check boxes.

Value property = 1

Value property = 2 | Value property = 0

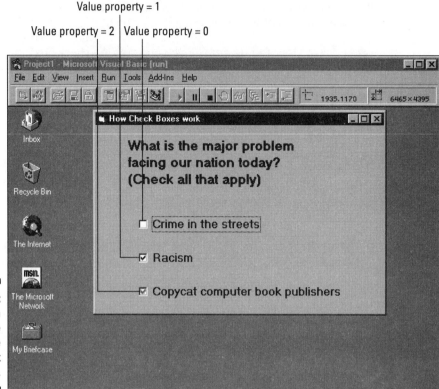

Figure 15-3:
Comparison
of three
possible
check box
values.

An unselected check box has its Value property set to 0. Clicking an unselected check box changes its Value property to 1.

A selected check box has its Value property set to 1. Clicking a selected check box changes its Value property to 0.

A grayed check box has its Value property set to 2. Clicking a grayed check box changes its Value property to 0.

A selected check box obviously means that the command represented by the check box has been chosen. Likewise, an unselected check box means that the command represented by the check box has not been chosen. However, a grayed check box can be used to show the user that the grayed check box's command is not applicable at this time.

There are only two ways to set a check box's Value property to 2 and have the check box appear grayed. The first way is to change the Value property in the Property window when you're designing your program. The second way is to use BASIC code. The following BASIC code sets the Value property to 2 for a check box named chkBold:

```
chkBold.Value = 2
```

To determine which check box the user chose, you have to review the Value properties of all your check boxes. For example, if a check box named `chkBold` is blank, it is equivalent to the following BASIC code:

```
chkBold.Value = 0
```

If the check box is selected, it is equivalent to

```
chkBold.Value = 1
```

If the check box is grayed, it is equivalent to

```
chkBold.Value = 2
```

Retrieving data from Drive, Directory, and File list boxes

When a user makes a selection from the Drive list box, Visual Basic stores the selection as a string in the Drive list box's Drive property. If a user clicks `c:` in a Drive list box named `drvWhichDrive`, for example, this is equivalent to the following BASIC code:

```
drvWhichDrive.Drive = "c:"
```

When a user makes a selection from the Directory list box, Visual Basic stores the selection as a string in the Directory list box's Path property.

If a user clicks `c:\dos` in a Directory list box named `dirFolder`, for example, this is equivalent to the following BASIC code:

```
dirFolder.Path = "c:\dos"
```

When a user makes a selection from a File list box, Visual Basic stores the file name as a string in the File list box's FileName property.

If a user clicks `autoexec.bat` in a File list box named `filGetFiles`, for example, this is equivalent to the following BASIC code:

```
filGetFiles.FileName = "c:\autoexec.bat"
```

Test your newfound knowledge

1. What does the following BASIC command do?

   ```
   WhatIsIt = chkBold.Value
   ```

   a. It tries to identify UFOs named chkBold.Value.

   b. It questions the need for anything named chkBold.Value.

   c. The command makes the computer ask, "What is it that you want me to do? Tell me and then leave me alone. I'm feeling bold today."

   d. The command yanks a number that's stored in the Value property of a check box named chkBold and stuffs the number in a variable named WhatIsIt. If the check box named chkBold were selected, the value of WhatIsIt would be 1.

2. Examine the following command and explain what it does.

   ```
   frmDataSheet!txtMessage.Text
   = "Warning!"
   ```

   a. It tells Visual Basic, "Okay, look for a form named frmDataSheet and on this form find a text box named txtMessage. When you find that, stuff its Text property with the string 'Warning!'"

   b. It tells Visual Basic, "Warning! This user is becoming a wee bit frustrated from using this program; if Microsoft doesn't make it easier to use, the user will erase all the disks and use them as coasters."

   c. The command tells everyone that the person who wrote this command probably had a good reason for not being present to help you interpret it.

   d. It warns you that your computer is about to explode and you had better take cover immediately.

A Drive list box's Drive property, the Directory list box's Path property, and the File list box's FileName properties can be changed only by using BASIC code.

Obtaining choices from a combo box

When a user chooses or types an item in a combo box, Visual Basic stores this information in the combo box's Text property (see Figure 15-4).

If the user types or selects an item named "High priority" in a combo box named cboPriorities, for example, this is equivalent to the following BASIC code:

```
cboPriorities.Text = "High priority"
```

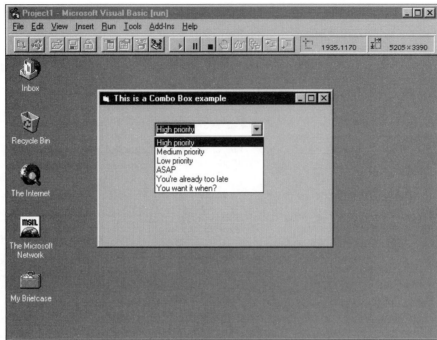

Figure 15-4:
A combo
box.

Getting values from horizontal and vertical scroll bars

Scroll bars that are not part of a text box, list box, or combo box represent a number. This number is stored in the scroll bar's Value property.

The value that a scroll bar can represent is determined by the scroll bar's Min and Max properties. The lowest possible value is –32,768. The highest possible value is 32,767.

Scroll bars let users visually represent a value, rather than typing a number from the keyboard. Ideally, you should use a scroll bar along with a label that shows the actual value of the scroll bar. That way, as users move the scroll box in the scroll bar, they can also see the value of the scroll bar changing, as shown in Figure 15-5.

Although scroll bars can represent a range of values, your program eventually will need to read a single value from the scroll bar. If you wanted to retrieve the value of a horizontal scroll bar named hsbSensitivity, for example, you would use the following command:

```
MouseSensitivity = hsbSensitivity.Value
```

Label and current value

Scroll box

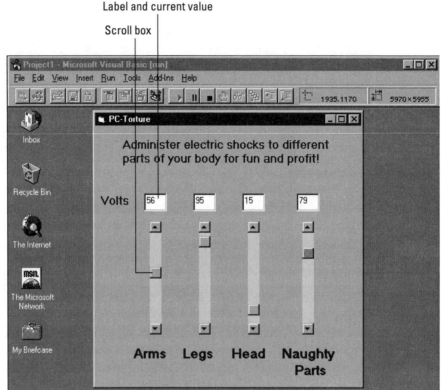

Figure 15-5:
Using a
label to
display the
value of a
scroll bar.

Retrieving data from a list box

A user can select one or more items from a list box depending on the list box's MultiSelect property. If the MultiSelect property is set to 0 (the default value) and a user selects an item, the list box stores the item in its Text property (as shown in Figure 15-6).

If the user selects an item named "Cat food" in a list box named `lstGroceries`, this is equivalent to the following BASIC code:

```
lstGroceries.Text = "Cat food"
```

If a list box's MultiSelect property is 1 or 2, users can select two or more items in the list box by holding down the Shift key and clicking on an item. Because a list box's Text property can hold only one string at a time, it's impossible to store all the selections made by a user in the list box's Text property.

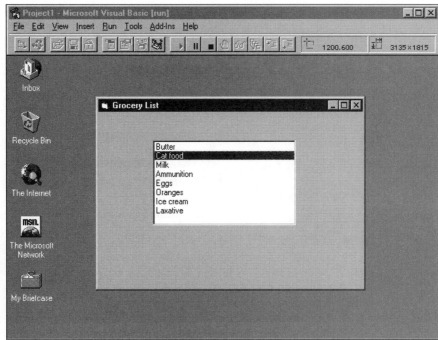

Figure 15-6:
A list box
with one
item
selected.

To retrieve data from a list box that allows multiple selections, you have to do the following:

1. Create a second list box to temporarily store any selected items from the first list box.

2. Set this second list box's Visible property to False so that the list box is invisible.

3. Every time a user selects an item from the first list box, copy it into the second (invisible) list box (see Figure 15-7).

The invisible list box contains only those items selected from another list box, and stores all items in a List property. Items in a list are assigned an index number. The first item in the list is given an index number of 0, the second item in a list is given an index number of 1, and so on. To better understand this concept, create on a blank form two list boxes and a command button with the following properties:

Invisible list box

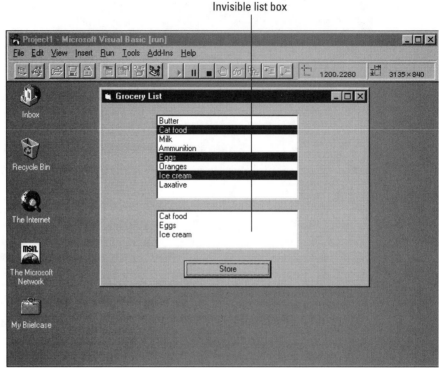

Figure 15-7:
Retrieving
multiple
items from
one list box
by using a
second
(invisible)
list box.

Object	*Property*	*Value*
First list box	Name	lstChoose
	MultiSelect	1 – Simple
Second list box	Name	lstTemp
	Visible	True
Command button	Name	cmdStore
	Caption	Store

Because the Visible property of the second list box is False, it's (obviously) invisible and you can't see what is happening. So, when you test the procedure, set the Visible property for the second list box to True so that you can see what happens. Then, after you've become "educated," change the Visible property back to False, as it would normally be.

The following procedure stores items in the lstChoose list box:

```
Private Sub Form_Load()
  lstChoose.AddItem "Butter"
  lstChoose.AddItem "Cat food"
  lstChoose.AddItem "Milk"
  lstChoose.AddItem "Ammunition"
  lstChoose.AddItem "Eggs"
  lstChoose.AddItem "Oranges"
  lstChoose.AddItem "Ice cream"
  lstChoose.AddItem "Laxative"
End Sub
```

This loads the lstChoose list box with items for the user to select.

An event procedure to retrieve multiple selected items from the lstChoose list box may look like the following:

```
Private Sub cmdStore_Click()
  Dim I
  lstTemp.Clear
  For I = 0 To lstChoose.ListCount - 1
    If lstChoose.Selected(I) Then
        lstTemp.AddItem lstChoose.List(I)
    End If
  Next I
End Sub
```

This is how Visual Basic responds to the code:

1. The first line tells Visual Basic, "Follow these instructions whenever the user clicks the command button named cmdStore."

2. The second line says, "Declare a variable called I and assume its data type is Variant."

3. The third line says, "Find a list box named lstTemp and clear out anything it might be storing."

4. The fourth line says, "Set the value of I to 0. Keep counting by one until the value of I equals the number of items displayed in the lstChoose list box."

5. The fifth line says, "If the user selected an item displayed in the lstChoose list box, follow the instructions in the sixth line."

6. The sixth line says, "Copy the item selected in the list box named lstChoose and put the copied item in the list box named lstTemp."

7. The seventh line says, "This is the end of all the instructions to follow for now."

8. The eighth line says, "Add one to the value of I and start back at line five."

9. The ninth line says, "This is the end of the instructions to follow when the user clicks the command button named cmdStore."

These instructions do nothing more than copy all selected items from one list box into a second list box, which is invisible.

Each item in a list box is identified by an index number. The top item of the list is assigned an index number of 0, the second item from the top is assigned an index number of 1, and so on.

To get at the items stored in the list box named lstTemp, you have to use index numbers. The following command retrieves the top item stored in the lstTemp list box:

```
lstTemp.List(0)
```

The following command retrieves the second item from the top in the lstTemp list box:

```
lstTemp.List(1)
```

Each increase in the index number retrieves the next item further from the top.

Chapter 16

Math 101: Arithmetic, Logical, and Comparison Operators

In This Chapter

▶ Adding, subtracting, multiplying, and dividing numbers

▶ Using the Not, And, Or, or Xor operators

▶ Comparing numbers and strings

▶ Comparing strings and operators

*A*fter a program gets data from the user (either as a number or as a string), the next step is to do something with that data. If your program mimicked an overworked clerical worker, the program might just lose the data and blame it on something else. But most likely, you want your program to calculate some sort of a result with the data it receives from the user.

To calculate a result, your program needs to get data from its user interface and then somehow change, modify, mutilate, or spindle that data. Changing anything involves an operation, so the special commands to work with data are called *operators*.

Visual Basic provides the following three types of operators:

✔ Arithmetic

✔ Logical

✔ Comparison

Arithmetic Operators

Arithmetic operators essentially turn your $2,000 computer into a $4.95 pocket calculator. These operators let you add, subtract, multiply, and divide numbers or variables that represent numbers. Table 16-1 shows the most common arithmetic operators.

Table 16-1	Arithmetic Operators
Operator	*What It Does*
+	Adds two numbers
–	Subtracts two numbers
*	Multiplies two numbers
/	Divides two numbers and returns a floating-point (decimal) number, such as 3.14, 16.2, or 392.2398
\	Divides two numbers and returns an integer, such as 8, 16,012, or 25
Mod (or modulo)	Divides two numbers and returns only the remainder
^	Raises a number to an exponential power
&	Adds (concatenates) two strings

Adding two numbers with the + operator

To add two numbers, use the + operator, as shown in the following example:

```
X = 10
Y = 15.4
SUM = X + Y
```

In case these three BASIC commands mystify you, here's how they work:

1. The first command says, "Create a variable called X and set its value to 10."

2. The second command says, "Create a variable called Y and set its value to 15.4."

3. The third command says, "Create a variable called Sum and set its value equal to the value of X plus the value of Y." In this case, the value of Sum equals 10 + 15.4, or 25.4.

Subtracting two numbers with the – operator

To subtract two numbers, use the – operator, as shown in the following example:

```
Income = 2000
Taxes = 1500
Real_Income = Income - Taxes
```

Here's how Visual Basic interprets these three BASIC commands:

1. The first command says, "Create a variable called Income and set its value to 2000."

2. The second command says, "Create a variable called Taxes and set its value to 1500."

3. The third command says, "Create a variable called Real_Income and set its value equal to the value of Income minus the value of Taxes." In this case, the value of `Real_Income` equals 2000 – 1500, or 500.

Negating numbers with the – operator

The – operator, used by itself, can turn a positive number into a negative number and vice versa. To negate a number, place the – operator in front of any number or variable, as shown in the following example:

```
Amount = 250
Balance = - Amount
```

This is how Visual Basic's tiny little brain interprets these BASIC commands:

1. The first command says, "Create a variable called Amount and set its value to 250."

2. The second command says, "Create a variable called Balance and set its value to the negative value of Amount." In this case, the value of `Balance` is –250.

Multiplying two numbers

To multiply two numbers, use the * operator, as shown in the following example:

```
Hours = 25
Wages = 5.75
Salary = Hours * Wages
```

To see how Visual Basic understands these three BASIC commands, this is how they work:

1. The first command says, "Create a variable called Hours and set its value to 25."

2. The second command says, "Create a variable called Wages and set its value to 5.75."

3. The third command says, "Create a variable called Salary and set its value equal to the value of Hours multiplied by the value of Wages." In this case, the value of Salary equals 25 * 5.75, or 143.75.

Dividing two numbers with the / operator

To divide two numbers and calculate a floating-point (decimal) number, use the / (forward slash) operator, as shown in the following example:

```
GamesWon = 104
TotalGames = 162
WinningPercentage = GamesWon / TotalGames
```

Visual Basic interprets these three BASIC commands as follows:

1. The first command says, "Create a variable called GamesWon and set its value to 104."

2. The second command says, "Create a variable called TotalGames and set its value to 162."

3. The third command says, "Create a variable called WinningPercentage and set its value equal to the value of GamesWon divided by the value of TotalGames." In this case, the value of WinningPercentage equals 104 / 162, or 0.6419753.

Dividing two numbers with the \ operator

To divide two numbers and calculate an integer, use the \ (backslash) operator, as shown in the following example:

```
CrateCapacity = 72
Bottles_in_Crate = 1900
FullCrates = Bottles_in_Crate \ CrateCapacity
```

So how does Visual Basic interpret these three BASIC commands? Glad you asked. Here's how:

1. The first command says "Create a variable called CrateCapacity and set its value to 72."

2. The second command says, "Create a variable called Bottles_in_Crate and set its value to 1900."

3. The third command says, "Create a variable called FullCrates and set its value equal to the value of Bottles_in_Crate divided by the value of CrateCapacity." In this case, the value of FullCrates equals 1900 / 72, or 26.

Dividing two numbers often calculates a floating-point (decimal) number, so how does Visual Basic handle rounding? Consider the following example:

```
Operand1 = 2.5
Operand2 = 1.5
Result = Operand1 \ Operand2
```

Before Visual Basic performs a calculation using the \ operator, the operands are rounded up to whole numbers. In this example, Operand1 is rounded up to 3 and Operand2 is rounded up to 2; therefore, Result = 3 \ 2, or 1.5. Because the \ operator must return an integer, the value of Result is rounded down to 1.

Dividing with mod (modulo)

To divide two numbers and calculate the remainder, use the Mod operator, as shown in the following example:

```
CrateCapacity = 72
Bottles_in_Crate = 1900
LooseBottles = Bottles_in_Crate Mod CrateCapacity
```

For those curiosity seekers, this is how Visual Basic interprets these commands:

1. The first command says, "Create a variable called CrateCapacity and set its value to 72."

2. The second command says, "Create a variable called Bottles_in_Crate and set its value to 1900."

3. The third command says, "Create a variable called LooseBottles and set its value equal to the remainder of the value of Bottles_in_Crate divided by the value of CrateCapacity." In this case, the value of `LooseBottles` equals 1900 Mod 72, or 28.

Calculating an exponential with the ^ operator

An *exponential* is a fancy mathematical term that means to multiply the same number by itself a certain number of times. For example, multiplying the number 2 four times would be represented by 2^4, or 2 * 2 * 2 * 2.

Because you can't type 2^4, and typing 2 * 2 * 2 * 2 is a bit cumbersome, Visual Basic provides the ^ (caret) operator, as shown in the following example:

```
2 ^ 4
```

Adding (concatenating) two strings

Adding or concatenating two strings means smashing them together. For this operation, use the & (ampersand) operator, as shown in the following example:

```
FirstName = "John "
LastName = "Doe"
FullName = FirstName & LastName
```

This is how Visual Basic follows these three BASIC commands:

1. The first command says, "Create a variable called FirstName and set its value to "John" (note the space at the end)."

2. The second command says, "Create a variable called LastName and set its value to "Doe"."

3. The third command says, "Create a variable called FullName and set its value equal to the value of FirstName and the value of LastName smashed together." In this case, the value of `FullName` equals `"John " & "Doe"`, or `"John Doe"`.

Logical Operators

Logical operators manipulate True and False values. Visual Basic represents a value of True as –1 and a value of False as 0. Table 16-2 shows the most-common arithmetic operators.

Table 16-2	Logical Operators
Operator	*How to Use*
And	Variable1 And Variable2
Or	Variable1 Or Variable2
Xor	Variable1 Xor Variable2
Not	Not Variable

Using the Not operator

It's a sad commentary on the negative impact that television has on children when their vocabulary degenerates to the monosyllabic utterance, "Not!"

Of course, the computer world laid claim to Not long before MTV materialized. The Not operator simply changes a True value to False and a False value to True, as in the following example:

Variable Name	*Value*
Another_Computer_Book	True
Not Another_Computer_Book	False

For clarity, cool programmers like to use parentheses. Using parentheses in the preceding example would result in this:

```
Not(Another_Computer_Book)
```

Using the And operator

The And operator compares the True or False values of two variables and calculates a new True or False value. This allows your program to make decisions, as the following example illustrates:

```
KicktheCat = CatPresent And CatMisbehaving
```

So when is the variable `KicktheCat` True or False? It depends on the True or False value of `CatPresent` and `CatMisbehaving`.

KicktheCat	CatPresent	CatMisbehaving
True	True	True
False	False	False
False	True	False
False	False	True

The `And` operator returns a True value only if both `CatPresent` and `CatMisbehaving` are True.

Using the Or operator

Like the `And` operator, the `Or` operator compares the True or False values of two variables and calculates a new True or False value. This allows your program to make decisions, as the following example illustrates:

```
LoafInside = GameOnTV Or WeatherBad
```

So when is the variable `LoafInside` True or False? It depends on the True or False value of `GameOnTV` and `WeatherBad`.

LoafInside	GameOnTV	WeatherBad
True	True	True
True	False	True
True	True	False
False	False	False

The `Or` operator returns a False value only if both `GameOnTV` and `WeatherBad` are False.

Using the Xor operator

As with the And and Or operators, the Xor operator compares the True or False values of two variables and calculates a new True or False value. This allows your program to make decisions, as the following example illustrates:

```
TellOffBoss = BossPresent Xor AtWork
```

So when is the variable TellOffBoss True or False? It depends on the True or False value of BossPresent and AtWork.

TellOffBoss	*BossPresent*	*AtWork*
True	True	False
True	False	True
False	True	True
False	False	False

The Xor operator returns a False value if both BossPresent and AtWork are True or if both are False.

Comparison Operators

Comparison operators compare two numbers or strings to see whether they're equal to, not equal to, greater than, or less than one another. Table 16-3 shows the most common arithmetic operators.

Table 16-3	**Comparison Operators**
Operator	*Meaning*
<	Less than
<=	Less than or equal to
>	Greater than
>=	Greater than or equal to
=	Equal to
<>	Not equal to

Comparing numbers and strings

As the following example illustrates, comparison operators compare the values of numbers and strings in order to return a value of True or False:

```
Age = 18
MinimumAge = 21
Pass = (Age >= MinimumAge)
```

This is how Visual Basic interprets these three BASIC commands:

1. The first command says, "Create a variable called Age and set its value to 18."

2. The second command says, "Create a variable called MinimumAge and set its value to 21."

3. The third command says, "Compare the value of Age and see if it is greater than or equal to the value of MinimumAge. If it is, create a variable called Pass and set its value to –1 (True). If it is not, set the value of Pass to 0 (False)."

Comparing numbers is fairly easy, but comparing strings is a bit trickier. When comparing strings, Visual Basic calculates the ANSI character code value of each letter.

ANSI character codes

At the simplest level, computers only understand two numbers: zero and one. You can represent all numbers with zeros and ones; such numbers are called *binary* numbers.

Unfortunately, computers don't understand what letters and punctuation marks mean. Instead, computers represent letters and punctuation marks (commas, periods, exclamation marks, and so on) as numbers. So the number 97 represents the letter *a*, the number 65 represents the letter *A*, and the number 33 represents an exclamation mark (!).

To make sure that all computers use the same numbers to represent the same letters and punctuation marks, the American National Standards Institute (ANSI) defined an ANSI Character Set that specifies which number represents which letter or punctuation mark.

Comparing strings with the = and <> operators

Two strings are equal only if they are absolutely identical. As you can see in the following example, the = operator always calculates a False value unless it compares two identical strings, such as `"a" = "a"`:

Operation	Value of Operation
`"a" = "a"`	True
`"a" = "A"`	False
`"a" = "aa"`	False

In the next example, however, you can see that the <> operator always calculates a True value unless it compares two identical strings, such as "Abott" <> "Abott":

Operation	Value of Operation
`"A" <> "a"`	True
`"Abott" <> "Abott"`	False

Comparing strings with the >, >=, <, and <= operators

When comparing strings, Visual Basic calculates the ANSI character code for each letter in each string, beginning with the first letter. The string whose character has the higher ANSI character code is considered greater.

For example, the letter *A* has an ANSI character code of 65 and the letter *a* has an ANSI character code of 97. So consider the following line:

```
Flag = ("Air" < "aardvark")
```

Because the first letter in `"Air"` has a lower character code number than the first letter in `"aardvark"`, Visual Basic considers the value of `"Air"` to be less than `"aardvark"`, so the value of `Flag` would be True.

Now consider the following example:

```
Flag = ("air" < "aardvark")
```

Here the value of `Flag` is False. How does Visual Basic decide if `"air"` is less than `"aardvark"`? First, Visual Basic calculates the ANSI character code for the first letter of each string. Because both begin with *a*, Visual Basic looks at the second letter. Because *i* has a higher ANSI character code than *a*, `"air"` is considered greater than `"aardvark"` and `Flag` is therefore False.

Consider one final example:

```
Flag = ("air" < "airplane")
```

In this example, the value of `Flag` is True. The first three letters of each string are identical, but the fourth letter is not. Because `"air"` doesn't have a fourth letter and `"airplane"` does, `"airplane"` is considered greater and `Flag` is therefore True.

Precedence

With all these operators crowding your BASIC commands, what happens if you lump them all together, like this:

```
Mess = 4 / 7 + 9 * 2
```

Test your newfound knowledge

1. What is the difference between the / operator and the \ operator?

   a. One is called a forward slash and one is called a backward slash. Other than that, they both look like typos.

   b. The / operator divides two numbers and the \ operator puts them back together again.

   c. The / operator calculates a floating-point (decimal) number, such as 3.54, and the \ operator calculates an integer, such as 5 or 34.

   d. The / operator doesn't work at all, so you have to use the \ operator instead.

2. Is the following statement True or False?

   ```
   "aeroplane" < "airplane"
   ```

   a. False, because I don't know what to think but the answer hasn't been *a* for a long time.

   b. True, because the second letter in *aeroplane* is less than the second letter in *airplane*.

   c. True and False because I'm hedging my bets.

   d. An aeroplane is an old-fashioned way of saying airplane, so they are exactly the same.

If you guessed that the value of Mess would be 18.57143 — congratulations! But how does Visual Basic handle this? First, it calculates those operators that have higher priority, or *precedence*.

Not all operators are equal. Some have a higher precedence than others, which means that they demand attention first. Table 16-4 lists the order in which Visual Basic pays attention to the various operators. The higher an operator appears in Table 16-4, the higher its precedence, so the equality operator (=) has higher precedence than the less than (<) operator.

Table 16-4	Precedence of Operators
Operator	*Type of Operator*
Exponential (^)	Arithmetic
Negation (–)	Arithmetic
Multiplication and Division (* and /)	Arithmetic
Integer division (\)	Arithmetic
Modulo (Mod)	Arithmetic
Addition and Subtraction (+ and –)	Arithmetic
String concatenation (&)	Arithmetic
Equality (=)	Comparison
Inequality (<>)	Comparison
Less than (<)	Comparison
Greater than (>)	Comparison
Less than or equal to (<=)	Comparison
Greater than or equal to (>=)	Comparison
Like	Comparison
Is	Comparison
Not	Logical
And	Logical
Or	Logical
Xor	Logical
Eqv	Logical
Imp	Logical

Think back to the example mentioned earlier. How does Visual Basic calculate the value of Mess in this equation:

```
Mess = 4 / 7 + 9 * 2
```

To help you understand how Visual Basic calculates a result, these are the steps it follows:

1. Multiplication and division have a higher precedence than addition, so Visual Basic looks at the multiplication and division operators first.

2. Because multiplication and division have the same precedence, Visual Basic starts with the one furthest to the left. So Visual Basic calculates the value of 4 / 7 and comes up with 0.57143. Now the equation has been simplified to

```
Mess = 0.57143 + 9 * 2
```

3. Visual Basic sees that the multiplication operator has a higher precedence than the addition operator, so it calculates the value of 9 * 2 and comes up with 18. The equation is now

```
Mess = 0.57143 + 18
```

The final value of Mess is 18.57143.

What if you really wanted Visual Basic to add the two numbers first before doing any division or multiplication? For clarity, and to make sure that calculations come out the way you intend, enclose particular operations in your equations in parentheses, as shown in the following example:

```
Mess = 4 / (7 + 9) * 2
```

This is how Visual Basic calculates the result:

1. The parentheses tell Visual Basic to add 7 + 9 first, which creates the following equation:

```
Mess = 4 / 16 * 2
```

2. Because the division and multiplication operators have the same precedence, Visual Basic begins with the leftmost operator. Visual Basic calculates 4 / 16, and comes up with 0.25. The equation is now

```
Mess = 0.25 * 2
```

3. Finally, Visual Basic multiplies these numbers and assigns the value of 0.5 to the variable Mess.

Whenever you use two or more operators, use parentheses for clarity and to ensure that Visual Basic calculates everything in the exact order you want.

Chapter 17
Strings and Things

*I*n addition to manipulating numbers, your program will probably manipulate strings as well. *Strings* are any combination of letters, numbers, or symbols that you want the program to treat literally.

For example, computers blindly interpret phone numbers and Social Security numbers as mathematical expressions. A typical computer would interpret the phone number 123-4567 as the expression, "Subtract 4567 from the number 123."

To tell your program to treat strings literally, always surround your strings with quotation marks, "like this." So if you want to assign the string 123-4567 to a variable, you use quotation marks, as in the following example:

```
Private Sub Count()
  Phone = "123-4567"
End Sub
```

If you forget to add the quotation marks, Visual Basic stupidly tries to interpret the string of numbers as an actual command.

After you have designated particular data as a string, Visual Basic provides all sorts of weird ways to examine, manipulate, and mutilate the string.

Manipulating Strings

You are not limited to using strings exactly as they originally appear. You can modify them in many ways. You can convert the case of a string, use parts of a string to look for and replace other strings, and shorten a string by removing extra spaces.

Counting the length of a string

A string is only as long as the number of characters (including spaces) that it contains. To count the length of a string, use the following BASIC command:

```
VariableName = Len("String")
```

For example:

```
Private Sub Form_Click()
Dim Name As String
Dim NameLength As Integer
  Name = "Bo the cat"
  NameLength = Len(Name)
End Sub
```

In this case, the length of the string `"Bo the cat"` is 10, so this value is assigned to the variable called `NameLength`.

Converting from uppercase to lowercase

To convert a string to all lowercase letters, use the following BASIC command:

```
LCase("String")
```

For example:

```
Private Sub Form_Click()
Dim Name, LowerCase As String
  Name = "DOESN'T THIS LOOK OBNOXIOUS?"
  LowerCase = LCase(Name)
End Sub
```

In this case, the value of LowerCase is the following string:

```
doesn't this look obnoxious?
```

Notice that the LCase command affects only letters. (How *do* you present a lowercase question mark, anyway?)

To convert a string to all uppercase letters, use the following BASIC command:

```
UCase("String")
```

For example:

```
Private Sub Form_Click()
Dim Name, UpperCase As String
   Name = "whisper when you speak"
   UpperCase = UCase(Name)
End Sub
```

In this case, the value of UpperCase is the following string:

```
WHISPER WHEN YOU SPEAK
```

Extracting characters from a string

Sometimes a string contains more information than you want. For example, you may have stored a person's full name in a variable called FullName, as in the following:

```
FullName = "John Doe"
```

To extract characters starting from the left of the string, use the following BASIC command:

```
Left(FullName, N)
```

The preceding command says, "See that string over there called FullName? Yank out N number of characters, starting from the left." For example:

```
Private Sub Form_Click()
   Dim FullName, First As String
   FullName = "John Doe"
   First = Left(FullName, 4)
End Sub
```

In the preceding example, the value of First is John.

To extract characters starting from the right of the string, use the following BASIC command:

```
Right(FullName, N)
```

This command says, "See that string over there called FullName? Yank out N number of characters, starting from the right." For example:

```
Private Sub Form_Click()
   Dim FullName, Last As String
   FullName = "John Doe"
   Last = Right(FullName, 3)
End Sub
```

In this example, the value of Last is Doe.

Finding part of a string with another string

If one string is buried in the middle of another string, you can find its location by using the following BASIC command:

```
InStr("TargetString", "WantedString")
```

This command returns a number defining the exact location from the left where the "WantedString" begins inside the "TargetString". For example:

```
Private Sub Form_Click()
   Dim FullName As String
   Dim Location As Integer
   FullName = "John Plain Doe"
   Location = InStr(FullName, "Plain")
End Sub
```

In this case, the value of Location is 6.

If the string you want isn't located inside the string you're searching for, the InStr command returns 0.

When you search for a string within another string, you have to search for the exact upper- or lowercase string. For example, the following command would return a value of 0:

```
InStr("John Plain Doe", "PLAIN")
```

In this case, "Plain" is not the same string as "PLAIN", so InStr returns 0. Essentially, a zero is Visual Basic's way of saying, "Sorry, I can't find your exact string anywhere."

Replacing part of a string with another string

In case you get the creative urge to challenge WordPerfect and write your own word processor in Visual Basic (complete with search and replace features), you can do so with the following BASIC command:

```
Mid("TargetString", Position) = "NewString"
```

This command says, "See that string called TargetString? Move to the position from the left, defined by Position, and insert the string called NewString."

Of course, you have to be careful when inserting a new string into an existing one. For example, consider the following code:

```
FullName = "John Plain Doe"
Mid(FullName, 6) = "Vanilla"
```

Here's how Visual Basic interprets this code:

First, Visual Basic assigns the string "John Plain Doe" to the variable called FullName.

Next, Visual Basic looks at the string "John Plain Doe", finds the sixth character from the left, and inserts the string "Vanilla" in it. So this is what happens:

```
John Plain Doe      (Original string)

     ^              (Sixth character from the left)

John Vanillaoe      (New string)
```

After you tell Visual Basic to replace part of a string with another one, it gets overzealous and wipes out anything that gets in the way of the new string.

Test your newfound knowledge

1. How do you tell your program to treat strings literally?

   a. Just say, "I'm not kidding, honest!"

   b. Add the word TreatLiterally to the line of code that the string resides in.

   c. Surround your strings with quotation marks.

   d. Speak clearly and slowly, so there's no misunderstanding.

2. What does the following line of code do?

   ```
   Found = InStr("TargetString",
   "WantedString")
   ```

   a. It shows a list of the ten most-wanted criminals, which you can also find at the post office.

   b. This line of code inserts a bull's-eye icon, showing where to aim your dart gun when you get frustrated.

   c. It returns a number, stored in the variable called Found, that defines the exact location from the left where the "WantedString" can be found inside the "TargetString."

   d. All of the above.

Trimming spaces from strings

Strings aren't always nice and neat. Sometimes there are spaces in front of or behind the string, as the following examples illustrate:

```
"           This is an example of leading spaces"
"This is an example of trailing spaces           "
```

To strip away leading spaces, use the following BASIC command:

```
LTrim("TargetString")
```

For example:

```
Private Sub Form_Click()
  Dim FullName As String
  FullName = "           John Doe"
  FullName = LTrim(FullName)
End Sub
```

The value of FullName would be "John Doe" with the leading spaces removed.

To strip away trailing spaces, use the following BASIC command:

```
RTrim("TargetString")
```

For example:

```
Private Sub Form_Click()
  Dim FullName As String
  FullName = "John          "
  FullName = RTrim(FullName)
  FullName = FullName & " " & "Doe"
End Sub
```

In the preceding example, the `RTrim` command removes the trailing spaces so the value of `FullName` is just plain `"John"`. Then the last command adds the value of `FullName` (`"John"`) to a blank space (`" "`) and the string `"Doe"` to create the string `"John Doe"`.

In case you have both leading and trailing spaces, you can combine the two commands like this:

```
LTrim(RTrim("TargetString"))
```

This command says, "First, remove all trailing spaces and then remove all leading spaces." For an even simpler method, use the following BASIC command instead:

```
Trim("TargetString")
```

For example:

```
Private Sub Form_Click()
  Dim FullName As String
  FullName = "      John Dull        "
  FullName = Trim(FullName)
  FullName = FullName & " " & "Doe"
End Sub
```

The `Trim` command removes both the leading and trailing spaces in one quick stroke, then the last command adds the string `"John Dull"` to a blank string (`" "`) and the string `"Doe"` to create `"John Dull Doe"`.

Converting Strings and Values

Visual Basic handles numbers and strings differently. There may come a time, however, when you need to convert a string into a number so that you can use it for calculations. Or you may need to convert a number into a string so that you can manipulate it. You also may need to convert a string into its ASCII or ANSI value.

Converting a string into a number

What if you have a text box in which users can type their hourly wages? Unfortunately, the Text property of any text box stores data as a string, not as a number. To convert this string into a number, you have to use one of the following BASIC commands:

```
CDbl("TargetString")

Csng("TargetString")
```

The first command says, "Take the string called TargetString and convert it to a Double number type."

The second command says, "Take the string called TargetString and convert it to a Single data type.

For example:

```
Private Sub Form_Click()
  Dim GetNumber As Double
  GetNumber = CDbl(txtHourlyWage.Text)
End Sub
```

Here's how Visual Basic interprets this code:

1. The first statement says, "Declare a variable called GetNumber as a Double data type."

2. The second statement says, "Get the string stored in the Text property of a text box called txtHourlyWage and convert it to a number."

3. Finally, the value stored in the `txtHourlyWage.Text` property is assigned to the `GetNumber` variable.

If the user typed 6.25 in the txtHourlyWage text box, the value of GetNumber would be 6.25.

If the user typed 6.25 Hourly wage or My hourly wage is 6.25 in the txtHourlyWage text box, Visual Basic chokes and screams about a type mismatch error because neither CDbl nor CSng knows how to handle characters.

Converting a number into a string

What if you have a number and need to convert it into a string so that you can do fancy string manipulations to it? Then you have to use the following BASIC command:

```
Str(Number)
```

This command says, "Take the number represented by Number and turn it into a string."

For example, Visual Basic considers these to be two completely different creatures:

```
10          ' This is a number
"10"        ' This is a string
```

The following converts a number into a string:

```
Str(10)    ' The string " 10"
Str(10.5)  ' The string " 10.5"
Str(-10)   ' The string "-10"
```

When Visual Basic converts a number into a string, the string has an extra leading space if it's a positive number or a minus sign (–) if it's a negative number.

Converting a string into its ASCII value

As a programmer, you'll have to practically memorize the ASCII table at some point, so you might as well find a copy of one and hang it near your computer somewhere so that you can find it easily.

An ASCII table shows the codes that computers use to represent most of the characters you will need. For example, the letter *A* has an ASCII value of 65, and the letter *a* has an ASCII value of 97.

Whenever you need the ASCII value of a one-character string, you can use this BASIC command:

```
Asc("Character")
```

The following shows how to convert a character into its ASCII value:

```
X = Asc ("A")    ' X = 65
X = Asc ("a")    ' X = 97
```

Converting an ANSI value into a string

Microsoft Windows doesn't use the ASCII table. Instead, it uses the ANSI table, which is practically the same as the ASCII table anyway. (You learned about the ANSI table in Chapter 16.)

To use an ANSI value, use the following BASIC command:

```
Chr("Character")
```

The only time you need to use the ANSI value of anything is for special control codes, such as for line feeds, carriage returns, and new lines.

The following commands shows common ANSI values:

```
LineFeed = Chr(10)
FormFeed = Chr(12)
Carriage = Chr(13)
```

By using all these fancy string manipulation commands, you can make sure that your strings look exactly the way you want before displaying them in a text box or label. Either that, or you can just have fun playing with words and numbers and pretend you're doing serious research for your job.

Chapter 18

Defining Constants and Using Comments

In This Chapter

▶ Naming and calculating constants

▶ Declaring the scope of constants

▶ Creating and using the three types of comments

A *constant* is a fixed value that never changes, no matter what happens to your program. Numbers, strings, and dates can all be constant values.

But why bother using constants? There are several good reasons, none of which make any sense until you start writing your own programs.

For example, suppose that you wanted to write a program that paid employees according to the current minimum wage. If the minimum wage were $5.95, you would have to use the number 5.95 everywhere in your program.

Unfortunately, the number 5.95 means nothing in itself. Even worse, if the minimum wage changes from $5.95 to $6.25, you have to change 5.95 to 6.25 everywhere in your program.

To overcome these problems, you can use constants. A constant is simply a word that represents a specific value. A constant not only uses plain English to describe what the value means, but it also lets you change its value quickly and easily.

Naming Constants

Constant names must meet the following criteria. They must

- ✔ Begin with a letter
- ✔ Be 40 characters or less
- ✔ Contain only letters, numbers, and the underscore character (_); punctuation marks and spaces are not allowed
- ✔ Be any word except a Visual Basic reserved keyword

To make constant names stand out, use all uppercase letters. For example, the following are acceptable constant names:

```
AGE
MY_BIRTHDAY
MINIMUM_WAGE
LIFEBOAT_CAPACITY
```

Declaring Constants

Before you can use a constant, you have to *declare* it. To declare a constant, you just give it a name and assign it a specific value, such as any of the following:

```
Numbers
Strings
Dates
```

The following code declares number, string, and date constants:

```
Private Sub Command1_Click()
  Const AGE = 21
  Const COMPANY = "Acme Manufacturing"
  Const CHRISTMAS = #25 December 1995#
End Sub
```

Place all constant declarations at the top of your event procedures. Instead of typing one constant declaration on each line, you can smash them all together and separate them with commas, as illustrated in the following code:

```
Private Sub Command1_Click()
  Const AGE = 21, COMPANY = "Acme Manufacturing"
End Sub
```

Note that number constants are only numbers, string constants are anything enclosed in quotation marks (" "), and date constants are dates surrounded by the pound sign (#).

Here are some of the ways in which dates can be displayed:

```
#12-25-95#
#December 25, 1995#
#Dec-25-95#
#25 December 1995#
```

Calculating constants

Constants normally represent a fixed value. However, constants can also be mathematic values based on other constants. For example:

```
Const RETIREMENT_AGE = 65
Const HALFWAY_THERE = RETIREMENT_AGE / 2
```

In this case, the value of the constant RETIREMENT_AGE is 65 and the value of the constant HALFWAY_THERE is 65 / 2, or 32.5.

Using constants

After you've declared a constant, you can use it just like any other value. Consider the following:

```
Const MINIMUM_WAGE = 5.75
Salary = MINIMUM_WAGE * 20
```

Here's how Visual Basic interprets this code:

1. The first command says, "Create a constant named MINIMUM_WAGE and set its value to 5.75."

2. The second command says, "Multiply the value of MINIMUM_WAGE by 20 and store this value in the variable called Salary." In this case, the value of MINIMUM_WAGE is 5.75, so you multiply 5.75 by 20, which equals 115. Then Visual Basic stores this value in Salary.

Scope of Constants

Visual Basic lets you declare the scope of constants in the following three ways:

- Local
- Module
- Public

Local constants

A *local* constant can be used only within the procedure in which it was de-clared. The purpose of local constants is to isolate specific constants in a single procedure where they are used.

Declare a local constant within an event procedure, as in the following:

```
Private Sub Command1_Click()
  Const SPEED_LIMIT = 55
End Sub
```

A local constant can be used only in the one event procedure in which it was declared. But what if you want to create a constant that two or more event procedures can share? In that case, you have to create a module constant.

Module constants

A *module* constant can be used only by an event procedure stored in the same file.

To declare a module constant, follow these steps:

1. Open the Code window by pressing F7.

2. Click the Object list box in the Code window and choose (General).

3. Click the Proc list box and choose (declarations).

4. Now type your constant declaration using the Const statement, as in the following:

```
Const DRINKING_AGE = 21
```

Module constants are useful for sharing a constant value among one or more event procedures, but isolating the constant to only those event procedures stored in the same file. If you want a constant that *any* procedure in your program can use, you need to create a public constant.

Public constants

A *public* constant can be the most convenient to use because every procedure in your Visual Basic program can access it. However, cool programmers use public constants only when absolutely necessary; it's considered bad programming practice to clutter up your program with public constants that only a few procedures will ever use.

Using public constants will never prevent your program from running properly; using them unnecessarily is just considered poor programming etiquette. Experienced programmers will blush in embarrassment for you if they catch you using public constants needlessly, and you'll probably never get invited to any of the really great programmer parties as a result. Public constants must be declared in a BAS (module) file. To declare a public constant, follow these steps:

1. Open the Project window by pressing Ctrl+R and click on the BAS (module) file where you want to put the public constant. (If you need to create a BAS file, click the Module icon or choose <u>M</u>odule from the <u>I</u>nsert menu.)

2. Open the Code window by pressing F7.

3. Click the Object list box in the Code window and choose (general).

4. Click the Proc list box and choose (declarations).

5. Type your public constant using the Public command, as in the following:

```
Public Const SPEED_LIMIT = 55
```

Using Comments

When you're coding your program (note the cool use of the word *coding*), the way your program works may be clear to you. Unfortunately, if you put your program aside and try to modify it five years later, you may have forgotten why you wrote certain commands and even how some of those commands work.

For just this reason, you should make it a habit to add plenty of comments to your programs. *Comments* are short descriptions that programmers add to their program to explain what certain commands mean or to indicate what is supposed to happen in the program.

As far as the computer is concerned, comments do absolutely nothing to help or hinder the way your program works. But from a programmer's point of view, comments help explain how and why a program functions.

Creating comments

Visual Basic lets you create comments by using the apostrophe (') symbol, followed by anything you care to type. The following, for example, is a valid comment:

```
Private Sub Command1_Click()
  ' This event procedure does absolutely nothing
End Sub
```

As far as Visual Basic is concerned, anything that appears to the right of the apostrophe symbol is ignored.

Comments can appear on separate lines or they can appear as part of another line, as in the following example:

```
Private Sub Command1_Click()
  X = Y * 2   ' Y represents the number of employees
End Sub
```

You can also cram several comments together on multiple lines:

```
Private Sub Command1_Click()
  Y = 200    ' Y represents the number of employees
  X = Y * 2
  ' X represents the number of employees who would like
  ' to slash the tires on the boss's car.
End Sub
```

Just remember that anything that appears to the right of the apostrophe symbol is ignored by the computer and is considered a comment.

Commenting for readability

The main reason for using comments is to make your programs easy to understand. For this reason, most cool programmers put comments at the beginning of every procedure.

Test your newfound knowledge

1. Why should you add comments to your program?

   a. To summarize and explain how your BASIC code works.

   b. To exercise your literary skills and prove that programmers can write, too.

   c. To prove that you have something to say besides BASIC commands.

   d. So that you can leave cryptic messages for other programmers to decipher.

2. Comment on the simplicity and brevity of this lesson.

   a. All right! Now I can quit and go home early.

   b. Why can't all the lessons in this book be this simple and short?

   c. I still can't write a program, but I know how to use comments. Maybe I should get a job as a commentator.

   d. Comments are cool. If we can write comments in our programs, does that mean we can write programs with our word processors?

These comments explain what data the procedure gets (if any) and what calculations it performs. By just looking at the comments, anyone can quickly see what the procedure does without needing to decipher several lines of cryptic BASIC code. For example, can you figure out what the following event procedure does?

```
Private Sub Command1_Click()
  A = SQR((B ^ 2 + C ^ 2))
End Sub
```

By adding a bunch of comments at the top of this procedure, you can make it much easier to understand the procedure's function:

```
Private Sub Command1_Click()
  ' The following equation uses the Pythagorean theorem
  ' for calculating the length of a sides of a right
  ' triangle if the lengths of two sides are known. In
  ' this case, the length of one side of the triangle is
  ' represented by B and the length of the second side of
  ' the triangle is represented by C.
  A = SQR((B ^ 2 + C ^ 2))
End Sub
```

If several people share the responsibilities for writing procedures, you can use comments to note the name of the programmer and the date each procedure was last modified. (That way you'll know who to blame when the procedure doesn't work.) For example:

```
Private Sub Command1_Click()
   ' Programmer: JOHN DOE
   ' Last modified: 1/1/80 (our computer clock doesn't work)
   A = SQR((B ^ 2 + C ^ 2))
End Sub
```

Of course, the drawback is that if you get too wordy, your comments can be more intrusive than helpful — like billboards along the highway. Just remember: Provide enough information to be helpful, but not so much that people drop off to sleep while reading your comments. You're not writing a classic novel here, just a brief description that other people can understand.

Comments for legibility

If your program contains lots of BASIC code, you can use comments and blank lines to make your code easy to read. For example, separating chunks of code can make it easier to see what each chunk does.

```
Private Sub Command1_Click()
   Const INTEREST_RATE = .055   ' 5.5% interest rate
   Const MB_ICONCRITICAL = 16   ' Displays icon Critical
                                     Message
   Dim Msg As String            ' Declares Msg as a string
                                     variable
BankBalance = 500
   BankBalance = BankBalance * INTEREST_RATE


   ' Subtract bank fees
   BankFees = BankBalance * 2
   BankBalance = BankBalance - BankFees


   ' Display a message box saying that the user owes the
   ' bank a certain amount of money.
   Msg = "Please pay this amount: " & -BankBalance
   MsgBox Msg, MB_ICONCRITICAL, "Amount You Owe"
End Sub
```

As you can see in the preceding example, you can insert hard returns to add blank lines between chunks of code, thereby making it easier to see what each chunk actually does.

Stripping out all comments and blank lines gives you the following equivalent but uglier version:

```
Private Sub Command1_Click()
  Const INTEREST_RATE = .055
  Const MB_ICONCRITICAL = 16
  Dim Msg As String
  BankBalance = 500
  BankBalance = BankBalance * INTEREST_RATE
  BankFees = BankBalance * 2
  BankBalance = BankBalance - BankFees
  Msg = "Please pay this amount: " & -BankBalance
  MsgBox Msg, MB_ICONCRITICAL, "Amount You Owe"
End Sub
```

Notice how this new version seems cramped and cluttered, much like your bathroom counter or your garage.

Comments for disability

With comments, you can not only add explanations about your program and visually break up your code but also temporarily disable one or more BASIC commands.

For example, as you're writing a program, you may find that a command isn't working as it should. To test how your program works without this command, you have two choices:

- ✔ Erase it.
- ✔ Comment it out.

If you erase a command and then decide you need it, you have to type it all over again. If you *comment it out*, however, you only have to erase the apostrophe symbol in order to put the command back in.

The following example contains a fairly long line of numbers:

```
Private Sub Command1_Click()
  X = 3.14 * 650 - (909 / 34.56) + 89.323
End Sub
```

If you had erased the second line, typing it again would be a real pain in the neck. However, you can just comment it out, as follows:

```
Private Sub Command1_Click()
   ' X = 3.14 * 650 - (909 / 34.56) + 89.323
End Sub
```

Remember, anything that appears to the right of the apostrophe symbol is ignored by the computer. So, to the computer, this procedure now looks like the following:

```
Private Sub Command1_Click()
End Sub
```

Placing the apostrophe in front of this statement turns it into a comment and disables it as a BASIC command. By removing the apostrophe symbol, you can quickly turn the comment back into a real-life BASIC command.

By using comments wisely, you can ensure that any programs you write can be easily understood by you or another programmer. Then again, if you really want to sabotage a programming project, add comments that don't make any sense or leave them out altogether and see what happens.

Chapter 19

Killing Bugs

● ●

In This Chapter

▶ Examining the various types of bugs

▶ Embarking on the big bug hunt

▶ Killing the bugs you find

● ●

*E*ven if you've written millions of different programs before, you'll probably make a mistake at one time or another. You may misspell a word or forget to type a command. So no matter how carefully you write your program, it may not work exactly as it should. The problems hindering it from working are called *bugs*.

Every program in the world has bugs, including MS-DOS, WordPerfect, Lotus 1-2-3, Paradox, and Microsoft Windows. The only difference between the bugs in your program and the bugs in a commercial program is that nobody is paying you to eliminate bugs in your program. With a fair amount of preplanning, application design, and just plain common sense, you can avoid quite a few bugs.

And don't worry. Many bugs are relatively harmless. These minor bugs normally won't prevent you from using a program correctly, but they may slow down your computer or display odd colors or objects on the screen at random times.

Major bugs are more devastating. For example, a major bug might cause a program to erase files when a user chooses the Save command. In the case of NASA, a major bug allegedly blew up a multimillion-dollar weather satellite because someone mistyped a single command in the program.

Nobody is perfect, so no program can be guaranteed to be completely bug-free. Even an experienced professional with a Ph.D. in computer science will regularly write bug-ridden programs.

Bugs are a fact of life, like cockroaches in a kitchen. You may never get rid of them all, but you can kill as many as possible along the way.

TECHNICAL STUFF

Why computer problems are called *bugs*

The first computer in the world used mechanical relays instead of modern electronics. One day the computer stopped working for no apparent reason. The scientists checked their programming (it should have worked), the electric cord (it was plugged in), and the wires inside the computer (they were still connected).

Eventually, someone noticed that a moth had gotten smashed in one of the relays, preventing the relay from closing all the way. Because the moth's dead body prevented the computer from working, problems with computers were henceforth known as *bugs* (which is a lot easier to say than *chihuahuas*, so it's a good thing a dog didn't get smashed in the first computer).

Types of Bugs

The art of killing bugs is known as *debugging*. Before you can kill a bug, you first have to find it. With small programs, such as ones that display `Hello, world!` on the screen, there are only so many places a bug can hide. With large programs, a bug can be hiding anywhere, and this can be as frustrating as trying to find a single tsetse fly in a high-rise apartment building.

To make it easier to hunt for bugs, computer scientists have classified bugs in three categories:

- Syntax errors
- Run-time errors
- Logic errors

Syntax errors

A *syntax* error is a bug that occurs when you misspell a command. If you typed *INTTEGER* instead of *INTEGER*, for example, Visual Basic would have no idea what INTTEGER meant and wouldn't even bother trying to run the rest of your program.

When Visual Basic runs across a syntax error, it politely highlights the misspelled word on the screen to show you exactly what the problem is. Just type the correct spelling and run your program again.

Even one syntax error will keep your program from running. When you finally get your program to run for the first time, you'll know that your program is completely free of syntax errors. Then you have to worry only about run-time and logic errors.

Run-time errors

A *run-time* error occurs when your program gets data that it doesn't quite know how to handle. A run-time error is more subtle than a syntax error. Your program may be riddled with run-time errors, but you may never know it until you actually run your program.

To simulate a run-time error in your own life, pull into the drive-thru window at your nearest Burger King. When the cashier asks, "May I help you?," order a Big Mac. Because the cashier expects you to order something from Burger King's menu, this person has no idea how to respond to your question and will suffer a run-time error.

For an example of a run-time error in a program, consider this formula for calculating a result:

```
TaxRate = TaxesOwed ÷ YearlyIncome
```

This equation normally works — unless the `YearlyIncome` equals 0. Because it's impossible to divide any number by 0, the program stops running if the value in `YearlyIncome` is 0.

To discover a run-time error, you must test your program for every possible occurrence: from someone pressing the wrong key to some idiot typing a negative number for his or her age.

Because the number of things that can ever go wrong is nearly infinite (Murphy's Law), you can understand why every large program in the world has bugs. (Now isn't this a comforting thought to remember the next time you fly in a computer-controlled airplane?)

Logic errors

The trickiest type of bug is a *logic* error. A logic error occurs when the program doesn't work correctly because you gave it the wrong commands or the commands you issued are out of sequence with other commands. Huh? How can you give it the wrong commands when you're the one writing the program? Believe it or not, it's easy.

Anyone raising teenagers knows that when you tell them to mow the lawn or clean up their rooms, they may do it — but not quite the way you wanted it accomplished. Instead of mowing the lawn in neat rows, a teenager may move around in circles and give up. Or instead of cleaning a room by picking up dirty clothes and tossing out papers, a teenager may shove the whole mess under the bed or out into the hallway.

In both cases, the teenager followed your instructions, but your instructions weren't specific enough. If a teenager can find a loophole in your instructions, he or she will, and a computer is no different.

Because you thought you gave the computer the right commands to follow, you have no idea why your program isn't working. Now you have to find the one spot where your instructions weren't clear enough. If you have a large program, this may mean searching the entire program, line by line. (Isn't programming fun?)

Bug Hunting

Basically, there are four steps to hunting down and killing bugs in your program:

1. Realizing that your program has a bug
2. Finding the bug
3. Finding what's causing the bug
4. Squashing the bug

Realizing that your program has a bug

The best way to discover bugs in your program is to let unsuspecting individuals use it. (In the world of commercial software, these unsuspecting individuals are called *paying customers*.)

The more people you find to test your program, the more likely it is that they will uncover bugs you never knew existed. Bugs can be as glaring as ones that cause the computer to crash, or they can be as sneaky as ones that round off numbers to the wrong decimal place.

After you've concluded that your program has a bug, you have to track the bug down. (For the optimists in the group, you can call your program's bugs *undocumented features*.)

Finding the bug

Finding where a bug is hiding is the toughest part. The simplest (and most tedious) way to find a bug's hiding place is to run your program and examine it line by line. The moment the bug appears, you know exactly which line caused it.

For small programs, this is acceptable. For large programs, this is crazy.

As a faster alternative, just examine the parts of your program in which you think the bug may be hiding. If your program doesn't print correctly, for example, the bug may be in your BASIC code that tells the computer how to print.

Finding what's causing the bug

When you've isolated where you think the bug is hiding, you have to figure out what is causing the bug in the first place.

Suppose that your program should print your name on the screen but is printing your Social Security number instead. The program may be *printing* everything correctly but is simply getting the wrong type of information to print.

By using your incredible powers of deductive reasoning, you realize that the bug is (probably) wherever your program first tries to get your name.

Squashing the bug

After you find the cause of your bug, it's time to correct your program. But be careful! Sometimes correcting one bug introduces two or three more by mistake. Huh? How can that be?

Compare this to repairing a problem with the plumbing in your house. The easiest solution may be to tear out a wall and put in new pipes. This may solve the plumbing problem, but tearing out a wall can also tear out electrical wires inside the wall. So now you've fixed your plumbing problems, but created a new electrical problem. If you put up a new wall with electrical wiring, you may inadvertently block a vent for the central air-conditioning. Move the wall back three feet, and now the roof may be too weak in the middle to hold up the wall. See — your small plumbing "bug" has just multiplied.

So when fixing a bug, be careful. Sometimes it is easier to rewrite a huge chunk of code than to try to fix a bug in it.

Killing Bugs at the Source

The best way to avoid bugs is to not have any in the first place. Of course, that's like saying to avoid money problems, just make sure you always have enough money.

Because bugs appear in even the best of programs, the most you can hope for is to reduce the number of bugs that can pop up in your programs. Here are some tips that might help:

- ✔ To avoid bugs, write lots of tiny programs and paste them together to make one huge program. The smaller your programs, the easier it is to isolate any bugs. In military terms, this is known as the *divide and conquer* method.

- ✔ Test your program each time you modify it. If your program worked fine until you changed three lines, the problem can be isolated to those three lines.

- ✔ Have someone you can pin the blame on. If your program refuses to work, blame your spouse, your dog, or your favorite deity. This won't help fix your program, but it will make you feel better for a moment or two.

How Visual Basic Tracks and Kills Bugs

Visual Basic provides two primary ways to help you track and kill bugs: stepping and watching.

- ✔ *Stepping* means that you go through your program line by line and examine each instruction. After each line runs, look to see what the program did. If your program works the way you wanted it to, the line is okay. If not, you just located a bug.

- ✔ *Watching* lets you see what data your program is using at any given time. By watching for specific data, such as a name or phone number, you can see whether your program is storing, printing, or modifying the specific data correctly.

By stepping through a program line by line and watching to see what data your program is using, you can find any bugs in your program.

Stepping through a program line by line

If you have absolutely no idea where your bug might be, you'll have to examine your entire program line by line. To step through a program, Visual Basic provides two commands:

> 🖝 Step Into (press F8)
>
> 🖝 Step Over (press Shift+F8)

The Step Into command runs through your entire program one line at a time, including every line stored in every procedure in your program.

In case you don't want to examine every line in every procedure, use the Step Over command instead. This command simply assumes that a procedure is working correctly and doesn't bother to run through that procedure line by line.

You can combine the two commands at any time. First use the Step Into command to examine your program line by line, then use the Step Over command to skip procedures that you're positive already work.

To use the Step Into or Step Over commands, follow these steps:

1. Press F8 or Shift+F8. Or choose Step Into or Step Over from the Run menu. Visual Basic displays and outlines a line in your program (see Figure 19-1).

2. Choose End from the Run menu when you want to stop.

Watching your variables

Stepping through your program line by line is useless unless you can see how your program is handling data at the same time. To help you see what values your variables contain at any given time, Visual Basic provides a debug window.

Test your newfound knowledge

1. What is a bug?

   a. A mistake that prevents a program from working correctly.

   b. An ugly little creature with six or more legs and a hard shell that crunches when you step on it.

   c. A moth that kills itself by crashing into your computer.

   d. Something little boys eat to frighten little girls.

2. How does Visual Basic help trap bugs?

   a. By coming loaded with several of its own.

   b. With glue and bug bait.

   c. By making programming so difficult that you couldn't write a bug if you wanted to.

   d. By stepping through your program and watching to see whether it handles data correctly.

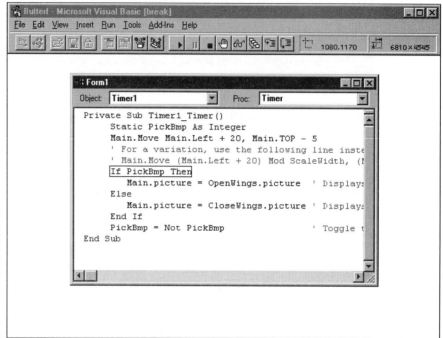

Figure 19-1:
What Visual
Basic looks
like when
it's stepping
through a
program.

The *debug window* tells Visual Basic, "These are the variables I want to examine. Show me the contents of these variables as I step through my program line by line."

To use the debug window to watch your variables, follow these steps:

1. Open up the Code window (by pressing F7) and find the variable that you want to watch.

2. Highlight that variable and choose <u>A</u>dd Watch from the <u>T</u>ools menu. An Add Watch dialog box appears, as shown in Figure 19-2.

3. Click OK.

4. Press F8 or Shift+F8 to choose the Step Into or Step Over commands. The Debug window displays the value of your watched variable each time you choose the Step Into or Step Over command (see Figure 19-3).

5. Choose <u>E</u>nd from the <u>R</u>un menu when you want to stop.

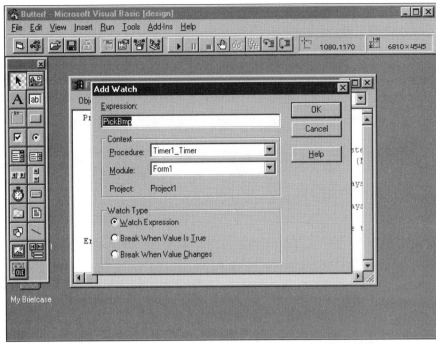

Figure 19-2:
The Add
Watch
dialog box.

Setting breakpoints

Both the Step Into and Step Over commands start from the beginning of your program and continue until they reach the end. This is acceptable for small programs, but it can get tedious for large programs.

To skip over large sections of your program that you know (or hope) already work, you can set a breakpoint. A breakpoint tells Visual Basic, "Run the program up until you reach the breakpoint. Then wait until I give you the Step Into, Step Over, or Run command."

To set a breakpoint, follow these steps:

1. Open the Code window (by pressing F7) and click on the line where you want to set your breakpoint.

2. Press F9 (or choose Toggle Breakpoint from the Run menu).

Once you've set a breakpoint, press F5. This runs your program until it reaches your breakpoint (see Figure 19-4). At this point, you can use the Step Into or Step Over commands along with the Add Watch command.

Pick Bmp variable and its value

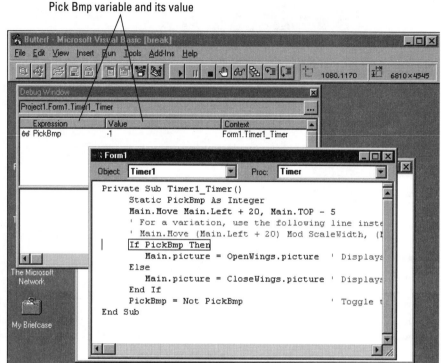

Figure 19-3:
The Debug
window.

To remove a breakpoint, follow these steps:

1. Open the Code window (by pressing F7) and click on the line where you want to remove your breakpoint.

2. Press F9 (or choose Toggle Breakpoint from the Run menu).

To quickly remove all breakpoints in your program, press Ctrl+Shift+F9 or choose Clear All Breakpoints from the Run menu.

Highlighted breakpoint

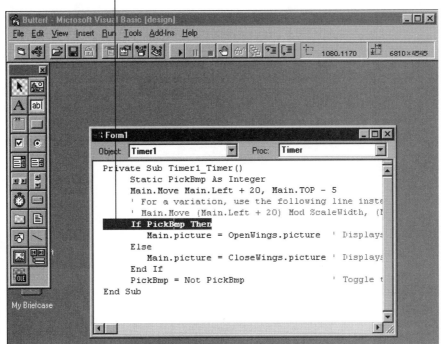

Part V
Making Decisions (Something You Stop Doing When You Get Married)

The 5th Wave   By Rich Tennant

MODERN MARRIAGE

©RICHTENNANT

WE'VE AGREED ON THE SILVER PATTERN, WALLPAPER AND CARPET SCHEME, BUT WE'RE STILL HASHING OUT THE CODE.

In this part . . .

Programs essentially contain instructions that tell the computer what to do next. The simplest programs just contain one massive list that the computer follows, one instruction after another.

But blindly following instructions doesn't make for a very useful program. Programs need to receive to the data they get and act accordingly.

This decision-making capability makes programs seem responsive, alive, and intelligent. (Well, alive anyway.) When your program can make decisions, it can begin doing something useful.

Chapter 20
The If-Then and If-Then-Else Statements

• •

In This Chapter

▶ Specifying a condition

▶ Using If-Then and If-Then-End If statements

▶ Using If-Then-Else and If-Then-ElseIf statements

• •

*W*e've all made decisions based on certain conditions, such as, "Don't worry, honey. If the ball game is over early, then I'll mow the lawn." Or "If you would stop feeding the cat, then maybe it wouldn't keep getting fatter." Visual Basic is no different when it comes to making decisions. It checks for certain conditions and then it responds.

Conditions

A *condition* must represent a value that is either True or False. Conditions can be

✔ A single variable

✔ An expression

If a condition is a single variable, that variable must have a value that is either True or False. You can check the value of a variable in two ways. The first way is to specifically check if a variable is equal to True. For example:

```
If TooHot = True Then
```

The second way (which is shorter to write) lets you eliminate = `True` and just write the following:

```
If TooHot Then
```

You don't have to specify whether this variable is equal to True because Visual Basic will check whether its value is True or False anyway.

If you want to specifically test whether a variable is False, you can do the following:

```
If TooCold = False Then
```

As a shortcut, eliminate = `False` and just write

```
If Not TooCold Then
```

If a condition is an expression, that entire expression must represent a value that is either True or False, such as

```
If Age >= 21 Then
```

In this condition, if the value of `Age` is greater than or equal to 21, the expression is True. Otherwise, it's False.

In the following example, if the string stored in the Text property of a text box called `txtName` contains the string `"Captain Mike"`, the expression is True. Otherwise, it's False.

```
If (txtName.Text = "Captain Mike") Then
```

In the following example, the expression `CatPresent And CatMisbehaving` evaluates to False:

```
CatPresent = False
CatMisbehaving = True
If CatPresent And CatMisbehaving Then
```

To make the condition in an If-Then statement easier to see, you can surround it with optional parentheses, as in the following line of code:

```
If (CatPresent And CatMisbehaving) Then
```

The parentheses don't affect your precious code one bit; they just help you identify the condition.

Now that you understand what and how conditions work, it's time to plug them into an If-Then statement.

The If-Then Statement

To make decisions, Visual Basic uses something called an If-Then statement. An If-Then statement is Visual Basic's way of checking whether a condition is True or False.

If the condition is True, Visual Basic follows a certain instruction. If the condition is False, Visual Basic ignores this instruction.

All of this may look rather wordy, so here's the condensed version of it:

```
If Condition Then Instruction
```

Essentially, this code tells Visual Basic that if a certain condition is True, it should obey the instruction that follows.

Whatever condition may be, it must always return a True or False value.

Here are a few real-life examples:

```
If Number > 25 Then txtNote.Text = "Full"
```

Here's how Visual Basic interprets this code:

1. This command says, "Check a variable called Number and see whether its value is greater than 25. If it is, then stuff the string "Full" into the Text property of a text box called txtNote."

2. "Otherwise, don't do anything and skip to the next instruction."

```
If Hungry Or Bored Then Message = "Let's eat."
```

Here's how Visual Basic interprets this code:

1. This command says, "Check the value of a variable called Hungry and check the value of a variable called Bored. If one or the other has a value of True, then create a variable called Message and set its value equal to the string Let's eat."

2. "Otherwise, don't do anything and skip to the next instruction."

The typical If-Then statement tests whether a certain condition is True or False and then follows a single instruction. But what happens if you want to test for a condition and then make the computer follow two or more instructions? In that case, you have to use a different form of the If-Then statement that is called the If-Then-End If statement.

The If-Then-End If Statement

The If-Then-End If statement lets Visual Basic check a single condition. If it's True, the program follows a bunch of instructions. Here's the proper If-Then-End If syntax:

```
If Condition Then
   Instruction1
   Instruction2
End If
```

Essentially, this code tells Visual Basic, "Check a condition; if it's True, then obey all the following instructions until you reach End If."

Here is an honest-to-goodness example:

```
If Electricity_is_Out = True Then
   Light_candles = True
   txtWarning.Text = "You just lost all your work."
End If
```

And here's how Visual Basic interprets this code:

1. The first line says, "Check the value for a variable called Electricity_is_Out. If it's True, then follow the next two instructions. If the value is False, then do nothing."

2. "Assign a value of True to the variable Light_candles."

3. "Assign the string "You just lost all your work." to the Text property of the txtWarning text box."

If-Then-Else Statement

The If-Then statement gives your program the capability to make decisions based on certain conditions. If this isn't the pinnacle of your computer programming career, hold on to your hats for the If-Then-Else statement.

The problem with using an If-Then statement or an If-Then-End If statement is that you may need too many of them to check for both True and False conditions. Is there an easier way? The answer, of course, is *yes*! Visual Basic offers something called an If-Then-Else statement.

Test your newfound knowledge

1. What is a condition?

    a. Something that makes you want to scratch your scalp or between your toes.

    b. An event that you use as an excuse for not doing something else, such as "My heart condition is bad today. I think I'll just stay inside and watch TV."

    c. Something your parents threaten you with. "If you don't behave yourself, you're going to bed without any supper."

    d. A variable or expression that evaluates to a True or False value.

2. What is the alternative to the following condition?

```
If MoneyGone = False Then
```

    a. If MoneyGone Then "Complain about overseas competitors."

    b. If MoneyGone Then "Reelect a new President."

    c. If Not MoneyGone Then

    d. If MoneyGone = True Or False Then

The simplest If-Then-Else statement looks like this:

```
If Condition Then
   Instructions1
Else
   Instructions2
End If
```

This statement tells Visual Basic, "If the condition is True, then follow the first batch of instructions. If the condition is False, then follow the second batch of instructions."

So how would you modify the following?

```
If Day > 15 Then txtReadMe.Text = "Bills are past due!"
If Day <= 14 Then txtReadMe.Text = "Pay your bills!"
```

Depending on the condition you use, you can rewrite these statements in two ways. If you use the condition Day > 15, you get the following:

```
If Day > 15 Then
   txtReadMe.Text = "Bills are past due!"
Else
   txtReadMe.Text = "Pay your bills!"
End If
```

But if you use the condition `Day <= 14`, you get the following:

```
If Day <= 14 Then
   txtReadMe.Text = "Pay your bills!"
Else
   txtReadMe.Text = "Bills are past due!"
End If
```

Both types of If-Then-Else statements are perfectly acceptable. It's just a matter of personal preference.

You can shove as many instructions as you want between the If-Then and Else lines and the Else and End If lines.

One possible drawback with an If-Then-Else statement is that if the first condition is False, Visual Basic blindly follows the second group of instructions. If you don't want this to happen, you have to specify a condition for the second set of instructions. To do that, you have to use an If-Then-ElseIf statement.

The If-Then-ElseIf Statement

An If-Then-ElseIf statement looks like the following:

```
If Condition1 Then
   Instructions1
ElseIf Condition2 Then
   Instructions2
End If
```

This code tells Visual Basic, "If Condition1 is True, then follow the first set of instructions. But if Condition1 is False, then check to see if Condition2 is True. If Condition2 is True, then follow the second set of instructions. If Condition2 is False, then don't do anything at all."

With an If-Then-Else statement, the computer always follows at least one set of instructions. But with an If-Then-ElseIf statement, it's possible that the computer won't follow any instructions — like a rebellious teenager.

For example:

```
If Day > 15 Then
   txtReadMe.Text = "Bills are past due!"
ElseIf Day > 10 Then
   txtReadMe.Text = "Pay your bills!"
End If
```

So what happens if the value of Day is 12?

1. Visual Basic checks the first condition and concludes that the expression 12 > 15 is False (because the value of Day is 12).

2. Then Visual Basic checks the second condition and concludes that the expression 12 > 10 is True, so it assigns the string, "Pay your bills!" to the Text property of a text box called txtReadMe.

Here's the tricky part. What happens if the value of Day is 6?

1. Visual Basic checks the first condition and concludes that the statement 6 > 15 is False, so it ignores the first set of instructions.

2. Next, Visual Basic checks the second condition and concludes that the statement 6 > 10 is False, so it ignores the second set of instructions.

3. Finally, Visual Basic reaches the end of the If-Then-ElseIf statement. Because none of the statements was True, none of the instructions was followed.

To handle multiple possibilities, you need more ElseIf conditions to check.

Making multiple choices with If-Then-ElseIf

For checking multiple conditions, use multiple ElseIfs, as follows:

```
If Condition1 Then
   Instructions1
ElseIf Condition2 Then
   Instructions2
ElseIf Condition3 Then
   Instructions3
End If
```

This tells Visual Basic, "If Condition1 is True, then follow Instructions1. But if Condition1 is False, check whether Condition2 is True. If Condition2 is True, then follow Instructions2. If Condition1 is False and Condition2 is False, then check to see whether Condition3 is True. If Condition3 is True, then follow Instructions3."

Once again, it's possible that all conditions will be False, so the computer may never follow any of the instructions.

You can use as many ElseIf lines as you need. Of course, the more you use, the more confusing your entire If-Then-ElseIf statement gets. ("Now if Condition3 is False but Condition4 is True, wait a minute, what's supposed to happen?")

Making sure that the computer follows at least one set of instructions

It's possible to have a huge If-Then-ElseIf statement and still not have a single instruction followed by the computer. To make sure that the computer follows at least one set of instructions, add an Else statement at the end, as shown in the following:

```
If Condition1 Then
   Instructions1
ElseIf Condition2 Then
   Instructions2
Else
   InstructionsDefault
End If
```

This tells Visual Basic, "If Condition1 is True, then follow the first set of instructions. But if Condition1 is False, check the value of Condition2. If Condition2 is True, then follow the second set of instructions. If all conditions are False, then go ahead and follow the last set of instructions."

Nesting If-Then statements

If you want, you can cram multiple If-Then statements inside one another such as:

```
If Age > 21 Then
  If Rating = 10 Then
    txtAction.Text = "Ask for a date."
  End If
Else
  txtAction.Text = "Sorry, you're too young."
End If
```

If the value of Age were 23 and the value of Rating were 10, Visual Basic would interpret this code as follows:

1. Visual Basic checks the first condition and concludes that the expression Age > 21 is True (because the value of Age is 23).

2. Then Visual Basic checks the second condition and concludes that the expression Rating = 10 is True, so it assigns the string, "Ask for a date." to the Text property of a text box called txtAction.

If the value of Age were 23 but the value of Rating were only 9, Visual Basic would interpret this code as follows:

1. Visual Basic checks the first condition and concludes that the expression Age > 21 is True (because the value of Age is 23).

2. Then Visual Basic checks the second condition and concludes that the expression Rating = 10 is False, so nothing happens.

Finally, if the value of Age were 13 and the value of Rating were 10, Visual Basic would interpret this code as follows:

1. Visual Basic checks the first condition and concludes that the expression Age > 21 is False (because the value of Age is 13).

2. Visual Basic skips to the Else part of the If-Then-Else statement and stuffs the string "Sorry, you're too young." in the Text property of the text box called txtAction. Notice that in this case, the value of Rating is irrelevant.

Be careful when nesting If-Then statements inside one another because nested If-Then statements might act in ways that you didn't expect. For example, in the preceding code, if the value of Age were 23 but the value of Rating were only 9, you might be surprised to find that this code won't put any string in the Text property of the text box called txtAction.

Chapter 21

Select Case and Nested Control Structures

. . . .

In This Chapter

▶ Examining the Select Case statement

▶ Making sure that the computer follows at least one set of instructions

▶ Using nested control structures

. . . .

*T*he main problem with using massive If-Then-ElseIf statements is that they're ugly, hard to read and understand, and cumbersome to write. Consider the following:

```
If Caller = "Frank" Then
    txtReply.Text = "Yes!"
ElseIf Caller = "Matt" Then
    txtReply.Text = "Okay, but only if you buy."
ElseIf Caller = "Jeff" Then
    txtReply.Text = "I'm washing my hair tonight."
ElseIf Caller = "Steve" Then
    txtReply.Text = "This is a recording."
End If
```

So what's the alternative to an endless proliferation of Elselfs?

One alternative is to toss your copy of Visual Basic out the window and find someone to write your programs for you. But the more practical alternative is to use something called the Select Case statement.

The Select Case Statement

The Select Case statement looks like the following:

```
Select Case VariableName
  Case X
      Instructions1
  Case Y
      Instructions2
  Case Z
      Instructions3
End Select
```

This statement tells Visual Basic, "Look at the value of the variable called VariableName. If this value is equal to X, then follow Instructions1. If this value is equal to Y, then follow Instructions2. If this value is equal to Z, then follow Instructions3."

Replacing the multiple If-Then-ElseIf statement at the beginning of this chapter with the Select Case statement would change the code to look like the following:

```
Select Case Caller
  Case "Frank"
      txtReply.Text = "Yes!"
  Case "Matt"
      txtReply.Text = "Okay, but only if you buy."
  Case "Jeff"
      txtReply.Text = "I'm washing my hair tonight."
  Case "Steve"
      txtReply.Text = "This is a recording."
End Select
```

Notice the cleaner look and the elimination of repetitive words such as ElseIf and Then.

Depending on how many values you need to check, you can sandwich as many Case lines in a Select Case statement as you want.

Using the Select Case Statement with Comparison Operators

Normally, the Select Case statement requires an exact value to examine. However, by using comparison operators, such as <, <=, or <>, you can make the Select Case statement examine whether a variable falls within a range of values.

To make a Select Case statement use comparison operators, you have to use the magic reserved word "is." Therefore, this Select Case statement

```
Select Case Day
  Case is > 15
    txtReadMe.Text = "Bills are past due!"
  Case is > 10
    txtReadMe.Text = "Pay your bills!"
End Select
```

is equivalent to the following If-Then statement:

```
If Day > 15 Then
  txtReadMe.Text = "Bills are past due!"
ElseIf Day > 10 Then
  txtReadMe.Text = "Pay your bills!"
End If
```

Making Sure That the Computer Follows at Least One Set of Instructions

Like the If-Then-ElseIf statement, it's possible that none of the instructions within the Select Case statement will be followed. To make sure that the computer follows at least one set of instructions, you have to use the magical Else command again.

The following code tells Visual Basic, "If the value of Day equals 1, then follow the first set of instructions. If the value of Day equals 2, then follow the second set of instructions. If the value of Day equals 3, then follow the third set of instructions. If the value of Day doesn't equal 1, 2, or 3, then follow the last set of instructions."

```
Select Case Day
  Case 1
     Instructions1
  Case 2
     Instructions2
  Case 3
     Instructions3
  Case Else
     InstructionsDefault
End Select
```

Nested Control Structures

Some of the simplest toys that amuse children to no end are those Chinese boxes stacked one inside the other. Each time you open a box, there's a smaller one inside. Eventually, you reach a point where there are no more boxes and you have to stop.

The same thing can happen with If-Then and Select Case statements. Normally, an If-Then statement contains one or more groups of instructions, such as the following:

```
If Cost > 45 Then
  txtDarkSide.Text = "Steal it."
Else
  txtGoodSide.Text = "Pay for it."
End If
```

And an ordinary Select Case statement contains one or more groups of instructions, such as the following:

```
Select Case ID
  Case 123
    chkFrank.Value = True
  Case 124
    chkBob.Value = True
  Case 125
    chkMartha.Value = True
End Select
```

Rather than shoving boring old instructions inside an If-Then or Select Case statement, however, you can shove If-Then and Select Case statements within other If-Then and Select Case statements, as the following example illustrates:

```
If IQ > 90 Then
   If Age < 10 Then
      txtAnalysis.Text = "Not bad for someone under 10."
   End If
End If
```

Visual Basic's brain interprets the code this way:

1. The first line says, "Check the value stored in a variable called IQ. If it's less than or equal to 90, then skip to the 5th line that says End If. But if the value of IQ is greater than 90, continue to the second line.

2. The second line says, "Check the value stored in the variable called Age. If it's greater than or equal to 10, then skip to the fourth line, which says End If. But if the value of Age is less than 10, continue to the third line.

3. The third line says, "Assign the string "Not bad for someone under 10." to the Text property of a text box called txtAnalysis."

4. The fourth line says, "This is the end of one If-Then statement. Continue to the fifth line."

5. The fifth line says, "This is the end of a second If-Then statement."

Notice that in this example, the only time the string "Not bad for someone under 10." is assigned to the Text property of the txtAnalysis text box is when both If-Then statements are True. If one of them is False, nothing happens.

Likewise, you can shove a Select Case statement inside another Select Case statement, such as:

```
Select Case IQ
   Case 120
      Select Case Age
         Case 9
            txtAnalysis.Text = "You must be a smart kid."
      End Select
End Select
```

Here's how Visual Basic interprets this code:

1. The first line says, "Check the value stored in a variable called IQ. Then continue to the second line."

2. The second line says, "If the value of IQ is exactly equal to 120, continue to the third line. If the value of IQ is anything else (such as 119, 121, or 3), skip to the seventh line.

3. The third line says, "Check the value stored in a variable called Age. Then continue to the fourth line."

4. The fourth line says, "If the value stored in the variable called Age is 9, then continue to the fifth line. If the value of Age is anything else (such as 3, 8, or 10), then skip to the sixth line."

5. The fifth line says, "Assign the string, "You must be a smart kid." to the Text property of a text box called txtAnalysis."

6. The sixth line says, "This is the end of one Select Case statement."

7. The seventh line says, "This is the end of another Select Case statement."

For kicks and grins, you can mix up these two and put an If-Then statement inside a Select Case statement or a Select Case statement inside an If-Then statement. (Some fun, huh?)

Nesting

Putting one or more If-Then or Select Case statements inside one another is known as *nesting*. Although there is no theoretical limit to how many If-Then or Select Case statements you can place inside one another, the fewer you use, the easier your code will be to figure out.

When nesting If-Then or Select Case statements, it's a good idea to indent statements so that it's easier to see where they begin and end. For example, notice how confusing the following program appears without indentation:

```
Select Case Salary
Case 1200
If Name = "Bob" Then
txtReview.Text = "No raise this year, ha, ha, ha!"
ElseIf Name = "Karen" Then
txtReview.Text = "Okay, how about a 5 percent raise?"
End If
End Select
```

Here's what it looks like with indentation:

```
Select Case Salary
  Case 1200
    If Name = "Bob" Then
      txtReview.Text = "No raise this year, ha, ha, ha!"
    ElseIf Name = "Karen" Then
      txtReview.Text = "Okay, how about a 5% raise?"
    End If
End Select
```

From the computer's point of view, both programs are the same. But from a programmer's point of view, the program using indentation is much easier to read and understand.

Test your newfound knowledge

1. What is the limit to the number of control structures (If-Then or Select Case statements) you can nest?

   a. The limit is determined by the programmer's willingness to type repetitive amounts of information without falling asleep at the keyboard.

   b. The limit is determined by the theoretical applications pursuant to the implications of Einstein's Theory of Relativity, as reworded by a lawyer.

   c. The limit is 55. If you go over that, you risk getting pulled over by a state trooper.

   d. There is no limit. But if you have too many nested control structures, your program will be harder to read and understand.

2. To make nested control structures easier to read and understand, what should you do?

   a. Avoid using nested control structures.

   b. Avoid programming altogether.

   c. Limit the number of nested control structures you use, and use indentation to make each If-Then or Select Case statement easy to find.

   d. Print in big, bold, block letters and use short statements like "See Dick run. Dick runs fast."

Part VI
Loops and Loops (or "Do I Have to Repeat Myself?")

5th Wave Power Tip: To increase application speed, punch the Command Key over and over and over as rapidly as possible. The computer will sense your impatience and move your data along quicker than if you just sat and waited. Hint: This also works on elevator buttons and cross walk signals.

In this part . . .

*E*very program contains instructions that tell the computer what to do. Sometimes these instructions are used only once, such as instructions that tell the computer what to do when the program loads.

But for most programs, certain instructions can be used over and over again. Rather than write these instructions multiple times, programmers have invented something magical called *loops*. Essentially a loop tells the computer, "See those instructions over there? Keep repeating them again and again a certain number of times, then stop." By using loops, programmers don't have to write the same instructions over and over again themselves.

Chapter 22

The Do While and Do-Loop While Loops

• •

In This Chapter

▶ Using the Do While loop

▶ Learning how often the Do While loop repeats itself

▶ Examining how the Do-Loop While loop works and when to use it

• •

Do While loops work like scared cats. Before doing anything, these loops tell Visual Basic, "Check whether a certain condition is True. If it is, go ahead and do something. Otherwise, sit tight, hide, and don't do a single thing."

You can find Do While loops in such everyday experiences as when parents tell their kids, "Look both ways before crossing the street. As long as there aren't any cars, you can walk across."

A Do While loop looks like this:

```
Do While Condition
   Instructions
Loop
```

The condition must be a variable or an expression that represents a True or False value. A Do While loop can hold one or more instructions.

How the Do While Loop Works

The first time Visual Basic sees a Do While loop, it says, "Okay, is the value of the condition True or False? If it's False, ignore all the instructions inside the Do While loop. If it's True, follow all the instructions inside the Do While loop."

For example, the following code has a Do While loop.

```
HomeAlone = True
Do While HomeAlone
  txtMessage.Text = "Have your parents come home yet?"
  If txtReply.Text = "Yes" Then HomeAlone = False
Loop
```

Visual Basic interprets the code like this:

1. The first line says, "Create a variable called HomeAlone and set its value to True."

2. The second line says, "As long as the value of the variable HomeAlone is True, keep repeating all the instructions sandwiched between the Do While line and the Loop line."

3. The third line says, "Assign the string, "Have your parents come home yet?" to the Text property of a text box called txtMessage."

4. The fourth line says, "If the string Yes appears in the Text property of a text box called txtReply, then set the value of HomeAlone to False."

5. The fifth line says, "This is the end of the Do While loop. Go back to the second line where the Do While loop begins as long as the variable HomeAlone is True."

How many times does the Do While loop repeat itself?

If the condition of a Do While loop is False, it's possible that none of the instructions inside the Do While loop will be run. In that case, the Do While loop repeats itself zero times.

If the condition of a Do While loop is True, the Do While loop repeats itself at least once.

If the condition of a Do While loop is always True, the Do While loop repeats itself an endless number of times until you turn off the computer or the universe explodes in another Big Bang.

When a loop repeats itself endlessly, it is called an *endless loop*.

Endless loops will send your program into infinity and keep it from working properly (because the loop never ends). To avoid an endless loop, make sure that at least one instruction inside your Do While loop changes the True or False value of the condition that the loop checks.

For example, the following is a typical Do While loop that can count:

```
Counter = 0
Do While Counter < 5
  Counter = Counter + 1
Loop
```

This code says the following:

1. The first line says, "Create a variable called Counter and set its value to 0."

2. The second line says, "As long as the value of Counter is less than 5, keep repeating all the instructions sandwiched between the Do While line and the Loop line."

3. The third line says, "Take the value of Counter and add one to it. Now store this new value in the Counter variable."

4. The fourth line says, "This is the end of the Do While loop. Go back to the second line where the Do While loop begins, but only if the value of Counter is less than 5."

Each time this loop runs, it increases the value of Counter by one. As soon as the value of Counter equals 5, the condition Counter < 5 suddenly becomes False and the Do While loop stops.

When to use a Do While loop

Use a Do While loop whenever you need to do the following:

✔ Loop zero or more times

✔ Loop as long as a certain condition remains True

How the Do-Loop While Loop Works

Do-Loop While loops work on the principle of laziness. Essentially, these loops tell Visual Basic, "Go ahead and do something until a certain condition tells you to stop."

You can find Do-Loop While loops in such everyday experiences as when parents tell their kids, "Go ahead and do what you want, just as long as you don't bother me."

A Do-Loop While loop looks like the following:

```
Do
   Instructions
Loop While Condition
```

The condition must be a variable or an expression that represents a True or False value. A Do-Loop While loop can hold one or more instructions.

The first time Visual Basic sees a Do-Loop While loop, it says, "Let me follow all the instructions inside the loop first. After this, check whether the value of the condition is True or False. If it's False, stop. If it's True, repeat all the instructions inside the Do-Loop While loop again."

For example, the following code has a Do-Loop While loop.

```
HomeAlone = True
Do
  txtMessage.Text = "Have your parents come home yet?"
  If txtReply.Text = "Yes" Then HomeAlone = False
Loop While HomeAlone
```

Visual Basic interprets the code like this:

1. The first line says, "Create a variable called HomeAlone and set its value to True.

2. The second line says, "This is the start of the Do-Loop While loop."

3. The third line says, "Assign the string "Have your parents come home yet?" to the Text property of a text box called txtMessage."

4. The fourth line says, "If the string Yes appears in the Text property of the text box called txtReply, then set the value of HomeAlone to False."

5. The fifth line says, "This is the end of the Do While loop. Check if the value of HomeAlone is True or False. If it's False, go to the next line. If it's True, go back to the second line and start all over again."

How many times does the Do-Loop While Loop repeat itself?

No matter what the condition of a Do-Loop While loop may be, it always runs at least once. As long as the condition remains True, the Do-Loop While loop can keep running until infinity (or until you neglect to pay your electricity bill).

To avoid an endless Do-Loop While loop, you have to make sure that at least one instruction inside your Do-Loop While loop changes the True or False value of the condition that the loop checks.

For example, the following is a typical Do-Loop While loop that can count:

```
Counter = 0
Do
   Counter = Counter + 1
Loop While Counter < 5
```

And here's what this code means:

1. The first line says, "Create a variable called Counter and set its value to 0."

2. The second line says, "This is the beginning of the Do-Loop While loop."

3. The third line says, "Take the value of Counter and add one to it. Now store this new value in the Counter variable."

4. The fourth line says, "This is the end of the Do-Loop While loop. As long as the value of Counter is less than 5, keep repeating all the instructions sandwiched between the Do line and the Loop While line. Otherwise, exit the loop."

Each time this loop runs, it increases the value of `Counter` by one. As soon as the value of `Counter` equals 5, the condition `Counter < 5` suddenly becomes False and the Do-Loop While loop stops.

When to use a Do-Loop While loop

Use a Do-Loop While loop whenever you need to do the following:

✔ Loop at least once

✔ Loop as long as a certain condition remains True

Choose your loops carefully because loops may look similar but act differently. To avoid confusion, try to stick with one type of loop throughout your program so that it will be easier for you to figure out how all your program's loops may work.

Test your newfound knowledge

1. What are two main differences between a Do While loop and a Do-Loop While loop?

   a. The words are in a different order, and they use a different number of consonants.

   b. The Do While loop runs zero or more times and repeats only if its condition is True. Regardless of its condition, the Do-Loop While loop runs at least once, and if its condition is True, it can run an infinite number of times.

   c. Both loops run endlessly, faster and faster, until your computer is flung up against a wall because they're running so fast.

   d. Four out of five dentists recommend the Do While loop, sugar-free chewing gum, and Crest toothpaste.

2. Why is it possible that a Do While loop runs zero or more times?

   a. Because it's the number one loop used by two out of three programmers employed at Microsoft, Borland, and Symantec.

   b. Nobody knows, but I remember seeing a segment on "Unsolved Mysteries," asking viewers to call in if they had any information that might help resolve this question.

   c. Because it checks its condition before it runs even once.

   d. Because it uses steroids: So not only does it run once, it runs faster than any other loop that isn't doped up.

Chapter 23

The Do Until and Do-Loop Until Loops

●●

In This Chapter

▶ Using the Do Until loop

▶ Learning how often the Do Until loop repeats itself

▶ Examining how the Do-Loop Until loop works and when to use it

●●

Do Until loops keep repeating until some condition becomes True, such as, "Keep stealing from the cash register until someone is watching."

A Do Until loop looks like this:

```
Do Until Condition
    Instructions
Loop
```

The condition must be a variable or an expression that represents a True or False value. A Do Until loop can hold one or more instructions.

How the Do Until Loop Works

The first time Visual Basic sees a Do Until loop, it says, "Let me check whether the value of the condition is True or False. If it's False, stop. If it's True, follow all the instructions inside the Do Until loop."

The following code has a Do Until loop.

```
WonLottery = False
Do Until WonLottery = True
  txtMessage.Text = "Did you win the lottery yet?"
  If txtAnswer.Text = "Yes" Then WonLottery = True
  Else BuyAnotherTicket()
Loop
```

This code tells the program the following:

1. The first line says, "Create a variable called WonLottery and set its value to False."

2. The second line says, "This is the beginning of the Do Until loop. Check whether the value of WonLottery is True or False. If it's False, go to the next line. If it's True, skip all the instructions in the loop and start on the line immediately following the loop."

3. The third line says, "Stuff the string "Did you win the lottery yet?" in the Text property of a text box called txtMessage."

4. The fourth line says, "If the user typed Yes in a text box named txtAnswer, set the value of WonLottery to True.

5. The fifth line says, "This is the end of the Do Until loop."

In this example, the Do Until loop keeps running until the value of `WonLottery` becomes True. (For most people, this Do Until loop is still running. . . .)

How many times does the Do Until loop repeat itself?

The Do Until loop can run zero or more times. This loop keeps repeating itself until its condition becomes True.

Notice that this is the opposite of the Do While and Do-Loop While loops. These two loops keep running as long as their condition is True. The Do Until loop keeps running until its condition *becomes* True. (This is the same thing as saying that the Do Until loop keeps running as long as its condition is False.)

To avoid an endless Do Until loop, make sure that at least one instruction inside your Do Until loop changes the True or False value of the condition that the loop checks.

For example, the following is a typical Do Until loop that counts:

```
Counter = 0
Do Until Counter > 4
  Counter = Counter + 1
Loop
```

Here's an explanation of the code:

1. The first line says, "Create a variable called Counter and set its value to 0."

2. The second line says, "This is the beginning of the Do Until loop. As long as the value of Counter > 4 is False, keep repeating all the instructions sandwiched between the Do line and the Loop line. Otherwise, if the value of Counter>4 is True, exit the loop."

3. The third line says, "Take the value of Counter and add one to it. Now store this new value in the Counter variable."

4. The fourth line says, "This is the end of the Do Until loop."

Each time this loop runs, it increases the value of Counter by one. As soon as the value of Counter equals 5, the condition Counter > 4 suddenly becomes True and the Do Until loop stops.

When to use a Do Until loop

Use a Do Until loop whenever you need to do the following:

✔ Loop zero or more times

✔ Loop until a certain condition becomes True

The Do Until loop works like the following two Do While loops:

```
Do While Not Condition        Do While Condition = False
   Instructions                  Instructions
Loop                          Loop
```

How the Do-Loop Until Loop Works

Do-Loop Until loops not only sound like you're stuttering, but they keep repeating until a condition becomes True.

A Do-Loop Until loop looks like this:

```
Do
   Instructions
Loop Until Condition
```

The condition must be a variable or an expression that represents a True or False value. A Do-Loop Until loop can hold one or more instructions.

The first time Visual Basic sees a Do-Loop Until loop, it says, "Follow all the instructions inside the loop once. Then check whether the value of the condition is True or False. If it's True, stop. If it's False, follow all the instructions inside the Do-Loop Until loop again."

The following code has a Do-Loop Until loop.

```
HomeAlone = False
Do
   txtMessage.Text = "Have your parents left yet?"
   If txtReply.Text = "Yes" Then HomeAlone = TrueLoop
Until HomeAlone
```

Here's what this code means:

1. The first line says, "Create a variable called HomeAlone and set its value to False."

2. The second line says, "This is the beginning of the Do-Loop Until loop."

3. The third line says, "Stuff the string "Have your parents left yet?" in the Text property of a text box called txtMessage."

4. The fourth line says, "If the string Yes appears in the Text property of a text box called txtReply, set the value of HomeAlone to True."

5. The fifth line says, "This is the end of the Do-Loop Until loop. Check whether the value of HomeAlone is True or False. If it's True, go to the next line. If it's False, go back to the second line and start all over again."

Test your newfound knowledge

1. If you need to loop until a certain condition becomes True, which type of loop would you use?

   a. Either a Do Until loop or a Do While Not loop.

   b. A loop twisted in the shape of a pretzel.

   c. A loop-the-loop.

   d. Have you noticed that if you stare at the word *loop* long enough, it starts to look funny?

2. When do you use a Do Until loop and when do you use a Do-Loop Until loop?

   a. Whenever I need to confuse myself on how different loops work.

   b. When I get mixed up and use the wrong loop by mistake.

   c. I use the Do Until loop if I need to loop zero or more times. I use the Do-Loop Until loop if I need to loop at least once.

   d. When I can't remember how to use a Do While loop. Can you explain it to me again?

How many times does the Do-Loop Until loop repeat itself?

No matter what the condition of a Do-Loop Until loop may be, it always runs at least once. As long as the condition remains False, it keeps running until its condition becomes True.

Notice that this is the opposite of the Do While loop and the Do-Loop While loop. These two loops keep running as long as their conditions are True. The Do-Loop Until loop, on the other hand, keeps running as long as its condition is False.

To avoid an endless Do-Loop Until loop, make sure that at least one instruction inside your Do-Loop Until loop changes the True or False value of the condition that the loop checks.

For example, the following is a typical Do-Loop Until loop that counts:

```
Counter = 0
Do
   Counter = Counter + 1
Loop Until Counter > 4
```

Here's what this code means:

1. The first line says, "Create a variable called Counter and set its value to 0."
2. The second line says, "This is the beginning of the Do-Loop Until loop."
3. The third line says, "Take the value of Counter and add one to it. Now store this new value in the Counter variable."
4. The fourth line says, "This is the end of the Do-Loop Until loop. As long as the value of Counter is 4 or less, keep repeating all the instructions sandwiched between the Do line and this Loop Until line. Otherwise, exit the loop."

Each time this loop runs, it increases the value of Counter by one. As soon as the value of Counter equals 5, the condition Counter > 4 suddenly becomes True and the Do-Loop Until loop stops.

When to use a Do-Loop Until loop

Use a Do-Loop Until loop whenever you need to do the following:

- ✔ Loop at least once
- ✔ Loop until a certain condition becomes True

The Do-Loop Until loop is equal to the following two Do-Loop While loops:

```
Do                                  Do
   Instructions                        Instructions
Loop While Not Condition            Loop While Condition = False
```

When creating loops, always make sure that they will eventually end and that they do exactly what you want them to do. If anything goes wrong with your program, look to see if your loops are causing the problem first.

Chapter 24

For Next Loops:
Loops That Can Count

● ●

In This Chapter

▶ Using the For Next loop

▶ Counting backward and forward

▶ Using the Step increment

● ●

*I*f you want to loop until a certain condition becomes True or False, use one of the following principles:

	As long as Condition = True	*As long as Condition = False*
Loop at least once	`Do` `Loop While condition`	`Do` `Loop Until condition`
Loop zero or more times	`Do While condition` `Loop`	`Do Until condition` `Loop`

All four of these types of loops keep running until a certain condition becomes True or False. But if you already know how many times you want a loop to run, use a For Next loop.

A For Next loop looks like the following:

```
For Counter = Start To End Step x
   Instructions
Next Counter
```

The counter is a variable that represents an integer. `Start` represents the first number assigned to the value of the counter. `End` is the last number assigned to the value of the counter. `Step` is the interval to count by. If `Step` is omitted, the interval defaults to 1.

How the For Next Loop Works

If you want to loop exactly three times, you can use the following code:

```
For X = 1 To 3
   Instructions
Next X
```

Here's what this code means:

1. The first line says, "Create a variable called X and set its value equal to 1. Keep looping as long as the value of X is either 1, 2, or 3. The moment the value of X is no longer one of these values, stop looping."

2. The second line is where you can shove one or more instructions (including additional For Next loops if you want).

3. The third line says, "Okay, add 1 to the value of X and go back to the first line. At this point, the value of X is now 2."

The following line tells Visual Basic to loop three times:

```
For X = 1 To 3
```

By default, Visual Basic counts by one. For grins and laughs, you can use any combination of numbers that you want, such as:

```
For X = 1209 To 1211
   Instructions
Next X
```

This For Next loop also loops three times, although it's not as easy to tell that just by looking at it:

```
The first time, X = 1209.
The second time, X = 1210.
The third and last time, X = 1211.
```

You can count by such bizarre numbers if these numbers somehow made sense to your program. For example, you could count by employee numbers:

```
For EmployeeNumber = 11250 To 11290
   ' Use the value of EmployeeNumber to search a database
   ' of employees and print their background information
Next EmployeeNumber
```

In this case, the instructions inside your For Next loop use the value of
`EmployeeNumber` to find a specific employee.

If you just need to loop a particular number of times, such as five, use the
simplest and most straightforward method, as shown in the following:

```
For X = 1 To 5
   Instructions
Next X
```

Only if your numbers must be used inside your For Next loop should you resort
to bizarre, hard-to-read counting methods, such as

```
For Counter = 3492 To 12909
Next Counter
```

Counting Backward and Forward

Normally, the For Next loop counts forward by 1s. However, if you want to
count by 5s, 10s, 13s, or 29s, you can. To count by any number other than 1,
you have to specify an increment. For example:

```
For counter = start To end Step increment
   Instructions
Next counter
```

Adding the `Step` increment instruction tells Visual Basic, "Instead of counting
forward by ones, count by the value of the increment." If you wanted to count
by 16s, you would use the following code:

```
For X = 0 To 32 Step 16
   Instructions
Next X
```

This For Next loop actually loops just three times:

The first time, $X = 0$

The second time, $X = 16$

The third time and last time, $X = 32$

If you want, you can even count backward. To count backward three times, you could use the following code:

```
For X = 3 To 1 Step -1
   Instructions
Next X
```

Here's what this code means:

1. The first line says, "Create a variable called X, set its value to 3, and count backward by –1."

2. The second line contains one or more instructions to follow.

3. The third line says, "Choose the next value of X. Because we're counting backward by –1, the new value of X will be X –1. The first time, X will be 2."

Although Visual Basic doesn't care about how you count, always choose the simplest method whenever possible. That way, you and any other programmers can quickly see how many times a For Next loop keeps looping.

Only count backward or by unusual numbers (increments of 3, 5, 16, and so on) if the numbers are needed by instructions in a For Next loop. Otherwise, you only make your program harder to read.

So what happens if you write a For Next loop like the following:

```
For J = 1 To 7 Step 5
   Instructions
Next J
```

Here's what this code means:

1. This For Next loop repeats itself twice. The first time, the value of J is 1.

2. The second time, the value of J is 1 + 5 (remember, the value of Step is 5), or 6.

3. Before it can repeat a third time, the loop changes the value of J to 6 + 5, or 11. Because 11 is greater than the specified range of J (1 To 7), the For Next loop refuses to loop a third time and quits.

When to Use a For Next Loop

Use a For Next loop whenever you want to loop a specific number of times.

Just to show you that it is possible, you can also use other types of loops to count. The following two loops will loop exactly five times:

```
X = 0                      For X = 1 To 5
Do While X < 6                 Instructions
    X = X + 1              Next X
    Instructions
Loop
```

Notice how simple and clean the For Next loop is compared to the Do While loop. You'll find that there are an infinite number of ways to write a program that works (and an even greater number of ways to write programs that don't work), but the simplest way is usually the best.

Use Caution When Using a For Next Loop with the Step Increment

A For Next loop must create its own variable to do its counting. For example, the following code creates a variable called XYZ that counts by 10s:

```
For XYZ = 1 To 50 Step 10
    Instructions
Next XYZ
```

Test your newfound knowledge

1. How many times will the following For Next loop repeat itself?

```
For ID = 15 To 1 Step -1
    Instructions
Next ID
```

a. Fifteen times.

b. One time, but fifteen times as fast.

c. Zero or more times, or something like that. Wait a minute. I think I'm in the wrong lesson.

d. None, because only history can repeat itself.

2. What is the main advantage of a For Next loop over a Do While loop?

a. A Do While loop is more complicated to use, and a For Next loop doesn't work at all.

b. It all depends on your point of view, man. Like, all things are good if we only love one another and live in peace and harmony.

c. You can specify how many times you want a For Next loop to repeat itself.

d. There is no advantage to learning Visual Basic. You should be learning C++ instead.

And the next code creates a variable called TUV that counts by increments of 1.5:

```
For TUV = 1 To 7 Step 1.5
    Instructions
Next TUV
```

For Next loops usually count by whole numbers, such as 1, 2, 5, or 58, so it's not difficult to determine the number of loops there will be. The first code example just shown counts by 10, so the number of times it will loop is pretty easy to figure out. (It loops five times.)

The second example, however, counts in increments of 1.5; because of this decimal increment, it's harder to tell how many times it will loop. (It loops four times.) When using the Step increment, use whole numbers so that you can see the number of loops more easily.

When using a For Next loop, *never* (and I repeat, *never*) change the value of the counting variable within the loop. The loop will get messed up, as the following example illustrates:

```
For X = 1 To 5
    X = 4
Next X
```

Here's what happens:

1. The first line says, "Create a variable called X and set its value to 1."

2. The second line says, "Assign the value of 4 to a variable called X."

3. The third line says, "Add 1 to the value of X. Because X is equal to 4, now make X equal to 5."

Because X now equals 5, this For Next loop becomes an endless loop, which never stops. So when using For Next loops, make sure that none of the instructions inside the loop changes the counting variable. Otherwise, you'll be sorry. . . .

Try It Yourself

This sample program runs through a For Next loop and prints the value of X on the screen each time it loops. To create this program for yourself, use the settings defined in the following table:

Property	Setting
	A For-Next Loop Example
	Next X
	cmdNext

window:

This program doesn't ... more exciting than loop five times and print the ... time.

Chapter 25

Nested Loops and Quick Exits

- -

In This Chapter

▶ Using nested loops

▶ Making nested loops work

▶ Exiting quickly from loops

- -

*F*or the ultimate in flexibility and complexity, you can jam loops inside other loops to create an endless series of loops. Whenever you have one loop stuffed inside another loop, it's called a *nested loop*. So which loop runs and completes first? The answer is simple.

Using Nested Loops

Instead of confusing you with a hard-to-follow explanation, followed by an example and then an explanation of the example, I'll start by showing you an example of a nested loop in action and then explain what it's doing:

```
Do While Employee = "Supervisor"
  For J = 1 To 5
    Instructions
  Next J
Loop
```

Now, here's what this code means:

1. The first line says, "Create a variable called Employee and check to make sure its value is equal to Supervisor. If it is, move to the second line. If it isn't, don't even bother looking at the For Next loop inside; simply skip to the fifth line."

2. The second line says, "Create a variable called J and set its value to 1."

3. The third line says, "Follow these instructions, whatever they may be."

4. The fourth line says, "Increase the value of J by 1. Keep doing this until the value of J is greater than 5."

5. The fifth line says, "This is the end of the Do While loop. Keep repeating as long as the variable Employee is equal to Supervisor."

Put simply, the inside loops always finish looping before the outer loops do.

Making Nested Loops Work

Naturally, Visual Basic gives you the complete freedom to cram as many loops inside one another as you want. When creating nested loops, indent each loop to make it easier to see where each loop begins and ends. For example, notice how confusing the following nested loops look without indentation:

```
Do While Name = "Sam"
Do
For K = 20 To 50 Step 10
Do
Do Until Sex = "Male"
'  Change some variables here
Loop
Loop While Age > 21
Next K
Loop Until LastName = "Doe"
Loop
```

This is what the same code looks like with indentations:

```
Do While Name = "Sam"
  Do
    For K = 20 To 50 Step 10
      Do
        Do Until Sex = "Male"
        '  Change some variables here
        Loop
      Loop While Age > 21
    Next K
  Loop Until LastName = "Doe"
Loop
```

From the computer's point of view, both nested loops work the same. But from a programmer's point of view, the nested loops using indentation are much easier to read and understand.

With so many nested loops, make sure that the inside loops don't accidentally mess up the conditions or counting variables of the outer loops. Otherwise, you may create an endless loop and have to examine all your loops to find the problem.

Another problem that can prevent nested loops from running is if they are tangled up, as in the following example:

```
For K = 1 To 4
  For J = 2 To 20 Step 2
Next K
  Next J
```

In this example, the two For Next loops intertwine because the first For Next loop ends before the second, inner For Next loop can end.

Fortunately, Visual Basic will catch this mistake before you can run it, so it's easy to correct this type of problem.

Quick Exits from Loops

A Do loop continues running until a certain condition becomes True or False. A For Next loop continues running until it finishes counting. But what if you need to exit a loop prematurely? In that case, you can bail out of a loop by using the magic Exit command.

Test your newfound knowledge

1. What is the limit to the number of loops you can nest?

   a. Theoretically, the number is infinity. Practically, the number is as many as you feel like typing, although the more nested your loops are, the harder it is to see what each one does.

   b. The number of loops is limited to your yearly allotment, as defined by Microsoft when you send in your registration card.

   c. Five.

   d. Discovered by Einstein, the limit to the number of nested loops is equal to the same value that measures the speed of light.

2. To make nested loops easier to read and understand, what should you do?

   a. Avoid using loops, control structures, variables, or anything else that requires thinking.

   b. Absolutely nothing. If people can't understand my nested loops, that's their problem.

   c. Avoid indentation, because only amateurs need to rely on such editing tricks to write programs.

   d. Use plenty of indentations to make the beginning and ending of each loop easy to find.

To bail out of a Do loop, use the command

```
Exit Do
```

as shown in the following example:

```
Do While Company = "Microsoft"
  QuitNow = optStop.Value
  If QuitNow = True Then
    Exit Do
Loop
```

This Do While loop continues looping as long as the value of a variable called Company equals "Microsoft". The moment the user clicks on a radio button called optStop, the program sets the value of QuitNow to True.

When this change occurs, the Exit Do command bails Visual Basic out of the loop, even if the value of Company still equals "Microsoft".

To bail out of a For Next loop, use the following:

```
Exit For
```

For example:

```
For Y = 1 To 100
  If chkStop.Value = True Then
    Exit For
Next Y
```

This For Next loop repeats 100 times unless the user selects a check box called chkStop. If that happens, the Exit For command bails Visual Basic out of the For Next loop — even if the value of Y is still less than 100.

It's *usually* (notice the emphasis on *usually*) a good idea to provide a way to bail out of a loop prematurely, just in case the user needs to do something else. However, make sure that using Exit Do or Exit For doesn't kick you out of the loop before you want it to. Otherwise, you'll have another bug to hunt and track down.

If you use the Exit Do/For commands within a loop nested inside another loop, the Exit Do/For commands exit out of only the current loop and then return control to the outer loop.

Part VII
Writing Subprograms (So You Don't Go Crazy All at Once)

By Rich Tennant

In this part . . .

Now it's time to learn how to divide event procedures (or subprograms) into even smaller programs so that they're easier to write, modify, and understand. Essentially, writing a program means writing lots of little subprograms and then pasting them together like building blocks until you have one complete and working program.

If you can understand the idea behind dividing a problem into smaller parts and conquering these parts one by one, you're ready to start writing subprograms.

Chapter 26

General Procedures (Subprograms That Everyone Can Share)

. . . .

. . . .

*P*rocedures are small programs that make up a single larger program, much like bricks make up an entire wall. Visual Basic has two types of procedures: event procedures and general procedures.

An *event procedure* is part of a user interface object, such as a command button, check box, or scroll bar. Event procedures run only when a certain event occurs to a certain object, such as clicking the mouse on a command button.

A *general procedure* isn't attached or connected to any specific objects on the user interface. A general procedure doesn't do anything until an event procedure specifically tells it to get to work.

So do you need event procedures? Yes. Event procedures make your user interface responsive. Do you need general procedures? No. General procedures exist solely for the programmer's convenience.

If two or more event procedures contain nearly identical instructions, it would be repetitive to type the same instructions over and over. Even worse, if you needed to modify the instructions, you would have to change these instructions in every event procedure.

As an alternative, you can use general procedures. The whole purpose of general procedures is to hold commonly used instructions in one place. That way, if you need to modify the instructions, you change them in just one place.

How to Create a General Procedure

After you've drawn all the objects that make up your user interface, Visual Basic automatically creates empty event procedures for all of your user interface objects.

Unfortunately, Visual Basic doesn't create a single general procedure for you; you have to create it yourself. You can create and save general procedures in two types of files:

- ✔ FRM (form) files
- ✔ BAS (module) files

When you save a general procedure in an FRM (form) file, the general procedure can be used only by event or general procedures stored in that same FRM file. When you save a general procedure in a BAS (module) file, however, the general procedure can be used by any event or general procedures that make up your Visual Basic program.

If you save your general procedures in a BAS file, you can create a library of useful general procedures that you can plug into any other Visual Basic programs you write. If your general procedures will be useful for only one specific program, store them in an FRM file.

To create and save a general procedure in an FRM (form) file, follow these steps:

1. Open the Code window by pressing F7 or selecting Code from the View menu.

2. Select (General) in the Object list box.

3. Select Procedure from the Insert menu. Visual Basic displays an Insert Procedure dialog box (see Figure 26-1).

4. Make sure that the Sub radio button is selected. Then type your procedure name in the Name box, and press Enter or click OK. Visual Basic displays an empty general procedure.

To create and save a general procedure to a new BAS (module) file, follow these steps:

1. Select Module from the Insert menu or click the Module icon. Visual Basic displays the Code window for your newly created BAS module file.

2. Select Procedure from the Insert menu. Visual Basic displays an Insert Procedure dialog box.

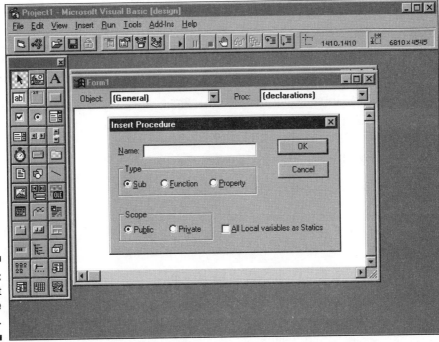

Figure 26-1:
The Insert
Procedure
dialog box.

3. Make sure the Sub radio button is selected. Then type your procedure name in the Name box, and press Enter or click OK. Visual Basic displays an empty general procedure.

To create a general procedure and save it to an existing BAS file, follow these steps:

1. Open the Project window by selecting Project from the View menu.

2. Highlight the BAS module file where you want to save your general procedure. Then press Enter or click the View Code button. Visual Basic displays the Code window for that particular BAS module file.

3. Select Procedure from the Insert menu. Visual Basic displays an Insert Procedure dialog box.

4. Make sure that the Sub radio button is selected. Then type your procedure name in the Name box, and press Enter or click OK. Visual Basic displays an empty general procedure.

Naming General Procedures

Unlike event procedure names, which identify the object name and the event, general procedures can be named anything you want, with the following restrictions:

- The name must be 40 characters or less.
- The name must begin with a letter and can consist of only letters, numbers, and the underscore character (_).
- The name can't be a reserved word.

Ideally, you should use names for your general procedures that describe what they do. For example:

```
CubeRoot
Ask4Password
DisplayWindow
```

These complete procedure names would appear in the Code window as follows:

```
Public Sub CubeRoot()
End Sub
```

and

```
Public Sub Ask4Password()
End Sub
```

and

```
Public Sub DisplayWindow()
End Sub
```

Notice that a complete general procedure name consists of four parts:

- `Public` (or `Private`)
- `Sub`
- Your general procedure name
- A pair of parentheses, ()

The word `Public` tells Visual Basic that the general procedure is public. This means that if the general procedure is stored in a BAS file, any event or general procedures stored in other FRM or BAS files can use it.

If you create a `Private` general procedure, that general procedure can be used only by other general procedures located in that same BAS file. There is no reason to create a `Private` general procedure and store it in an FRM file. All general procedures stored in an FRM file can be used only by other general procedures stored in that same FRM file.

The word `Sub` identifies your procedure as a Sub procedure. Your procedure name is the name that event procedures and other general procedures use to call your general procedure. *Calling* a procedure means telling a particular procedure, "Okay, do something now!"

The pair of parentheses is called the argument list (which you learn about in Chapter 27). The simplest general procedures have an empty argument list, represented by an empty pair of parentheses.

How to Use a General Procedure

A general procedure contains one or more instructions. When another procedure wants to use those instructions stored in a general procedure, it calls this general procedure by name.

There are two ways to call a procedure. You can state the procedure's name:

```
ProcedureName
```

or you can state the procedure's name along with the word `Call`:

```
Call ProcedureName
```

Your computer doesn't care which method you use. But whatever method you choose, use it consistently to make your programs easier to read.

Stating only the procedure name is simpler than using the word `Call`, but the latter helps identify all the procedure calls in your program. For example, consider the following general procedure:

```
Public Sub Warning()
  txtDisplay.Text = "Warning!"
End Sub
```

This general procedure simply assigns the string `"Warning!"` to the Text property of a text box called `txtDisplay`.

Test your newfound knowledge

1. Why would you need to use a general procedure?

   a. Because a more specific procedure wouldn't do the job.

   b. To store commonly used instructions in one place so that the procedure is easy to modify.

   c. To keep your event procedures from getting lonely.

   d. There's no reason to use general procedures — cool programmers have no need of such crutches.

2. What are the two ways to use, or call, a general procedure?

   a. Pick up the telephone and ask for MCI, AT&T, or Sprint.

   b. State the general procedure's name or insert the word Call before the general procedure's name.

   c. See your favorite psychic and participate in a séance.

   d. Get your local hog-calling contest winner to shout real loud for you.

If an event procedure wanted to use or call this general procedure, it would look like the following:

```
Public Sub cmdAlert_Click()
  Warning
End Sub
```

If the event procedure used the Call method of calling a procedure, it would look like this:

```
Public Sub cmdAlert_Click()
  Call Warning
End Sub
```

Both of these event procedures are equivalent to the following:

```
Sub cmdAlert_Click()
  txtDisplay.Text = "Warning!"
End Sub
```

Chapter 27

Passing Arguments

∙ ∙

In This Chapter

▶ Sending arguments to a procedure

▶ Passing arguments by value

▶ Quitting a procedure early

∙ ∙

*W*hen a procedure calls a general procedure, it does so by name. This tells the general procedure, "Hey, I better get busy and start doing something."

Many times, the called general procedure needs no further instructions when its name is called. Sometimes, though, the called general procedure needs additional information before it can do anything.

The procedure can call a general procedure and give it data to work with. This data is called an *argument*. Essentially, the first procedure is saying, "Don't argue with me. Here's all the information you need to get busy. Now get to work."

Why Use Arguments?

An argument is data — numbers, strings, or variables (which represent a number or string) — that a general procedure needs to work with. By using arguments, you can write a single, nonspecific procedure that can replace two or more specialized general procedures.

For example, you could create two general procedures, as follows:

```
Public Sub DisplayWarning()
  txtReadMe.Text = "Warning! Nuclear meltdown has occurred!"
End Sub
```

and

```
Public Sub DisplayCaution()
  txtReadMe.Text = "Caution! Turn off the reactors now!"
End Sub
```

To use either procedure, you would call them in one of two ways:

- DisplayWarning or Call DisplayWarning
- DisplayCaution or Call DisplayCaution

However, creating two procedures that do almost the same thing is tedious and wasteful.

Instead, you can replace both of those procedures with a single one, such as the following:

```
Public Sub Display(Message As String)
  txtReadMe.Text = Message
End Sub
```

This new procedure says, "Create a variable called Message that holds any information that another procedure will give me. Whatever this value may be, stuff it in the Text property of the text box called txtReadMe."

Sending Arguments to a Procedure

To call a procedure and send an argument to it, you can use one of three methods:

- ProcedureName Argument
- ProcedureName (Argument)
- Call ProcedureName (Argument)

Suppose you had the following general procedure:

```
Public Sub Display(Message)
  txtReadMe.Text = Message
End Sub
```

To call the preceding procedure and display the message `"Warning! Nuclear meltdown has occurred!"`, you could use one of three methods:

- ✔ `Display "Warning! Nuclear meltdown has occurred!"`
- ✔ `Display ("Warning! Nuclear meltdown has occurred!")`
- ✔ `Call Display ("Warning! Nuclear meltdown has occurred!")`

All three methods are equivalent, as shown in Figure 27-1.

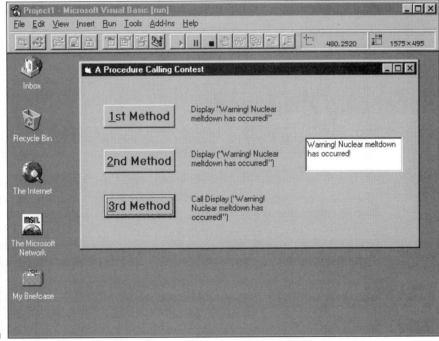

Figure 27-1:
Calling the procedure with different arguments produces the same result.

Now here's what the preceding general procedure does:

1. First it tells Visual Basic, "Find a procedure named Display and send it one argument." In this case, the one argument is the string, `"Warning! Nuclear meltdown has occurred!"`

2. Visual Basic finds a general procedure called `Display`. The `Display` procedure says to assign whatever argument it gets to the variable `Message`.

3. Then the Display procedure says, "Stuff the value of Message into the Text property of the text box called txtReadMe. Because the value of Message is the string "Warning! Nuclear meltdown has occurred!", stuff this value into the Text property."

If you had called the procedure in the following way:

```
Display ("Caution! Turn off the reactors now!")
```

the Text property of the text box called txtReadMe would get stuffed with the string "Caution! Turn off the reactors now!".

By using the same procedure but feeding it different arguments, we've replaced two specialized general procedures with a single general procedure.

Accepting Arguments

Before a general procedure can accept arguments, you have to define the procedure's argument list. Essentially, this list defines how many arguments the general procedure can take.

For example, to define a general procedure that won't take any arguments, you use an empty parentheses, as follows:

```
Public Sub NoBackTalk()
End Sub
```

To call this procedure, you could choose one of two ways:

- NoBackTalk
- Call NoBackTalk

To define an argument list that takes one argument, you would do the following:

```
Public Sub BackTalk(Something)
End Sub
```

In this case, the variable called Something is by default a Variant data type, which can represent a number or string. To call this procedure and give it the argument 4, you could do one of the following:

✔ BackTalk 4
✔ BackTalk(4)
✔ Call BackTalk(4)

To define an argument list that takes two or more arguments, you have to specify a variable for each argument and separate each by a comma. For example, the following defines three arguments:

```
Public Sub Chatty(Message, Reply, Gossip)
End Sub
```

This argument list defines three arguments that can represent a number or a string. To call this procedure and give it the arguments 30, "Hello", and 12.9, you would do one of the following:

✔ Chatty 30, "Hello", 12.9
✔ Call Chatty(30, "Hello", 12.9)

There is no practical limit to the number of arguments a procedure can accept. However, the longer your argument list is, the more complicated your procedure must be and the more likely you'll get confused trying to understand what your procedures do exactly.

Defining argument types

Besides defining the number of arguments in an argument list, you have the option of defining the type of data each argument must represent.

For example, you can define an argument to represent only one of the following:

✔ Integer
✔ Long
✔ Single
✔ Double
✔ Currency
✔ String

Argument types have to be defined in the argument list, for example:

```
Public Sub Convert(Fahrenheit As Integer, Celsius As Integer)
```

This defines two arguments, both of which must represent an Integer. The following code shows the only procedure call that would work:

```
Public cmdTest_Click()
Dim X, Y As Integer
Dim A, B As String
Dim M, N As Single
  Call Convert(X, Y)       ' This would work
  Call Convert(A, B)       ' Neither A nor B are Integers
  Call Convert(M, N)       ' Neither M nor N are Integers
  Call Convert("Hello", X) ' "Hello" is not an Integer
End Sub
```

The main reason to specify an argument's type is to prevent your procedure from trying to work with incorrect data. For example, if your procedure expects a string but gets an integer, your program could crash. Even worse, it might run correctly but contain the wrong information. In this case, you would have created a bug called a logic error. (Remember those?)

Although you don't have to declare an argument's type, it's always a good idea to do so, just to prevent any bugs from breeding inside your precious code.

Problems with sending arguments

There are two problems that may occur when calling procedures. One problem is when the number of arguments sent doesn't match the number or arguments defined by the procedure. The other problem occurs when the types of arguments sent don't match the types of arguments defined by the procedure.

Giving the wrong number of arguments

When you define a procedure with an argument list, the argument list defines the number of arguments it needs to run. If you call this procedure and don't give it the correct number of arguments, it won't work. For example:

```
Public Sub ArgueWithMe(Flame)
End Sub
```

This procedure expects one argument, which can be a number or a string. None of the following calls to this procedure works, because the number of arguments is not one:

✔ ArgueWithMe

✔ ArgueWithMe 9, "Shut up!"

✔ Call ArgueWithMe("Why?", "Go away!", 4500, "Okay.")

Giving the wrong type of arguments

Likewise, when calling a procedure, always make sure that the arguments have the same data type as the types defined in the argument list. For example:

```
Public Sub ArgueWithMe(Flame As String)
End Sub
```

This procedure expects one argument, which must be a String data type. None of the following calls to this procedure works because the arguments are not String data types.

- ✔ ArgueWithMe(78.909)
- ✔ ArgueWithMe(9)
- ✔ Call ArgueWithMe(34)

Passing arguments by value

To further protect your procedures from messing around with each other's variables, you can pass arguments by value. Normally, when you pass an argument to a procedure, the new procedure can change the argument's value. This is like giving somebody a drink and having them spit in it and hand it back to you.

If another procedure needs certain data, but you don't want that data to change in other parts of your program, you can pass an argument by value. This means that you give a procedure an argument and the procedure can change the argument all it wants. However, any changes it makes to this variable are limited within that particular procedure. This is like pouring part of your drink into another cup and giving it to another person. If that person decides to spit in his or her cup, your drink will still be uncontaminated.

To define an argument as passed by value, you would define it with the ByVal keyword in the argument list, like this:

```
Public Sub Switch(ByVal Name As String)
```

You never need to use the ByVal keyword to CALL a procedure. To call the preceding Switch procedure, you would use one of the following three methods:

- ✔ Switch "John Doe"
- ✔ Switch("John Doe")
- ✔ Call Switch("John Doe")

To specify that an argument be passed by value, you must put the `ByVal` keyword in front of each argument:

```
Public Sub BlackBox(ByVal X As Integer, Y As Integer)
```

In the preceding example, only the argument X is passed by value. The Y variable is not. To specify that the Y argument also be passed by value, you have to do the following:

```
Public Sub BlackBox(ByVal X As Integer, ByVal Y As Integer)
```

Test your newfound knowledge

1. Explain why argument passing is useful in writing programs.

   a. Argument passing is like passing the buck. Programmers do this all the time to avoid taking responsibility when their project is behind schedule.

   b. Passing arguments lets you write one general-purpose procedure to replace two or more specialized procedures.

   c. Arguments let you give wrong information to your procedures, so they have twice as many chances of wrecking your entire project.

   d. Argument passing is like scream therapy. Each side argues for its own point until both sides are exhausted. This prevents people from shooting each other at work.

2. Explain what the following argument list means:

```
Public Sub Confusion(ByVal Catch
   As String, X As Integer, Z)
End Sub
```

   a. I haven't learned my lesson and I have to review this section all over again.

   b. Now I finally understand why programmers look and act the way they do, if they have to spend eight hours a day deciphering cryptic commands like this.

   c. Someone didn't comment the code correctly to make this argument easy to understand.

   d. The procedure expects three arguments. The first argument is called Catch, is passed by value, and must be a String data type. The second argument is called X and must be an Integer data type. The third argument is called Z and can be any data type.

Quitting a Procedure Prematurely

Normally, a procedure runs until all of its instructions have been followed. However, you may want to exit a procedure before it's finished.

To exit a procedure prematurely, you have to use the following code:

```
Exit Sub
```

For example, you might have a procedure like the one that follows:

```
Public Sub EndlessLoop()
  X = 0
  Do
    X = X + 1
    If (X = 13) And (txtMessage.Text = Bad luck") Then
      End Sub
  Loop Until chkQuit.Value = 0
End Sub
```

If the value of chkQuit.Value were never equal to 0, the preceding procedure would keep looping until the value of X was equal to 13 and the Text property of a text box called txtMessage was equal to the string "Bad luck".

Try It Yourself

The following sample program lets you click two command buttons. Clicking the Hello button displays "Hello, world!" on the screen. Clicking the Good-bye button displays "Good-bye, cruel world!"

In case you have to try everything for yourself before you're convinced, the following table creates a simple program for you to play with.

Object	Property	Setting
Form	Caption	Argument Passing
Command1	Caption	Hello
	Height	495
	Left	1920
	Name	cmdHello
	Top	3000
	Width	1335
Command2	Caption	Good-bye
	Height	495
	Left	3720
	Name	cmdBye
	Top	3000
	Width	1335
Label1	Caption	(Empty)
	Height	495
	Left	2280
	Name	lblMessage
	Top	2040
	Width	2535

Type the following in the Code window:

```
Public Display(Message As String)
  lblMessage.Caption = Message
End Sub

Public cmdHello_Click()
  Display ("Hello, world!")
End Sub

Public cmdBye_Click()
  Display ("Good-bye, cruel world!")
End Sub
```

Chapter 28
Functions, a Unique Type of Subprogram

· ·

In This Chapter

▶ Calling functions

▶ Defining argument types

▶ Quitting a function early

· ·

*F*unctions return a single value. Procedures on the other hand, return zero or more values. Think of a function as a simpler version of a procedure. When you need to calculate only a single value, use a function instead of a procedure.

A typical function looks like the following:

```
Public Function FunctionName(ArgumentList)
   FunctionName = SomeValue
End Function
```

The word `Public` tells Visual Basic that if the function is stored in a BAS file, it can be used by all event and general procedures in your Visual Basic program. (If the function is stored in an FRM file, it can be used only by event and general procedures stored in that same FRM file.)

The word `Function` defines the subprogram as a function. The `FunctionName` can be any valid Visual Basic name, preferably one that describes what the function does. The argument list can contain zero or more arguments.

Assigning a Function to a Value

Somewhere inside the function, you must assign the function's name to a value or an expression, such as the following:

```
Public Function YardsToMeters(Yards)
Const Conversion = 0.9
  YardsToMeters = Yards * Conversion
End Function
```

If you don't assign the function's name to a value, the function won't return any value — and the whole point of using functions is to return a value.

You can also define the specific data type of the value that a function returns, such as Integer, String, or Currency.

The three main differences between a function and a procedure are as follows:

- A function can return only one value. A procedure can return zero or more values.

- Somewhere inside the function, the function's name must be assigned a value. You never have to do this with a procedure.

- You can define the data type that a function represents. You cannot define a procedure to represent a data type. (You can define only the data types of a procedure's argument list.)

Calling Functions

Calling a function is different than calling a procedure. Because functions represent a single value, you call a function by assigning the function name to a variable:

```
Public Function YardsToMeters(Yards As Single)
Const Conversion = 0.9
  YardsToMeters = Yards * Conversion
End Function

Private Sub cmdConvert_Click()
Dim Meters As Single
  Meters = YardsToMeters(Val(txtYards.Text))
  txtMetric.Text = Str$(Meters)
End Sub
```

This event procedure says, "When the user clicks on a command button called cmdConvert, do the following:"

1. Create a variable called `Meters` and define it to hold only Single data types.

2. Take whatever value is stored in the Text property of a text box called `txtYards` and use the value as an argument for the `YardsToMeters` function.

3. The `YardsToMeters` function takes `txtYards.Text` as its argument, multiplies it by 0.9, and stores this new result in the `YardsToMeters` function name. The result stored in the `YardsToMeters` function name gets stuffed into the `Meters` variable.

4. The value stored in the `Meters` variable gets converted into a string and stuffed into the Text property of a text box named txtMetric.

Note the differences in calling procedures and calling functions. When calling a procedure, you can use one of three methods:

- ✔ `ProcedureName ArgumentList`
- ✔ `ProcedureName(ArgumentList)`
- ✔ `Call ProcedureName(ArgumentList)`

You have only one way to call a function:

```
Variable = FunctionName(ArgumentList)
```

Because a function name represents a single value, you can use a function name in any mathematical expression, such as

```
Variable = FunctionName(ArgumentList) + Variable
```

So a procedure that calls a function could look like this:

```
Private Sub cmdConvert_Click()
Dim Meters As Single
  NewValue = (YardsToMeters (txtMetric.Text) + Meters) * 4
End Sub
```

Defining Functions as a Certain Data Type

Because a function returns a single value, you can specify what data type that value represents.

For example:

```
Public Function YardsToMeters(Yards) As Single
Const Conversion = 0.9
   YardsToMeters = Yards * Conversion
End Function
```

This defines the value of `YardsToMeters` as a Single data type. That means the only possible values `YardsToMeters` could represent are decimal numbers. You can define a function to represent any one of the following:

- ✔ Integer
- ✔ Long
- ✔ Single
- ✔ Double
- ✔ Currency
- ✔ String

No matter what data type a function represents, any variables assigned to it must be of the same data type. For example:

```
Public Function YardsToMeters(Yards) As Single
Const Conversion = 0.9
   YardsToMeters = Yards * Conversion
End Function

Private Sub cmdConvert_Click()
Dim Meters As Single
   Meters = YardsToMeters(Val(txtYards.Text))
   txtMetric.Text = Str$(Meters)
End Sub
```

In this example, the variable `Meters` is defined as a Single data type and the `YardsToMeters` function is also defined as a Single data type.

If `Meters` were defined as the following:

```
Dim Meters As String
```

the line

```
Meters = YardsToMeters(Val(txtYards.Text))
```

would not work because `Meters` is a String data type, and YardsToMeters returns a Single data type value.

(If you're still confused, think of pulling into the drive-thru window of Burger King and asking for a Big Mac. In that case, the Burger King cashier won't know what to do with your order. In the preceding example, `Meters` expects a string but `YardsToMeters` gives it a number, so the program won't work.)

Defining argument types

Arguments are data (numbers; strings; or variables, which represent a number or a string) that a function needs to work.

Besides defining the number of arguments in an argument list, you have the option of defining the type of data each argument must represent.

For example, you can define an argument to represent only one of the following:

- ✔ Integer
- ✔ Long
- ✔ Single
- ✔ Double
- ✔ Currency
- ✔ String

To define an argument type, you have to define its type in the argument list:

```
Public Function Convert(Fahrenheit As Integer, Celsius As
        Integer)
```

Test your newfound knowledge

1. When would you use a function and when would you use a procedure?

   a. In Chapter 26, we learned about procedures, so that's where you would use a procedure. In this chapter, you'd use only functions, because that's what this lesson covers.

   b. Use a function when you need to calculate a single value. Use a procedure to calculate zero or more values.

   c. Functions and procedures are identical except they use different names, have different purposes, and don't look the same.

   d. You use a function only if you're too wimpy to use a procedure, like a real programmer would.

2. Which line is a function call and which line is a procedure call?

```
Private Sub cmdDisplay()
Dim Alex, Pete, George As Double
Pete = 3
George = 0
```

```
Alex = ClockworkOrange(Pete,
  George) ' Line 5
ConditionedBehavior(Alex) ' Line
  6
End Sub
```

   a. Line five is a function call, because a variable is assigned to the value represented by the function name. Line six is a procedure call, because its name is not assigned to a variable.

   b. Both lines five and six are procedure calls, because I think this is a trick question and because guessing wrong 99 percent of the time since the start of this book still hasn't convinced me that the right answer is always the most obvious one.

   c. Line six is a function call because it looks different from line five, which is also a function call.

   d. I don't know the answer, but this question looks as odd as a clockwork orange. Have you seen the movie of the same name by Stanley Kubrick?

This example defines two arguments and both must represent an Integer. The following shows the only procedure call that would work:

```
Private Sub cmdTest_Click()
Dim X, Y, Z As Integer
Dim A, B, C As String
Dim L, M, N As Single
  Z = Convert(X, Y)        ' This would work
  C = Convert(A, B)        ' Neither A nor B are Integers
  L = Convert(M, N)        ' Neither M nor N are Integers
  Z = Convert("Hello", X)  ' "Hello" is not an Integer
End Sub
```

The main reason to specify an argument's type is to prevent a function from working with the wrong type of data. For example, if your function expects an integer but gets a string, your program could crash. Even worse, it might create a logic error.

Although you don't have to declare an argument's type, it's always a good idea to do so, just to prevent any bugs.

Problems sending arguments

There are two problems that may occur when calling procedures. One problem is when the number of arguments sent doesn't match the number of arguments defined by the function.

Another problem is when the types of arguments sent don't match the types of arguments defined by the function.

Giving the wrong number of arguments

When you define a function with an argument list, the list specifies the number of arguments that the function needs to run. If you call this function and don't give it the right number of arguments, it won't work. For example:

```
Public Function Flame(Mail)
End Function
```

This function expects one argument, which can be a number or a string. None of the following calls to this function works, because the number of arguments is not one:

- ✔ X = Flame
- ✔ X = Flame(9, "Shut up!")
- ✔ X = Flame("Why?", "Go away!", 4500, "Okay.")

Giving the wrong type of arguments

Likewise, when calling a procedure, always make sure that the arguments have the same data type as the types defined in the argument list:

```
Public Function Flame(Mail As String)
End Function
```

This procedure expects one argument, which must be a String data type. None of the following calls to this function will work because the arguments are not String data types:

✔ X = Flame(78.909)

✔ X = Flame(9)

✔ X = Flame(34)

Quitting a Function Prematurely

Normally, your function runs until all of its instructions have been followed. However, you may want to exit a procedure before it's finished.

To exit a procedure prematurely, you have to use the following code:

```
Exit Function
```

Before you exit a function, make sure that you also assign a value to the function name; otherwise, your program may not work correctly.

Chapter 29

File Management

Most Visual Basic programs consist of four types of files:

✔ VBP project files (previous versions of Visual Basic called them MAK project files)

✔ FRM (form) files

✔ BAS (module) files

✔ OCX or VBX custom control files

VBP Project Files

A VBP project file contains a list of all the FRM, BAS, and OCX or VBX custom control files that make up a single Visual Basic program. The following are the partial contents of a typical project file:

```
BIBLIO.FRM
BIBLIO.BAS
FRMABOUT.FRM
Object={F9043C88-F6F2-101A-A3C9-08002B2F49FB}#1.0#0;
        COMDLG16.OCX
Object={FAEEE763-117E-101B-8933-08002B2F4F5A}#1.0#0;
        DBLIST16.OCX
ProjWinSize=103,443,191,255
```

```
ProjWinShow=2
IconForm="Form1"
HelpFile="BIBLIO.HLP"
Title="BIBLIO"
ExeName="BIBLIO.exe"
```

Earlier versons of Visual Basic called project files MAK files. To maintain compatibility with Visual Basic 4.0 and to keep from getting confused, you should rename all your MAK files as VBP files. Aren't you glad you upgraded to Visual Basic 4.0?

To create a new VBP project file, follow these steps:

1. Select New Project from the File menu. Visual Basic displays a blank form.

2. Select Save Project from the File menu.

To load an existing VBP or MAK project file, follow these steps:

1. Select Open Project from the File menu. (As an alternative, you can press Ctrl+O or click the Open Project icon.) Visual Basic displays an Open Project dialog box.

2. Type or click the name of the VBP or MAK project file you want to load and then click Open.

Whenever you load a VBP or MAK project file, Visual Basic automatically loads all the files listed in the VBP or MAK project file.

Adding files to a project file

The more Visual Basic programs you write, the more useful certain parts of them will be for future programs you may write. Fortunately, Visual Basic makes it easy to take FRM and BAS files that are created for other programs and add them to a new program you're working on.

To add the capabilities of a new FRM or BAS file to your program, just add the FRM or BAS file to your VBP project file.

To add a file to a VBP project file, follow these steps:

1. Press Ctrl+D or select Add File from the File menu. Visual Basic displays an Add File dialog box.

2. Type or click the name of the FRM or BAS file you want to add to the VBP project file.

Removing files from a project file

Sometimes you may want to remove a file permanently from a project file. To remove an FRM file or a BAS file from a VBP or MAK project file, follow these steps:

1. Press Ctrl+R or select Project from the View menu. The Project window appears.

2. Highlight the FRM, BAS, CLS, or RES file that you want to remove.

3. Select Remove File from the File menu.

When you remove a file from a project file, the removed file still exists on your floppy or hard disk. Removing a file simply tells Visual Basic, "See that file over there? I don't want it to be part of this particular program anymore, so get rid of it, but keep it saved on disk in case I want it back again." To erase or delete a file from your floppy or hard disk, use the Windows Explorer or the DOS `Delete` or `Erase` command.

FRM (Form) Files

A FRM file contains the user interface of a Visual Basic program. A Visual Basic program can have zero or more FRM files. If the program has zero FRM files, however, it won't have a user interface.

Creating a form file

Whenever you run Visual Basic, it automatically displays a blank form on the screen. If you want to create another form, click the Form icon in the Toolbar (see Figure 29-1) or select Form from the Insert menu. Visual Basic displays a new blank form.

Saving a form file

When you add a new form file to your project, Visual Basic displays its name in lowercase in the Project window. The moment you save the form file, its name appears in uppercase in the Project window.

To save a form, follow these steps:

1. Press Ctrl+R or select Project from the View menu. The Project window appears.

2. Click on the FRM file you want to save.

Form icon

Figure 29-1:
The Form
icon in the
Toolbar.

3. Press Ctrl+S or select <u>S</u>ave File from the <u>F</u>ile menu. Visual Basic displays a Save File As dialog box if you haven't saved this file before.

4. Type a name for your FRM file and click the OK button.

Printing a form file

Visual Basic, in its spirit of democracy, gives you three ways to print a form file:

✔ Print an exact image of the form as it appears on the screen

✔ Print the object names and properties that appear on the form

✔ Print all the event procedures (BASIC code) stored on the form

Usually you'll want to print an exact image of a form so that you can show people what your program looks like, rather than dragging them to your computer and forcing them to stare at your monitor.

To print an exact visual image of a form, follow these steps:

1. Press Ctrl+R or select P<u>r</u>oject from the <u>V</u>iew menu. The Project window appears.

2. Click on the FRM file you want to print.

3. Press Ctrl+P or select Print from the File menu. Visual Basic displays a Print dialog box, as shown in Figure 29-2.

4. Click the check box labeled Form Image.

5. Click the OK button. Visual Basic prints the form exactly as it appears to a user.

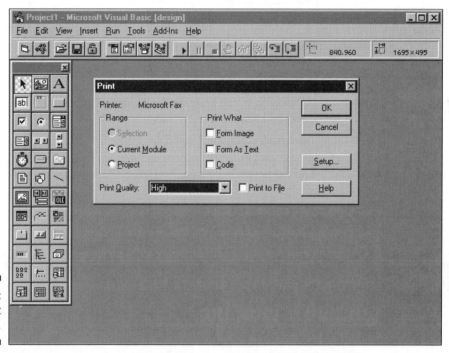

Figure 29-2:
The Print
dialog box.

Sometimes a visual image of a form isn't as useful as knowing the property values of the form and each object on the form. Usually you'll want to print all the object names and properties so that you and your fellow programmers can better understand how the program's user interface works.

To print all the object names and properties that appear on the form, do the following:

1. Press Ctrl+R or select Project from the View menu. The Project window appears.

2. Click on the FRM file you want to print.

3. Press Ctrl+P or select Print from the File menu. Visual Basic displays a Print dialog box.

4. Click the check box labeled Form As Text.

5. Click the OK button. Visual Basic prints all the properties of the form and all the objects on the form.

Finally, you may want to print your form file's BASIC code, which is entombed in the form. This can be especially useful so you and your fellow programmers can dissect a program to see how it works.

To print all the event procedures of a form and each object on the form, follow these steps:

1. Press Ctrl+R or select Project from the View menu. The Project window appears.

2. Click on the FRM file you want to print.

3. Press Ctrl+P or select Print from the File menu. Visual Basic displays a Print dialog box.

4. Click the check box labeled Code.

5. Click the OK button. Visual Basic prints all the code stored on the form.

BAS (Module) Files

A BAS (module) file can contain global or module general procedures, along with constant and variable declarations that are used by other parts of your program, such as other BAS or FRM files.

A module general procedure, constant, or variable can be used by any procedure that is stored in any file listed in the same VBP project file.

You can declare global constants and variables only in a BAS module. You cannot declare a global constant or variable in an FRM file or inside a procedure in a BAS module. If you try, Visual Basic won't let you and will radiate your eyeballs as punishment.

Most cool programmers use BAS files for storing top secret BASIC code that they can use over and over in different programs. That way, instead of rewriting their program each time, they can just add the BAS file to your project file.

Creating a BAS file

Visual Basic programs can contain zero or more BAS files. For short programs, you may not need any BAS files. But for larger programs, you may have several BAS files.

To create a new BAS file, click the Module icon in the Toolbar (see Figure 29-3) or select <u>M</u>odule from the <u>I</u>nsert menu. Visual Basic displays the code window for your newly created BAS file.

Module icon

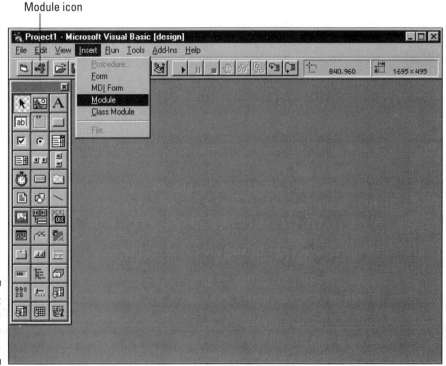

Figure 29-3:
The Module
icon on the
Toolbar.

Saving a BAS file

When you add a new BAS file to your project, Visual Basic displays its name in lowercase in the Project window. The moment you save the module file, its name appears in uppercase in the Project window.

To save a BAS file, follow these steps:

1. Press Ctrl+R or select P<u>r</u>oject from the <u>V</u>iew menu. The Project window appears.

2. Click on the BAS file you want to save.

3. Press Ctrl+S or select <u>S</u>ave File from the <u>F</u>ile menu. Visual Basic displays a Save File As dialog box if you haven't saved this file before.

4. Type the name of the BAS file and click the OK button.

Printing a BAS file

Visual Basic lets you print all the code stored in a BAS file. Because Visual Basic can only display, at most, a screenful of your precious BASIC code, printing it all on paper lets you see and review the whole thing at one time.

To print a BAS file, follow these steps:

1. Press Ctrl+R or select Project from the View menu. The Project window appears.

2. Click on the BAS file you want to print.

3. Press Ctrl+P or select Print from the File menu. Visual Basic displays a Print dialog box.

4. Click the check box labeled Code.

5. Click the OK button. Visual Basic prints all the procedures stored in the BAS file

OCX and VBX Custom Control Files

Visual Basic can use two types of custom controls: VBX and OCX. If you're writing programs for Windows 3.1 (considered a 16-bit operating system), use a VBX. If you're writing programs for Windows NT or Windows 95 (considered 32-bit operating systems), use an OCX.

Both VBX and OCX custom controls can add features to the capabilities of your Visual Basic program. Visual Basic itself comes with several custom controls. Some of the more common ones are

- GRID16.OCX, GRID32.VBX, and GRID.VBX
- COMDLG16.OCX, COMDLG32.OCX, and CMDIALOG.VBX

The GRID16.OCX, GRID32.VBX, and GRID.VBX custom controls let you draw a grid on a form, similar to a spreadsheet grid (see Figure 29-4). The COMDLG16.OCX, COMDLG32.OCX, and CMDIALOG.VBX custom controls let your programs use the standard Windows Open, Save As, Print, Color, and Font dialog boxes.

If you're writing programs for Windows 3.1, use either the VBX custom control or the OCX with the number 16 in its file name, such as GRID16.OCX. If you're writing programs for Windows 95 or Windows NT, use the OCX with the number 32 in its file name, such as GRID32.OCX.

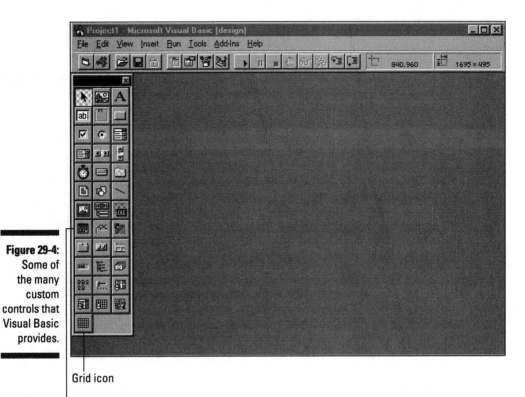

Figure 29-4:
Some of
the many
custom
controls that
Visual Basic
provides.

Grid icon

Common dialog box icon

If you want to extend the capabilities of Visual Basic, you can also buy custom controls from many commercial publishers. These custom controls offer such diverse capabilities as telecommunications, database access, and word processing features. Then again, if you believe advertisements for custom controls, you might believe also that a custom control can wash your dishes, mow your lawn, and do your laundry.

Besides buying commercial custom controls, you can also find many shareware custom controls through local BBSs and major on-line services such as CompuServe, GEnie, and America Online.

Whenever you add a custom control to a VBP project file, the custom control icon appears in the Visual Basic Toolbox.

To add a particular OCX or VBX file to a VBP project file, follow these steps:

1. Press Ctrl+T or select Custom Controls from the Tools menu. Visual Basic displays a Custom Controls dialog box (see Figure 29-5).

2. Click in the check box of the OCX or VBX file that you want to add and then click OK.

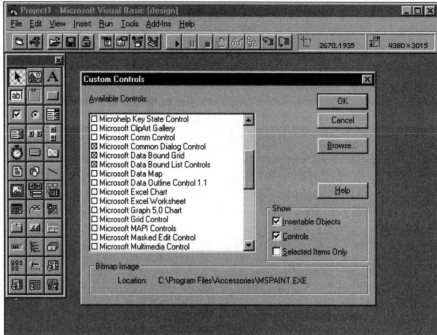

Figure 29-5:
The Custom
Controls
dialog box.

For more information on the most popular and useful VBX and OCX custom controls available, browse through Chapter 32.

Part VIII
Database Programs and Printing

In this part . . .

Most people don't care about learning a database
program, and even more people don't care about all
the different file formats that data may be trapped in. To
cater to these people, Visual Basic can cheerfully read,
write, and modify information that is in a variety of database
file formats, including Microsoft Access, dBASE, and Paradox.

Besides providing employment for hundreds of computer
book authors and publishers, the purpose of most programs
is to store information and then print it. After all, what good
would a word processor be if you had to type everything in
and it then refused to print anything out? In this part, you
learn all about storing and printing information for your own
Visual Basic programs.

Chapter 30

Using Files from Database Programs You'd Rather Not Use

••

In This Chapter

▶ Connecting to a database file

▶ Displaying different records

▶ Searching for specific records

••

*I*f you're planning to store a great deal of data, you might as well store it in a database file. Visual Basic can store and retrieve data in any one of the following five database formats:

- ✔ Microsoft Access MDB files
- ✔ Borland dBASE or Microsoft FoxPro DBF files
- ✔ Borland Paradox DB files
- ✔ Novell Btrieve DDF files
- ✔ Open DataBase Connectivity (ODBC) databases

If you have no clue as to what any of these files or databases are, consider yourself lucky.

Visual Basic comes with a separate program called the Data Manager, which lets you create Microsoft Access database (MDB) files without shelling out the money to buy a real copy of Microsoft Access. Unfortunately, if you want to create database files for dBASE, Btrieve, ODBC, or Paradox, you must own a program that can create these files for you. This is Microsoft's subtle attempt to coerce the whole world into switching to Microsoft Access.

What Are Database Files?

Whenever one of those fancy database programs such as Paradox, Access, or dBASE saves information, the program stores the information in a disk file. Because the disk file contains a bunch of data that somebody thinks is important, it's called a *database file*. Essentially, a database file is like a shoe box jammed with junk.

To organize its data, a database file is made up of one or more records. A record is like a 3 × 5 index card. Each record contains fields, which contain the specific information (names, addresses, and stuff like that). Figure 30-1 shows an example of a record.

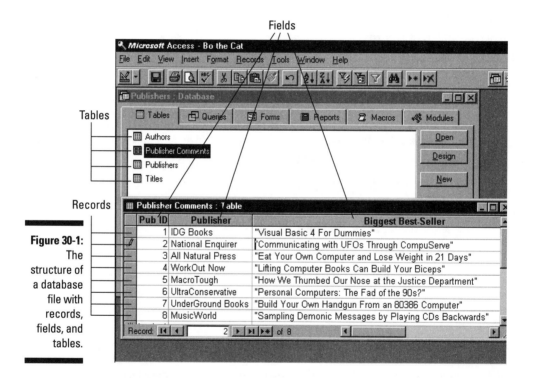

Figure 30-1: The structure of a database file with records, fields, and tables.

To organize this information further, database files let you organize data into tables. A table is a subset of your entire database. It contains only specific information, such as the names of all the people who live in Oregon or the phone numbers of everyone you can't stand.

How to Connect to a Database File

When you want Visual Basic to read and modify a database file, you have to specify the following:

- ✔ Which database file to use
- ✔ Which recordset type to use
- ✔ Which database table to use
- ✔ Which database fields to display

To connect your program to a database file, follow these steps:

1. Make sure that the database file that you want to connect exists. If not, you'll have to create it, using a database program or the Data Manager program.

2. Select the Data Control icon from the Visual Basic Toolbox and draw it on your form. Figure 30-2 shows this icon and the drawn data control.

3. Press F4 or select Properties from the View menu to open the Properties window.

4. Choose the DatabaseName property and click the gray ellipsis button (. . .) in the settings box. Visual Basic displays a DatabaseName dialog box.

5. Select the database file that you want to use, such as BIBLIO (which is the sample database that comes with Visual Basic) and click Open.

6. Click the Recordset Type property and click the gray down-arrow button in the settings box. Visual Basic displays a list of recordset types to choose from.

7. Select a recordset type, such as Table.

8. Choose the RecordSource property and click the gray down-arrow button in the settings box. Visual Basic displays a list of database tables you can choose from.

9. Select a database table (such as Titles, if you chose the BIBLIO sample database that comes with Visual Basic).

If you're just using Microsoft Access MDB files, choose the Table recordset type in step 7. If you're using any other type of database, choose the Dynaset recordset type. If you need to read data but not update it, go ahead and choose the Snapshot recordset type.

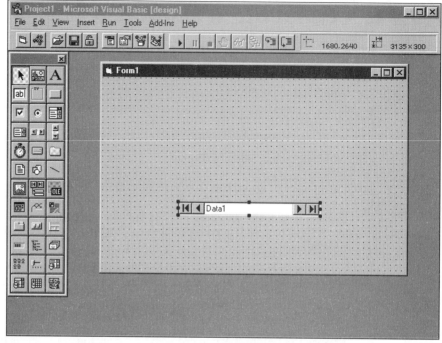

Figure 30-2:
The Data
Control icon
and the data
control,
drawn as a
horizontal
scroll bar.

Displaying Data Fields on the Screen

After you connect your program to a database file, the next step is to display
the information stored in the fields of the database. Visual Basic gives you
seven ways to display database fields:

- ✔ Check boxes
- ✔ Image boxes
- ✔ Labels
- ✔ List boxes
- ✔ Combo boxes
- ✔ Picture boxes
- ✔ Text boxes

Check boxes display Yes and No or True and False values. If a field has a Yes or
True value, the check box appears selected on the screen. If the field has a No
or False value, the check box appears blank.

Image and picture boxes enable you to display graphics, as long as the database file itself contains graphics.

List and combo boxes enable you to display multiple choices. The combo box gives users a chance to type in something that's not included in the combo box's list.

Text boxes and labels display information such as names, addresses, phone numbers, and quantities.

Use a text box if you want to give the user the ability to change the displayed data. Use a label when you want to prevent a user from changing data.

To create a text box, label, check box, image box, combo box, list box, or picture box to display a database field, follow these steps:

1. Draw the text box, label, check box, image box, combo box, list box, or picture box on the form that contains the data control.

2. Press F4 or select Properties from the View menu to display the Properties window.

3. Choose the DataSource property and click the gray down-arrow button in the settings box. Visual Basic lists all the data control names on the form.

4. Select a data control name.

5. Choose the DataField property and click the gray down-arrow button in the settings box. Visual Basic lists all the field names you can display.

6. Select a field name.

When selecting a field name for a check box, make sure that the database field contains only Yes/No or True/False values. When selecting a field name for an image or a picture box, make sure that the database field contains only graphics images. Otherwise, Visual Basic will get confused and stop.

Choosing Different Records

When Visual Basic loads a database, it makes the first record of the database the current record. Any commands you issue affect only that first database record.

Choosing different records is like thumbing through a library card catalog. (For those younger people who have never seen a library card catalog, think of thumbing through a CD music collection in a music store.)

Visual Basic provides two ways to make a different record the current record:

- ✔ Using the data control object
- ✔ Using BASIC code

The data control object has four arrows that let the user scroll through different records. Figure 30-3 shows these arrows.

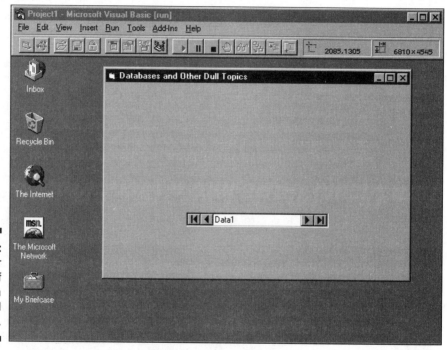

Figure 30-3:
The four
arrows of
the data
control
object.

The data control object is designed to look like the controls on a tape cassette or VCR. (Then again, how many people know how to program their VCR?)

The arrows on the far left and far right move to the first and last database record. The other two arrows move forward or backward, one record at a time.

The data control object lets a user choose a record. Just make sure that you have a text box or label on the screen to display the data from the current record. If you don't, the user will have no idea which record is current.

Displaying the records in a database

To display the *first record* using BASIC code, you have two choices:

- ✔ Data1.Refresh
- ✔ Data1.Recordset.MoveFirst

In all these commands, Data1 refers to the name of your data control object. If you change the name of the data control, you'll have to use your new name instead.

To display the *last record* in the database, use the following command:

```
Data1.Recordset.MoveLast
```

To display the *next record* in the database, use the command that follows:

```
Data1.Recordset.MoveNext
```

To display the *previous record* in the database, use the following command:

```
Data1.Recordset.MovePrevious
```

Deleting a record

To delete a record from a database, find the record that you want to obliterate from the face of the earth and then use the following two commands:

```
Data1.Recordset.Delete
Data1.Recordset.MoveNext
```

This command says, "See the currently displayed record? Delete it now and then display the next record so that the deleted record won't be visible anymore."

Adding a record

To add a record to a database, follow these steps:

1. Create a new record, using the following code:

```
Data1.Recordset.AddNew
```

2. Put data in the fields of this newly created record by using the following code:

```
Data1.Recordset.Fields("FieldName") = "NewData"
```

(FieldName is the specific field you want to change in your database, and yes, you need the quotation marks surrounding the field name. NewData is the new information you want to store in the field, and can be a string or a number. If the information is a string, it needs quotation marks around it. If the information is a number, you don't need the quotation marks.)

3. Save the record to the database with the following code:

```
Data1.Recordset.Update
```

Visual Basic always adds new records to the end of a database file.

Editing a record

To edit an existing record in a database, follow these steps:

1. Display the record that you want to edit.

2. Use the following command to tell Visual Basic that you want to edit this record:

```
Data1.Recordset.Edit
```

3. Assign the new data to the specific field whose contents you want to change:

```
Data1.Recordset.Fields("FieldName") = "NewData"
```

4. Save the record to the database:

```
Data1.Recordset.Update
```

Counting the number of existing records

Sometimes it's nice to know how many records a database file contains. To calculate this value, use the commands that follow:

```
Dim TotalRecords As Integer
Data1.Recordset.MoveLast
TotalRecords = Data1.Recordset.RecordCount
```

The first line says, "Create a variable called TotalRecords, and define it as an Integer data type." The second line says, "Move to the last record in the database." The third line says, "Count the number of records and store this value in the variable called TotalRecords."

Test your newfound knowledge

1. What are the steps you must follow to make your Visual Basic program use a database file?

   a. First, create a database file using a separate database program such as Access or Paradox. Then draw the Data Control icon on a form, choose the database file name for the DatabaseName property of the Data Control icon, and choose a database table for the RecordSource property of the Data Control icon.

   b. Buy a computer, take it back to the store because it doesn't work, hire a database programmer, fire the database programmer, and throw up your hands in despair.

   c. Visual Basic can use database files? Hey, where can I learn more about this?

   d. None. This is a trick question and I refuse to reveal my ignorance by selecting any of these choices.

2. What do the following four lines of BASIC code do?

```
Data1.Recordset.AddNew
Data1.Recordset.Fields("Question")
  = "Did you ever smoke anything
  illegal?"
```

```
Data1.Recordset.Fields("Answer")
  = "Yes, but I never inhaled."
Data1.Recordset.Update
```

   a. The first line erases any existing databases on your hard disk, the second and third lines are superfluous, and the fourth line wipes out the rest of the files stored on your hard disk.

   b. The first line adds a new record to a database file; the second line stores the string "Did you ever smoke anything illegal?" in the database field called "Question"; the third line stores the string "Yes, but I never inhaled." in the database field called "Answer"; and the fourth line updates the database with this new information, adding this new record at the end of the database file.

   c. The first line confuses Visual Basic, the second line asks Visual Basic a question, the third line displays Visual Basic's answer as given under the advice of a lawyer, and the fourth line ignores the whole problem and hopes that everyone will forget what really happened.

   d. Hey! You're making fun of somebody important, aren't you?

Finding a Specific Record

To find a specific record in a database, you have to use one of the following commands:

- `Data1.Recordset.FindFirst "criteria"`
- `Data1.Recordset.FindNext "criteria"`
- `Data1.Recordset.FindPrevious "criteria"`
- `Data1.Recordset.FindLast "criteria"`

The search criteria (or criterion, in case you think the singular form of criteria doesn't look silly) specifies which field to search and the specific data you want to find. For example, to find all the records containing information on people with the last name Quayle, your search criteria would look like the following:

```
"LastName = 'Quayle'"
```

Notice that the data you're searching for (`'Quayle'`) must appear surrounded by single quotation marks. If you fail to use single quotation marks, Visual Basic won't know what you want to find and won't do anything, out of spite. Of course, this example assumes that a field called `LastName` exists.

If you try searching for data in a nonexistent field, you'll get an error message.

To find the *first record* that meets your search criteria, use a command like the following:

```
Data1.Recordset.FindFirst "LastName = 'Quayle'"
```

After you've found one record that meets your search criteria, you can search for another record that meets your criteria. To find the *next record* that meets your search criteria, use a command like the following:

```
Data1.Recordset.FindNext "LastName = 'Quayle'"
```

To find the *previous record* that meets your search criteria, use a command like the following:

```
Data1.Recordset.FindPrevious "LastName = 'Quayle'"
```

To find the *last record* that meets your search criteria, use a command like this:

```
Data1.Recordset.FindLast "LastName = 'Quayle'"
```

Yanking data from a database field

Before you yank out information from a database field, find the record that you want by using the `FindFirst`, `FindNext`, `FindLast`, or `FindPrevious` command. Then yank information from the database field using one of two methods:

- ✔ Create a text box or label and set its DataField property to the field you want.
- ✔ Use BASIC code to yank information out of a database and assign it to a variable:

```
Dim Store As String
Store = Data1.Recordset.Fields("Fieldname").Value
```

The first line says, "Create a variable called Store and define it as a string data type." The second line says, "Yank the data stored in the field called Fieldname and store its value in the Store variable."

Changing data in a database

To change the contents of a database field when the field is displayed in a text box, check box, image, or picture box, just type or paste new information inside.

To change the contents of a database field by using BASIC code, use the following commands:

```
Data1.Recordset.Edit
Data1.Recordset.Fields("Fieldname").Value = NewValue
Data1.Recordset.Update
```

The first command tells Visual Basic, "I'm getting ready to change some data in a database." The second command replaces the current value of the field Fieldname with the value stored in NewValue. The third command says, "Save my changes to the database."

Placing a bookmark on a specific record

You can put a bookmark on a record so that you can quickly jump back to it anytime. To create a bookmark, you have to create a variable and define it as a Variant or String data type. For example:

```
Dim BookMark1 As Variant
```

or

```
Dim BookMark2 As String
```

Each bookmark can point to only one record at a time.

To place a bookmark, display the record where you want to put it and then use the following command:

```
BookMark1 = Data1.Recordset.Bookmark
```

To jump back to a bookmark, use the following command:

```
Data1.Recordset.Bookmark = Bookmark1
```

Note: Not all database files let you use bookmarks. Microsoft Access MDB files are always bookmarkable (is that a real word?), but other database types may not be, depending if an index exists for that particular database. (If you have no idea what an index is, you don't have to worry about it.) To determine whether a database file supports bookmarks, examine the Bookmarkable property, as in the following:

```
If Data1.Recordset.Bookmarkable = True Then
   ' Can place bookmarks
ElseIf Data1.Recordset.Bookmarkable = False Then
   ' Cannot use bookmarks
End If
```

Be careful about database formats. Each time a company such as Microsoft upgrades their database program (such as Access), the new version of that database program may use a different file format. This means that Visual Basic may not be able to use the new, updated file format.

Chapter 31

Making Your Program Print Stuff

In This Chapter

▶ Printing a form

▶ Using the printer object to print lines and circles

▶ Counting pages

A program can suck in data, manipulate it, and display it on the screen. But eventually, your program may need to print stuff out.

Visual Basic provides two ways to print stuff:

✔ Display data on a form and then print the form

✔ Send data directly to the printer using the Printer object

Printing a Form

Printing a form is the simplest method. To print a form, use this syntax:

```
FormName.PrintForm
```

This tells Visual Basic, "Find the form named FormName and send it to the printer."

To print a form named `frmAbout`, you would use the following command:

```
frmAbout.PrintForm
```

You can print any form in your program, including invisible forms and mini-mized forms. The only drawback with printing forms is that the print resolution may not be very high.

When you use the PrintForm command, Visual Basic sends each pixel of the form to your printer. So if you have a fuzzy, grainy monitor, your form is going to look fuzzy and grainy, even if you use the best laser printer in the world.

Most screens display a resolution of 96 dots per inch. Most laser printers can print at resolutions of 300 dots per inch. For quick printing, the PrintForm command works well. But for higher resolution printing, print using the Printer object instead.

Printing with the Printer Object

The Printer object is a temporary storage space that intercepts data, cleans it up, then sends the clean version to the printer. To print a form using the Printer object, you essentially have to redraw your form on the Printer object, using BASIC code.

The advantage of the Printer object is that it uses the resolution of your printer. The disadvantage is that you have to write lots of BASIC code, just to print a simple form.

Before you print anything using the Printer object, you have to define the top/bottom page margins and the right/left page margins.

To define the *top* page margin, use this following syntax, where `TopValue` measures the size of the top margin:

```
Printer.ScaleTop = TopValue
```

To define the *bottom* page margin, use the syntax that follows, where `BottomValue` measures the size of the bottom margin:

```
Printer.ScaleBottom = BottomValue
```

To define the *left* page margin, use the following syntax, where `LeftValue` measures the size of the left margin:

```
Printer.ScaleLeft = LeftValue
```

To define the *right* page margin, use the following syntax, where `RightValue` measures the size of the right margin:

```
Printer.ScaleRight = RightValue
```

Printing text on the printer object

Before you can print text through the Printer object, you have to define the X and Y location where you want the text to appear.

To define this location, use this syntax:

```
Printer.CurrentX = XValue
Printer.CurrentY = YValue
```

These commands say, "Start printing all text at the location defined by the CurrentX and CurrentY properties.

To start printing at the upper-left corner of a page, use the following commands:

```
Printer.CurrentX = 0
Printer.CurrentY = 0
```

Test your newfound knowledge

1. Why would you ever want to have your Visual Basic program print anything?

   a. To waste paper and help contribute to global deforestation in Third World countries.

   b. So I can justify buying a $1000 laser printer.

   c. To provide hard copies of any important information that my Visual Basic program may create.

   d. There's never a reason to print anything. Hasn't watching American politics taught you to never put down on paper anything that might implicate you in the future?

2. Why do you need to specify x- and y-coordinates when printing text or drawing lines or circles?

   a. To make you feel like you actually learned something useful in high school geometry class.

   b. So you can tell Visual Basic exactly where you want your lines, circles, or text to appear on the printed page. Is that too much to ask?

   c. The x- and y-coordinates define the location of your printer in relation to your computer. If you define the x- and y-coordinates incorrectly, your documents may start printing out from your toaster or air conditioner.

   d. No reason. It's just another ploy by Microsoft to make you think Visual Basic programming is a lot more complicated than it really is.

After you define where to start printing, the next step is to actually print some text. To print text on the printer object, follow this syntax:

```
Printer.Print "Text string"
```

This command says, "Put a text string on the printer object and print it at the location previously defined by the CurrentX and the CurrentY properties."

Printing lines and circles on the printer object

Printing plain text can be boring, so Visual Basic gives you the option to spice up your printouts with lines and circles. If this sounds like Visual Basic is turning your $2000 computer and $1000 laser printer into an Etch-A-Sketch, you're right.

Defining line thicknesses

Before you start drawing lines and circles, you have to define the draw width. The smaller the draw width, the thinner your lines will look.

To define the draw width, use the syntax that follows:

```
Printer.DrawWidth = Value
```

To define the skinniest draw width possible, use this command:

```
Printer.DrawWidth = 1
```

To define a fatter draw width, use this command:

```
Printer.DrawWidth = 5
```

For those who really care, the values of DrawWidth can vary from 1 to 32,767. A value of 1 specifies a line one pixel wide. A value of 32,767 specifies a line of 32,767 pixels wide, which is probably wider than you will ever need.

Drawing lines on the printer object

To draw a line, use the syntax that follows, where x1 and y1 define the starting point of the line and x2 and y2 define the ending point:

```
Printer.Line (x1,y1) - (x2,y2)
```

Drawing circles on the printer object

To draw a circle, use this syntax, where x and y are the center of the circle and Radius defines the circle's radius:

```
Printer.Circle(x,y), Radius
```

Printing Multiple Pages

Usually Visual Basic keeps printing your data until it runs out of room on the page. Then it cuts your text off and starts printing a new page automatically.

However, if you want to control when Visual Basic starts printing a new page, use the following command:

```
Printer.NewPage
```

This tells Visual Basic to start printing on a new page. (Wow! What will they think of next?)

Defining the Print Quality

Depending on your printer, you can specify a range of resolutions for printing. The magic command to control print resolution is

```
Printer.PrintQuality = x
```

where x represents a negative number between -4 and -1, or a positive number representing the specific resolution you want to use, measured in dots per inch (dpi). For example, the following table shows the print resolution of the negative numbers -4 to -1:

`Printer.PrintQuality = -1`	Draft resolution
`Printer.PrintQuality = -2`	Low resolution
`Printer.PrintQuality = -3`	Medium resolution
`Printer.PrintQuality = -4`	High resolution

If you're the type who likes to specify the exact print resolution to use, just specify a positive number. To define 300 dots per inch, which is what most cheap laser printers can produce these days, you would use the following command:

```
Printer.PrintQuality = 300
```

Keeping a Page Count

When you're printing multiple pages, Visual Basic automatically keeps track of the page count in a property called Page. To use this page count, use the following BASIC command:

```
Printer.Page
```

When You've Finished Printing

Use the following command to tell Visual Basic you've finished printing:

```
Printer.EndDoc
```

If you neglect to use this command, guess what? Visual Basic assumes that it exists anyway, so you really don't need to use this after all. However, for good programming practice, use this command so that it's clear exactly when you've finished printing.

In case you want to stop printing, you can tell Visual Basic, "Hey, I changed my mind. Stop printing." To stop the printer right away, use the following BASIC command:

```
Printer.KillDoc
```

Try It Yourself

The following sample program prints a short message when you click the Click to Print command button. To create this program, use the settings specified in the following table:

Object	Property	Setting
Form	Caption	Print Example
Command1	Caption	Click to Print
	Name	cmdPrint

Type the following in the Code window:

```
Private Sub cmdPrint_Click()
Dim TotalPages As Integer
Dim PageCount As String
  ' Specifies the text position to print
  Printer.CurrentX = 100
  Printer.CurrentY = 100
  Printer.Print "This appears at the top of the page"

  ' Specifies a line width and location
  Printer.DrawWidth = 3
  Printer.Line(100, 100)-(10000, 100)
  Printer.Line(100, 350)-(10000, 350)
  TotalPages = Printer.Page

  ' Specifies where to print the page count
  Printer.CurrentX = 1000
  Printer.CurrentY = 400
  PageCount = "TotalPages = " & Str$(TotalPages)
  Printer.Print PageCount
  Printer.EndDoc
End Sub
```

For simple printing tasks, writing some BASIC code won't be too tough. But if you want to do fancy printing and write your own desktop publishing program in Visual Basic, good luck. It's possible; it just may take a really long time to write all the BASIC code to tell the printer how to work.

Part IX
The Part of Tens

"GENTLEMEN, I SAY RATHER THAN FIX THE 'BUGS', WE CHANGE THE DOCUMENTATION AND CALL THEM 'FEATURES'."

In this part . . .

Now that you've made it this far in the book (unless you cheated and skipped to here while standing in a bookstore, trying to decide whether this book is worth the money), you're ready for a few ideas to help you write the best Visual Basic programs possible without losing your mind in the process.

Chapter 32
The Ten Most Useful Visual Basic Add-On Programs

. . . .

In This Chapter

▶ Using custom controls

▶ Turning Visual Basic into a spreadsheet

▶ Turning Visual Basic into a word processor

▶ Turning data into pretty charts

▶ Hunting and squashing bugs

▶ Adding your own VBA macros

. . . .

*A*lthough Microsoft tried to make Visual Basic the most powerful Windows programming tool around (so they can continue their quest for worldwide dominance in the software market), the standard edition of Visual Basic still has some glaring limitations.

For example, if you want to create your own telecommunications program, you can't. If you want to create objects that have a three-dimensional appearance, too bad. And if you want to develop Visual Basic programs for the mythical pen-computing market, you're out of luck.

To make up for these flaws, Microsoft offers a Professional Edition of Visual Basic. Although the price for this Professional Edition is several hundred dollars more than the Standard Edition (depending on where you buy it), the Professional Edition gives you many features that the Standard Edition lacks.

However, the Professional Edition also has its share of flaws. Although it has a custom control that enables you to write Visual Basic telecommunications programs, it lacks the all-important XModem, YModem, ZModem, and Kermit transfer protocols. Using the Professional Edition's communications custom control is about as useful as buying a telephone that lets you dial out but won't let you talk or hear anything from the other line.

Similarly, the other features of the Professional Edition *seem* to offer a great deal, but in reality, they only offer stripped-down or limited capabilities. If the Professional Edition of Visual Basic still seems too tame for you hard-core, dedicated programmers, take a look at the following third-party Visual Basic add-on programs.

If you're writing programs for Windows 3.1, you must use VBX custom controls. If you're writing programs for Windows NT or Windows 95, you can use either VBX or OCX custom controls, although only OCX custom controls will take full advantage of Windows NT or Windows 95.

Some publishers sell both VBX and OCX versions of their programs in one package; others sell them separately (and usually charge much more for the OCX versions).

Add-Ons to Keep Visual Basic Programmers from Going Completely Insane

The more you use Visual Basic, the more you'll get aggravated by all the repetitive, tedious mouse clicks, menu pulling, and typing that you have to do just to define the properties of the many objects you create. To help you avoid the inherent repetition of designing a Visual Basic user interface, look at a program called VBAssist.

Among its other features, VBAssist lets you design an object once and then use that same object as a template for creating new ones. So if you prefer that all your check boxes have green backgrounds, red foregrounds, borders, and blank captions, VBAssist cheerfully allows you to create and store such odd designs.

Another problem occurs if you write a huge Visual Basic program and then want to know which procedure stored in which FRM or BAS file contains the one variable you want to modify. Normally, searching for this type of information can be as enjoyable as trying to find your car in a mega-shopping mall's multilevel parking structure.

So that's why you need MicroHelp's VBXRef program. This program cross-references all your procedures so that you can quickly find, organize, and move your procedures around without tearing your hair out and wishing you had studied psychology instead of computer science in college.

VBAssist
Sheridan Software Systems, Inc.
35 Pinelawn Road
Melville, NY 11747
Tel: 516-753-0985
Fax: 516-753-3661
BBS: 516-753-5452
Web: `http://www.shersoft.com`

MicroHelp VBXRef
MicroHelp
211 J.V.L. Industrial Park Drive, NE
Marietta, GA 30066
Tel: 770-516-0899
Fax: 770-516-1099
BBS: 770-516-1497
Web: `http://www.microhelp.com`

Make Visual Basic a Little Less Wimpy as a Programming Language

Visual Basic provides the standard objects that you need to create a halfway decent user interface, such as command buttons, check boxes, radio buttons, combo boxes, and scroll bars. However, real programmers demand more power. If you want the ability to display ASCII files and search through them for user-defined strings, you need MicroHelp's VBTools.

In addition to giving you a custom control for displaying ASCII files, MicroHelp's VBTools also includes custom controls for displaying playing cards or dice (great for writing your own games), the ability to create business presentation graphics (useful if you want to write a Visual Basic version of Harvard Graphics), and gauges that appear on a form, such as a thermometer or fuel gauge.

Then there's Crescent Software's QuickPak Professional add-on, which also gives you many custom controls to spruce up Visual Basic. QuickPak Professional includes custom controls for displaying hypertext documents (like the Windows Help System), calendars (so the user can visually choose a date instead of typing something boring like 1/1/80), and even a special custom control for inputting and displaying currency values (so you can keep track of all the money you have to spend on Visual Basic add-on programs).

Anytime you think that Visual Basic's Toolbox is too limited, get one of these add-on programs to beef up Visual Basic's programming capabilities so that you can write more-powerful programs even faster than someone struggling with C++.

MicroHelp VBTools
MicroHelp
4211 J.V.L. Industrial Park Drive, NE
Marietta, GA 30066
Tel: 770-516-0899
Fax: 770-516-1099
BBS: 770-516-1497
Web: `http://www.microhelp.com`

QuickPak Professional
Crescent Division of Progress Software
14 Oak Park
Bedford, MA 01730
Tel: 617-280-3000
Fax: 617-280-4025
Web: `http://www.progress.com/crescent`

Turn Visual Basic into a Spreadsheet

One of Visual Basic's inventions in the software industry is the spreadsheet grid, which lets you display numbers and words in columns and rows, or perform calculations on numbers using formulas.

If you need to have 2 billion rows by 2 billion columns, look at the FarPoint Spread custom control, which Microsoft used so that they could write their Microsoft Profit accounting program in Visual Basic. (Microsoft Profit has since been sold to another company after Microsoft decided to bail out of the accounting software market.)

For those who need to read and write to Excel files, look at Formula One. Besides letting you modify Excel files, this spreadsheet grid also provides most of Excel's formulas. If you know how to use Excel, you can easily plop Formula One into your Visual Basic programs and create anything in Visual Basic and Formula One that might otherwise require Excel.

Formula One
Visual Components
15721 College Boulevard
Lenexa, KS 66219
Tel: 913-599-6500
Fax: 913-599-6597
BBS: 913-599-6713
Web: http://www.visualcomp.com

Spread
FarPoint Technologies, Inc.
133 Southcenter Court, Suite 1000
Morrisville, NC 27560
Tel: 919-460-4551
Fax: 916-460-7606
Web: http://www.fpoint.com/fpoint

Turn Data into Pretty Charts

It's one thing to display rows and columns of mind-numbing numbers that nobody can make any sense of, but it's an entirely different thing to display that same data in eye-catching pie charts, 3-D bar graphs, or hi-lo financial charts so that you can show everyone exactly why your company is going bankrupt and who's fault it really is.

So the next time you need to convert raw numbers into easy-to-understand charts, or you need to confuse people in power with pretty pictures that look good but don't explain a thing, plug one of these charting custom controls in your Visual Basic program.

First Impression
Visual Components
15721 College Boulevard
Lenexa, KS 66219
Tel: 913-599-6500
Fax: 913-599-6597
BBS: 913-599-6713
Web: http://www.visualcomp.com

Graphics Server
Pinnacle Publishing, Inc.
P.O. Box 888
Kent, WA 98035-0888
Tel: 206-251-1900
Fax: 206-251-5057
Web: http://www.pinpub.com

Let Visual Basic Break into Computers by Modem

With the Standard Edition of Visual Basic, you can't write a telecommunications program without great amounts of grief. With the Professional Edition of Visual Basic, you can write a weak telecommunications program that can dial out but can't transfer files using the common XModem, YModem, or ZModem protocols.

But don't worry. The PDQComm program and the MicroHelp Communications Library give Visual Basic a variety of transfer protocols and terminal emulations to choose from. Now you, too, can write Visual Basic programs to rival the features of CrossTalk, ProComm Plus, or HyperAccess. With a little luck, you might even try writing a demon dialer to hunt out all the unlisted phone numbers connected to military computers and see whether you can steal any important information.

MicroHelp Communications Library
MicroHelp
4211 J.V.L. Industrial Park Drive, NE
Marietta, GA 30066
Tel: 770-516-0899
Fax: 770-516-1099
BBS: 770-516-1497
Web: http://www.microhelp.com

PDQComm
Crescent Division of Progress Software
14 Oak Park
Bedford, MA 01730
Tel: 617-280-3000
Fax: 617-280-4025
Web: http://www.progress.com/crescent

Turn Visual Basic into a Word Processor

Just in case you think Microsoft, Lotus, and WordPerfect couldn't design a decent word processor if their lives depended on it, here's your chance to prove your point. Normally Visual Basic provides text boxes with weak editing and word-wrapping capabilities. However, you can create your own word processor with Visual Basic by using Visual Writer.

Visual Writer can work with another add-on program called Visual Speller, so you can quickly add word processing and spell-checking capabilities to any of your Visual Basic programs. If you feel really creative, see if you can write a Visual Basic program that knocks Microsoft Word, WordPerfect, or WordPro (the word processor formerly known as Ami Pro) out of the word processing market altogether.

Visual Writer and Visual Speller
Visual Components
15721 College Boulevard
Lenexa, KS 66219
Tel: 913-599-6500
Fax: 913-599-6597
BBS: 913-599-6713
Web: http://www.visualcomp.com

Display Graphics and Other Pretty Pictures

Visual Basic's picture and image boxes can easily handle WMF metafiles, BMP bitmapped files, and ICO icons. But the computer world is full of other types of graphics file formats, including TIFF, WPG, PCX, EPS, GIF, GEM, TARGA, DIB, DRW, and other acronyms that nobody can ever remember.

In a world swimming with graphics images stored in different formats, you need to buy a special graphics file converter or find a way to get Visual Basic to display these different file formats.

If you choose the latter approach, get ImageMan or LeadTools. Both these add-ons let you import, export, and modify all these different types of graphics file formats. So if your idea of fun is scanning in your dog's face and displaying it in a Visual Basic program, now you can do so, without worrying about which file format your dog's face may be stored in.

ImageMan
Data Techniques, Inc.
300 Pensacola Road
Burnsville, NC 28714
Tel: 704-682-4111
Fax: 704-682-0025
BBS: 704-682-4356
Web: http://www.data-tech.com

LeadTools
Lead Technologies, Inc.
900 Baxter Street
Charlotte, NC 28204
Tel: 704-332-5532
Fax: 704-372-8161
Web: http://www.leadtools.com

Squash Bugs in Your Visual Basic Programs

Visual Basic provides simple debugging tools to help you step through your code line by line, set breakpoints to stop your program from running at certain points, and watch your variables to see when and how they may change.

Such simple debugging tools can get your program working correctly, but what if you want to optimize your program by seeing which procedures are used most often? Or what if you want to see exactly how your program is affecting your computer's memory requirements? Then you need a more specialized debugging tool, such as PinPoint or SpyWorks.

These debugging tools let you peer into the guts of your Visual Basic program and see more than you might ever care to learn about. If you're a hard-core programmer, these debugging tools are not just lifesavers; they're also essential when impressing other programmers with your ability to write programs that actually work.

PinPoint
Avanti Software, Inc.
385 Sherman Avenue, Suite #3
Palo Alto, CA 94306
Tel: 415-329-8999
Fax: 415-329-8722
Web: http://www.avantisoft.com

SpyWorks
Desaware, Inc.
1100 E. Hamilton Avenue, Suite #4
Campbell, CA 95008
Tel: 408-377-4770
Fax: 408-371-3530
Web: http://www.vbxtras.com/~desaware

Add Your Own VBA Macros

In an effort to standardize the software industry (and make a few bucks for itself in the process), Microsoft has proclaimed that all of their programs will use Visual Basic as its primary macro language. Unlike the old days when you had to learn Excel's macro language and then learn a new macro language to write Word macros, the new macro version of Visual Basic (dubbed Visual Basic for Applications, or VBA) uses Visual Basic to do everything.

So what happens if you write a program and you want to add a macro language? You could create your own macro language from scratch (good luck) or just plug in BasicScript or the Sax Basic Engine.

Either BasicScript or the Sax Basic Engine will let your users write their own macros using the standard VBA language. Not only will this make it easier for people to write macros for your program, but it also helps Microsoft's standard dominate the world software market just a little bit further.

BasicScript
Summit Software Company
4933 Jamesville Road
Jamesville, NY 13078-9428
Tel: 315-445-9000
Fax: 315-445-9567
Web: `http://www.summsoft.com`

Sax Basic Engine
Sax Software Corporation
950 Patterson Street
Eugene, OR 97401
Tel: 541-344-2235
Fax: 541-344-2459
Web: `http://www.saxsoft.com`

Combine Computer Telephony with Visual Basic

Computer telephony looks like a misprint or a really stupid phrase. Yet to thousands of people, computer telephony means the marriage of fax machines, answering machines, and voice mail. If you need to set up your own voice mail, paging system, or order entry line and don't mind losing customers who can't stand waiting on hold while listening to endless series of instructions ("Push 1 to repeat this message in sixteen different languages..."), use your Visual Basic skills to create your own phone system.

Contact Parity Software or Stylus Innovation, Inc. for information on their series of computer telephony products that can turn any business phone into a computer-controlled barrier to a real human being.

Visual Voice
Stylus Product Group, Artisoft, Inc.
201 Broadway
Cambridge, MA 02139
Tel: 617-621-9545
Fax: 617-621-7862
Web: `http://www.stylus.com`

CallSuite
Parity Software
One Harbor Drive, Suite 110
Sausalito, CA 94965
Tel: 415-332-5656
Fax: 415-332-5657
Web: `http://www.paritysw.com`

Chapter 33

Ten Sources for More Visual Basic Information

· ·

In This Chapter

▶ Finding magazines and newsletters

▶ Utilizing CompuServe

▶ Finding local BBSs

▶ Joining a user group

▶ Attending technical conferences

▶ Attending Microsoft University

· ·

*N*ow that you've reached the end of this book (even if you just skipped to this section while browsing through this book in the bookstore), you may be wondering where you can learn more about Visual Basic without going through the process of trial and error and driving yourself crazy in the process.

Visual Basic is exploding in popularity, so there's help virtually everywhere you turn. Best of all, many sources of information are free.

Buy, Read, or Steal *Visual Basic Programmer's Journal*

Every month, look for a fresh copy of *Visual Basic Programmer's Journal* at your favorite magazine stand or bookstore. This magazine comes loaded with articles exploring the intricate details of Visual Basic, reviews of Visual Basic add-ons, and sample Visual Basic code that you can copy (steal) for your own use. For more information about this magazine, contact:

Visual Basic Programmer's Journal
Fawcette Technical Publications
209 Hamilton Avenue
Palo Alto, CA 94301-2500
Tel: 415-833-7100
Fax: 415-853-0230
CompuServe: GO WINDX
Web: http://www.windx.com

Beg Microsoft for a Copy of "The Microsoft Developer's Network News"

To keep developers firmly wedded to the Microsoft camp, Microsoft publishes a monthly newsletter called "The Microsoft Developer's Network News." This newsletter comes jam-packed with information about Visual C++, Visual Basic, Windows, Excel, and other products that Microsoft feels like promoting at any given time. (Notice that you'll never find any mention about Microsoft's failed languages in this newsletter, such as Microsoft QuickPascal or Microsoft LISP.)

Because Microsoft is loaded with cash, they freely mail "The Microsoft Developer's Network News" to people they think will help promote the cause of Microsoft by using Microsoft products. If you can convince Microsoft that you'll swear undying loyalty to them, you too can receive this newsletter for free. Just contact:

"The Microsoft Developer's Network News"
Microsoft Corporation
One Microsoft Way
Redmond, WA 98052-6399
Fax: 206-936-7329
Internet: devnetwk@microsoft.com

Spend a Bundle of Money and Get a Visual Basic Newsletter

A company called The Cobb Group publishes a bunch of monthly newsletters for a variety of programs, including Paradox, Lotus 1-2-3, and Visual Basic. Although a year's subscription is about $60, the "Inside Visual Basic" newsletter provides plenty of source code examples that you can study, modify, and claim you wrote yourself to impress your boss, who doesn't know any better.

Another company, Pinnacle Publishing, also publishes a monthly newsletter that comes with source code examples on an enclosed floppy disk. Of course, this newsletter costs a bit more ($179 a year), but if you can get your company to buy this for you, who cares about the price?

"Inside Visual Basic"	**"Visual Basic Developer"**
The Cobb Group	Pinnacle Publishing, Inc.
9420 Bunsen Parkway, Suite 300	P.O. Box 888
Louisville, KY 40220	Kent, WA 98035-0888
Tel: 800-223-8720	Tel: 206-251-1900
Fax: 502-491-8050	Fax: 206-251-5057
Web: http://www.cobb.com	Web: http://www.pinpub.com

Join CompuServe

CompuServe (often abbreviated as CIS) provides many Visual Basic files for downloading, along with access to Visual Basic experts, programmers, and people who don't have any idea what they're doing.

Just dial into CompuServe and use the GO MSBASIC command. This dumps you in the Microsoft Basic forum, where you can post messages for others to read, provide advice for people crying for help, and download the latest information from Microsoft along with the latest shareware Visual Basic programs, add-ons, and text files.

If you want to visit the Visual Basic Programmer's Journal forum, use the GO VBPJ command. In this forum you can download files from the magazine or contact different Visual Basic third-party companies that seem to have sprouted up faster than independent countries in Eastern Europe.

CompuServe
P.O. Box 20212
5000 Arlington Centre Boulevard
Columbus, OH 43220
Tel: 614-457-8650
Web: http://www.compuserve.com

Find a Local BBS Dedicated to Visual Basic

As a less expensive alternative (depending on where you live), you can often find a local *bulletin board system* (BBS) dedicated to supporting Visual Basic. If your city has such a Visual Basic BBS, you're in luck. If you live outside the city or your city doesn't have such a BBS, you'll have to make many long-distance calls to another city or start your own Visual Basic BBS.

One of the larger Visual Basic BBSs is located in Cleveland, Ohio. Called WIND (for *Windows Information Network for Developers*), this BBS provides files for Visual Basic, Visual C++, and Access. In addition to any long-distance phone charges you may rack up calling the WIND BBS, be prepared to pay for access to the BBS itself (approximately $40 a year).

For another Visual Basic BBS, contact the Atlanta VB BBS (don't you just love acronyms?), which also focuses on Visual Basic freeware, shareware, and demos.

WIND
200 Public Square, #26-4600
Cleveland, OH 44114
Voice: 216-861-0467
BBS: 216-694-5734

Atlanta VB BBS
Advanced Digital Solutions, Inc.
430 10th Street, NW, Suite N-205
Atlanta, GA 30318
Voice: 404-872-8728
BBS: 404-872-0311

Join a Local Visual Basic User Group

User groups consist of friendly, fanatical people dedicated to one specific type of program, computer, or special interest. Many cities have a local Visual Basic user group, where Visual Basic enthusiasts (fanatics) can get together, share ideas, swap files, sell stuff, make friends, and infect one another with their general enthusiasm for Visual Basic.

Because Microsoft makes money as more people use their products, Microsoft cheerfully encourages people to create Visual Basic user groups wherever they may be. You can often find Visual Basic user groups listed in local computer magazines, newsletters, or BBSs. If you want to start a Visual Basic user group, give Microsoft a call at 800-228-6738 and they'll happily include your name and phone number in their Visual Basic user group directory. Or ask for their user group directory and see if there's a Visual Basic user group near you.

Attend a Visual Basic Technical Conference

Every year, Microsoft and *Visual Basic Programmer's Journal* sponsor a Visual Basic Technical Summit in a major city along both the East and West coasts of the United States (as well as a few overseas).

These conferences are great places to learn techniques from real-life Visual Basic programming experts, listen to the latest propaganda talks from Microsoft representatives, buy Visual Basic add-ons cheaply from vendors, and make lots of contacts in the Visual Basic world. For more information about these technical conferences, contact:

Visual Basic Programmer's Journal
Fawcette Technical Publications
209 Hamilton Avenue
Palo Alto, CA 94301-2500
Tel: 415-833-7100
Fax: 415-853-0230
CompuServe: GO WINDX
Web: http://www.windx.com

When All Else Fails, Call Microsoft's Technical Support

Microsoft, out of the goodness of its heart, supplies various phone numbers that you can call for help. However, Microsoft, unlike WordPerfect, refuses to offer toll-free technical support.

Here's a short list of the different Microsoft phone numbers that you can call when you need help and your favorite Visual Basic guru isn't around.

Visual Basic Startup Service: 206-646-5105

Call this number any time you have trouble installing or setting up Visual Basic on your computer. Call between 6:00 a.m. and 6:00 p.m. Pacific time, Monday through Friday (except holidays).

Microsoft FastTips: 206-646-5107

This number connects you to recorded answers to common problems encountered when using Visual Basic. Because this number connects to an answering machine, it's available 7 days a week, 24 hours a day.

Microsoft OnCall for Visual Basic: 900-896-9876 or 206-646-5106

This number connects you to a real live Visual Basic technician, available 6:00 a.m. to 6:00 p.m. Pacific time, Monday through Friday (except holidays). Unlike psychic hotlines, Microsoft OnCall won't start charging you until you finally connect to a person who can start answering your questions. There is a flat fee for this service, billed to your VISA, MasterCard, or American Express card.

Microsoft Product Support Download Service: 206-936-6735

This number connects you to Microsoft's BBS, available 7 days a week, 24 hours a day. Connect with your modem using 9600/2400/1200 baud, no parity, 8 data bits, and 1 stop bit. For no charge (except for the phone call), you can download technical notes from Microsoft.

Go Back to School (at Microsoft University)

Knowing that traditional universities and schools are usually 10 years behind the rest of the world, Microsoft created their own school and dubbed it Microsoft University. Although Microsoft University lacks a football team, cheerleaders, and a liberal arts program, it does offer three courses geared toward Visual Basic programmers:

- ✔ Introduction to Programming for Microsoft Windows Using Microsoft Visual Basic
- ✔ Programming in Microsoft Visual Basic
- ✔ Building Applications for Microsoft SQL Server using Microsoft Visual Basic

For class schedule and course fee information, call Microsoft University at 206-828-1507.

When All Else Fails, Read the Microsoft Visual Basic Manual

Yes, everyone agrees that computer manuals are notoriously dull, confusing, and incomplete. But if you can discipline yourself to wade through the scattered information, you'll likely find exactly what you're looking for (although you may have to read the information several times to understand exactly what the writer is trying to tell you).

Microsoft supplies two types of manuals: the *Programmer's Guide* and the *Language Reference*. The *Programmer's Guide* is part tutorial and part introductory guide to Visual Basic programming. The more you learn about Visual Basic, the less you'll come to depend on the *Programmer's Guide*.

The *Language Reference* is more like a dictionary. When you want to know what a particular Visual Basic command or keyword can do, look in this book. This manual is more complete but is completely user-hostile when it comes to helping you understand the nuances of Visual Basic.

If reading manuals is against your religion, Microsoft pretty much copied the manual into the Visual Basic help system. Just click the Help menu and choose Contents. Then choose the topic that you want more help on.

Chapter 34

Visual Basic Topics That Didn't Fit Anywhere Else

● ●

In This Chapter

▶ Using Microsoft Access

▶ Shopping from mail-order dealers

▶ Using C++ or Delphi

▶ Using the Windows API

● ●

*F*inally, here are some tidbits that you may find useful and interesting as you develop the next killer application using Visual Basic.

Buy a Software Suite

Ever since Microsoft got the bright idea of combining several programs together under the name of a *suite*, and charging much less for the combined bundle, other companies have gotten into the act. As a result, you can often buy a single suite for several hundred dollars, which includes thousands of dollars worth of Visual Basic custom controls.

One of the better Visual Basic suites is called Visual Components. This suite combines an Excel-compatible spreadsheet (called Formula One), a charting custom control (called First Impression), a word processor (called Visual Writer), a spell checker (called Visual Speller), and a Web browser (called Web Viewer).

Because all of these custom controls are designed to work together, you'll find it easy to display data in Formula One and then chart it using First Impression, or write something in Visual Writer and then spell check it with Visual Speller.

Other companies sell similar suites as well, so the next time you're about to buy a Visual Basic custom control, ask the company if they also bundle it in a suite. If so, you might find the suite a much better deal than buying custom controls individually.

Visual Suite
Visual Components
15721 College Boulevard
Lenexa, KS 66219
Tel: 913-599-6500
Fax: 913-599-6597
BBS: 913-599-6713
Web: http://www.visualcomp.com

Buy a Copy of Microsoft Access

Visual Basic comes with an add-on program called Data Manager that lets you create Microsoft Access databases, but you might want a copy of Microsoft Access anyway. With Microsoft Access, you can convert database files stored in other formats and save them as Access MDB files.

Because Microsoft designed Visual Basic to work with Access database files, you might as well shell out the money and buy a copy of Microsoft Access. (Anyone studying business should study Microsoft's slick marketing campaigns.)

Learn Visual Basic for Applications (VBA)

As part of Microsoft's dream of software domination, all Microsoft products — Word, Excel, PowerPoint, and Access — will eventually share a common macro language called Visual Basic for Applications (VBA). Essentially, VBA will give you complete control over all Microsoft programs. Instead of writing your own word processor from scratch, VBA would let you customize Word instead.

For the future, learn Visual Basic now. Then as Microsoft products and VBA start dominating the software market, you'll be far ahead of everyone else when it comes to developing unique applications for specialized markets.

Shop from Mail-Order Dealers

Don't buy Visual Basic or any Visual Basic add-on programs direct from the publisher. Most software publishers cheerfully charge full retail price for their programs, which makes as much sense as paying full sticker price for a used car.

Local computer dealers often sell software at a 10 to 30 percent discount. Most local dealers sell Visual Basic, but few local dealers sell Visual Basic add-on programs.

Rather than buy direct from the software publisher, shop by mail-order instead. Mail-order dealers give you even steeper discounts (up to 50 percent in some cases), with the added advantage of saving you from having to pay sales tax.

One popular mail-order dealer that specializes in selling programming tools, compilers, and add-ons is The Programmer's Paradise. Besides selling plenty of Visual Basic tools, they also sell all sorts of tools and compilers for oddball languages like Ada, C++, COBOL, Prolog, xBase, and LISP. Give them a call and they'll send you a free catalog.

In case you want a mail-order house that specializes in Visual Basic products, contact VBxtras. Besides distributing a quarterly catalog of the more common Visual Basic add-on products, the VBxtras catalog also provides a one-page description of each product to help you decide what it actually does.

The Programmer's Paradise
1163 Shrewsbury Avenue
Road, Suite 100
Shrewsbury, NJ 07702-4321
Tel: 800-445-7899
Fax: 908-389-9227
Web: http://www.pparadise.com

VBxtras
1901 Powers Ferry
Atlanta, GA 30339
Tel: 770-952-6356
Fax: 770-952-6388
Web: http://www.vbxtras.com

Extend Visual Basic by Writing Your Own DLL Files Using C++ or Delphi

If you plan to write lots of Visual Basic programs, you should organize your commonly used procedures in separate BAS module files. That way you can quickly plug in BAS module files to any Visual Basic programs you write.

Unfortunately, BAS module files can contain only Visual Basic commands. Because languages such as C++ and Pascal can be more flexible in digging into the guts of your computer and manipulating individual bits and bytes, many programmers write commonly used procedures in C++ or Pascal and store them in separate *Dynamic Link Library* (DLL) files. A DLL file contains commonly used procedures that you can share among different programs.

Writing a DLL file requires learning C++ or Pascal, which most Visual Basic programmers try to avoid in the first place. But because there are hoards of C++ and Pascal programmers out there writing useful procedures, you can take advantage of these procedures by adding DLL files to your own Visual Basic programs. It won't be easy, but at least it's easier than your other alternative, which is to use the Windows Application Programming Interface (see the following section).

Extend Visual Basic's Capabilities Using the Windows Application Programming Interface (API)

Visual Basic makes programming so easy because it insulates you from all the messy details needed to write Windows programs. But the price you pay for this insulation is a loss of flexibility that C++ programmers love to flaunt (as they slowly go mad, dealing with the complexities of Windows programming).

Eventually, you'll find Visual Basic's ease of use frustrating because you can't perform certain tasks. The quickest and easiest alternative is to buy an add-on program to give Visual Basic the features you want. But if you can't find such an add-on program, you'll have to dig into the guts of Windows itself.

To help programmers write programs for Windows, Windows has many commands called the Microsoft Windows *Application Programming Interface* (API). Although they're complicated to learn and understand, they give you the ability to manipulate (and of course, crash) Windows to your heart's content.

If you like living dangerously, take the time to learn about the Windows API. Otherwise, just pretend this section never existed and skip to another section of the book.

Convert Your Visual Basic Programs into Another Language

Visual Basic can compile your programs into a pseudo-EXE file that requires a separate run-time DLL file to work. Besides the inconvenience of having to distribute this separate DLL file with every program you pass out, this feature of Visual Basic also causes Visual Basic programs to run slower than programs created with real compilers, such as C++ or Pascal.

To remedy this situation, you have several choices. If you're really masochistic, use Visual Basic to create a prototype of your program and then rewrite the whole thing from scratch using your favorite C++ compiler.

As an easier alternative, try using a program called Velocity/VB, which converts your Visual Basic programs into Visual C++ source code. From there (as long as you have a copy of Visual C++) you can compile your program into a true EXE or DLL file.

In case you don't like the thought of learning anything remotely related to C++, try using either Conversion Assistant or VB2D, which are programs that convert Visual Basic programs into Delphi source code. As long as you have a copy of Delphi, you can then compile your program into a real EXE or DLL file as well.

Since this is the world of computers, it's likely that neither Velocity/VB, Conversion Assistant, or VB2D will ever work 100 percent correctly, so be prepared for some headaches in the conversion process. Still, if you absolutely need a real EXE file and you don't want to give up Visual Basic, Velocity/VB, Conversion Assistant, or VB2D can keep you and Microsoft happy by keeping you firmly wedded to using Visual Basic.

Conversion Assistant
EarthTrek
79 Montvale Avenue, #5
Woburn, MA 01801
Tel: 617-273-0308
Fax: 617-270-4437

VB2D
Eagle Research
360 Ritch Street, Suite 300
San Francisco, CA 94107
Tel: 415-495-3136
Fax: 415-495-3638
Web: `http://www.xeaglex.com`

Velocity/VB
Crescent Division of Progress Software
14 Oak Park
Bedford, MA 01730
Tel: 617-280-3000
Fax: 617-280-4025
Web: `http://www.progress.com/crescent`

Rival BASIC Compilers That Bill Gates Doesn't Want You to Know About

From the early days of personal computers (the mid-70s), Microsoft has always been associated with the BASIC programming language. Just in case you don't like Visual Basic, here's a list of rival BASIC compilers that compete directly with Microsoft's Visual Basic.

First there's PowerBASIC, formerly sold as Turbo Basic by Microsoft's arch-rival, Borland International. PowerBASIC is available for DOS and Windows. Even better, the Windows version lets you convert your DOS programs to Windows programs with fairly minor modifications.

Then there's a new Visual Basic clone called PowerObjects, developed by the Oracle Corporation. Oracle is one of the largest software companies in the world that most personal computer owners have never heard about because Oracle tends to focus on high-end (translate that to mean "really complicated") database and programming tools for mainframe and mini-computers.

While you can't take a Visual Basic program and run it under PowerObjects (or vice versa), PowerObjects lets you draw your user interface and write BASIC code just like Visual Basic. So if you know Visual Basic, learning PowerObjects should be fairly simple. Best of all, PowerObjects can run under Windows or the Macintosh, which means you can write one PowerObjects program on the Macintosh and then compile it to run under both Windows and the Macintosh.

If you wait a little longer, IBM and Apple might have a trick or two to spring on the BASIC programming community. Both companies are rumored to be working on a Visual Basic clone that runs under Windows, OS/2, and the Macintosh operating system. Code-named "Bart" by IBM and "DeNali" by Apple, this new programming tool will be able to run (and compile) your Visual Basic programs for OS/2 and the Macintosh.

Just don't hold your breath waiting for this IBM/Apple Visual Basic clone to emerge any time soon. Given the glacial pace of software development for something as radically useful as "Bart/DeNali," there's a real good chance this project will die long before it reaches the general public.

PowerBASIC
PowerBasic
316 Mid Valley Center
Carmel, CA 93923
Tel: 408-659-8000
Fax: 408-659-8008
BBS: 408-659-7401
Web: http://www.powerbasic.com

CA-Realizer
Oracle Corporation
500 Oracle Parkway
Redwood Shores, CA 94065
Tel: 415-506-7000
Fax: 415-506-7200
Web: http://www.oracle.com

Buy a Program to Create Help Files

Every good Windows program has an on-line help system so that panicky users can browse through a hypertext reference on the screen instead of wading through hundred-page manuals that don't make any sense anyway. If you're serious about writing Visual Basic programs, you'll need to provide a help system with your programs, too.

Creating a help system isn't difficult, just incredibly dull and tedious. You can, however, get a special program to make the process a little more enjoyable. Many of these help file creation programs let you design your help screens as easily as writing a document in a word processor. Then when you're finished, these programs let you test it by showing you exactly how your help screens will look when added to your own Visual Basic programs.

In today's competitive world of software development, a good help file is crucial to your program's professional appearance. Then again, if you don't care about making your programs easier to use, go work for any of the major software companies instead.

VaporWare — Visual Basic for the Mac

Ever since Microsoft introduced Visual Basic for Windows in 1991, there have been persistent rumors that Microsoft would release versions of Visual Basic for other operating systems as well. The original 1991 documentation for Visual Basic version 1.0 even dropped hints of a Visual Basic for OS/2. Since then, Microsoft and IBM broke up over OS/2 development, so you can forget about ever seeing any Microsoft products supporting OS/2.

In 1992, Microsoft did release a version of Visual Basic for MS-DOS and then promptly let it languish. Although Microsoft won't confirm or deny it, rumors continue about a Visual Basic for the Mac.

Because Microsoft's original venture with QuickBasic for the Mac met with little more than stifled yawns, don't expect to hear about Visual Basic for the Mac anytime soon. To develop a complete Macintosh version of Visual Basic, Microsoft would also have to create a Macintosh version of their Access database program.

Not even Microsoft has all the resources to pursue multiple projects in several directions simultaneously, so most of Microsoft's Macintosh projects get pushed aside in favor of the more profitable Windows projects.

But if or when a Macintosh version of Visual Basic comes out, you'll be able to write Visual Basic programs for Windows and the Macintosh, essentially doubling the potential market for your programs.

Index

• C •

Title	Author	ISBN	Price
INTERNET / COMMUNICATIONS / NETWORKING			12/20/94
CompuServe For Dummies™	by Wallace Wang	1-56884-181-7	$19.95 USA/$26.95 Canada
Modems For Dummies™, 2nd Edition	by Tina Rathbone	1-56884-223-6	$19.99 USA/$26.99 Canada
Modems For Dummies™	by Tina Rathbone	1-56884-001-2	$19.95 USA/$26.95 Canada
MORE Internet For Dummies™	by John R. Levine & Margaret Levine Young	1-56884-164-7	$19.95 USA/$26.95 Canada
NetWare For Dummies™	by Ed Tittel & Deni Connor	1-56884-003-9	$19.95 USA/$26.95 Canada
Networking For Dummies™	by Doug Lowe	1-56884-079-9	$19.95 USA/$26.95 Canada
ProComm Plus 2 For Windows For Dummies™	by Wallace Wang	1-56884-219-8	$19.99 USA/$26.99 Canada
The Internet For Dummies™, 2nd Edition	by John R. Levine & Carol Baroudi	1-56884-222-8	$19.99 USA/$26.99 Canada
The Internet For Macs For Dummies™	by Charles Seiter	1-56884-184-1	$19.95 USA/$26.95 Canada
MACINTOSH			
Macs For Dummies®	by David Pogue	1-56884-173-6	$19.95 USA/$26.95 Canada
Macintosh System 7.5 For Dummies™	by Bob LeVitus	1-56884-197-3	$19.95 USA/$26.95 Canada
MORE Macs For Dummies™	by David Pogue	1-56884-087-X	$19.95 USA/$26.95 Canada
PageMaker 5 For Macs For Dummies™	by Galen Gruman	1-56884-178-7	$19.95 USA/$26.95 Canada
QuarkXPress 3.3 For Dummies™	by Galen Gruman & Barbara Assadi	1-56884-217-1	$19.99 USA/$26.99 Canada
Upgrading and Fixing Macs For Dummies™	by Kearney Rietmann & Frank Higgins	1-56884-189-2	$19.95 USA/$26.95 Canada
MULTIMEDIA			
Multimedia & CD-ROMs For Dummies™, Interactive Multimedia Value Pack	by Andy Rathbone	1-56884-225-2	$29.95 USA/$39.95 Canada
Multimedia & CD-ROMs For Dummies™	by Andy Rathbone	1-56884-089-6	$19.95 USA/$26.95 Canada
OPERATING SYSTEMS / DOS			
MORE DOS For Dummies™	by Dan Gookin	1-56884-046-2	$19.95 USA/$26.95 Canada
S.O.S. For DOS™	by Katherine Murray	1-56884-043-8	$12.95 USA/$16.95 Canada
OS/2 For Dummies™	by Andy Rathbone	1-878058-76-2	$19.95 USA/$26.95 Canada
UNIX			
UNIX For Dummies™	by John R. Levine & Margaret Levine Young	1-878058-58-4	$19.95 USA/$26.95 Canada
WINDOWS			
S.O.S. For Windows™	by Katherine Murray	1-56884-045-4	$12.95 USA/$16.95 Canada
MORE Windows 3.1 For Dummies™, 3rd Edition	by Andy Rathbone	1-56884-240-6	$19.99 USA/$26.99 Canada
PCs / HARDWARE			
Illustrated Computer Dictionary For Dummies™	by Dan Gookin, Wally Wang, & Chris Van Buren	1-56884-004-7	$12.95 USA/$16.95 Canada
Upgrading and Fixing PCs For Dummies™	by Andy Rathbone	1-56884-002-0	$19.95 USA/$26.95 Canada
PRESENTATION / AUTOCAD			
AutoCAD For Dummies™	by Bud Smith	1-56884-191-4	$19.95 USA/$26.95 Canada
PowerPoint 4 For Windows For Dummies™	by Doug Lowe	1-56884-161-2	$16.95 USA/$22.95 Canada
PROGRAMMING			
Borland C++ For Dummies™	by Michael Hyman	1-56884-162-0	$19.95 USA/$26.95 Canada
"Borland's New Language Product" For Dummies™	by Neil Rubenking	1-56884-200-7	$19.95 USA/$26.95 Canada
C For Dummies™	by Dan Gookin	1-878058-78-9	$19.95 USA/$26.95 Canada
C++ For Dummies™	by Stephen R. Davis	1-56884-163-9	$19.95 USA/$26.95 Canada
Mac Programming For Dummies™	by Dan Parks Sydow	1-56884-173-6	$19.95 USA/$26.95 Canada
QBasic Programming For Dummies™	by Douglas Hergert	1-56884-093-4	$19.95 USA/$26.95 Canada
Visual Basic "X" For Dummies™, 2nd Edition	by Wallace Wang	1-56884-230-9	$19.99 USA/$26.99 Canada
Visual Basic 3 For Dummies™	by Wallace Wang	1-56884-076-4	$19.95 USA/$26.95 Canada
SPREADSHEET			
1-2-3 For Dummies™	by Greg Harvey	1-878058-60-6	$16.95 USA/$21.95 Canada
1-2-3 For Windows 5 For Dummies™, 2nd Edition	by John Walkenbach	1-56884-216-3	$16.95 USA/$21.95 Canada
1-2-3 For Windows For Dummies™	by John Walkenbach	1-56884-052-7	$16.95 USA/$21.95 Canada
Excel 5 For Macs For Dummies™	by Greg Harvey	1-56884-186-8	$19.95 USA/$26.95 Canada
Excel For Dummies™, 2nd Edition	by Greg Harvey	1-56884-050-0	$16.95 USA/$21.95 Canada
MORE Excel 5 For Windows For Dummies™	by Greg Harvey	1-56884-207-4	$19.95 USA/$26.95 Canada
Quattro Pro 6 For Windows For Dummies™	by John Walkenbach	1-56884-174-4	$19.95 USA/$26.95 Canada
Quattro Pro For DOS For Dummies™	by John Walkenbach	1-56884-023-3	$16.95 USA/$21.95 Canada
UTILITIES / VCRs & CAMCORDERS			
Norton Utilities 8 For Dummies™	by Beth Slick	1-56884-166-3	$19.95 USA/$26.95 Canada
VCRs & Camcorders For Dummies™	by Andy Rathbone & Gordon McComb	1-56884-229-5	$14.99 USA/$20.99 Canada
WORD PROCESSING			
Ami Pro For Dummies™	by Jim Meade	1-56884-049-7	$19.95 USA/$26.95 Canada
MORE Word For Windows 6 For Dummies™	by Doug Lowe	1-56884-165-5	$19.95 USA/$26.95 Canada
MORE WordPerfect 6 For Windows For Dummies™	by Margaret Levine Young & David C. Kay	1-56884-206-6	$19.95 USA/$26.95 Canada
MORE WordPerfect 6 For DOS For Dummies™	by Wallace Wang, edited by Dan Gookin	1-56884-047-0	$19.95 USA/$26.95 Canada
S.O.S. For WordPerfect™	by Katherine Murray	1-56884-053-5	$12.95 USA/$16.95 Canada
Word 6 For Macs For Dummies™	by Dan Gookin	1-56884-190-6	$19.95 USA/$26.95 Canada
Word For Windows 6 For Dummies™	by Dan Gookin	1-56884-075-6	$16.95 USA/$21.95 Canada
Word For Windows For Dummies™	by Dan Gookin	1-878058-86-X	$16.95 USA/$21.95 Canada
WordPerfect 6 For Dummies™	by Dan Gookin	1-878058-77-0	$16.95 USA/$21.95 Canada
WordPerfect For Dummies™	by Dan Gookin	1-878058-52-5	$16.95 USA/$21.95 Canada
WordPerfect For Windows For Dummies™	by Margaret Levine Young & David C. Kay	1-56884-032-2	$16.95 USA/$21.95 Canada

Fun, Fast, & Cheap!

CorelDRAW! 5 For Dummies™ Quick Reference
by Raymond E. Werner

ISBN: 1-56884-952-4
$9.99 USA/$12.99 Canada

Windows "X" For Dummies™ Quick Reference, 3rd Edition
by Greg Harvey

ISBN: 1-56884-964-8
$9.99 USA/$12.99 Canada

Word For Windows 6 For Dummies™ Quick Reference
by George Lynch

ISBN: 1-56884-095-0
$8.95 USA/$12.95 Canada

WordPerfect For DOS For Dummies™ Quick Reference
by Greg Harvey

ISBN: 1-56884-009-8
$8.95 USA/$11.95 Canada

Title	Author	ISBN	Price
DATABASE			
Access 2 For Dummies™ Quick Reference	by Stuart A. Stuple	1-56884-167-1	$8.95 USA/$11.95 Canada
dBASE 5 For DOS For Dummies™ Quick Reference	by Barry Sosinsky	1-56884-954-0	$9.99 USA/$12.99 Canada
dBASE 5 For Windows For Dummies™ Quick Reference	by Stuart J. Stuple	1-56884-953-2	$9.99 USA/$12.99 Canada
Paradox 5 For Windows For Dummies™ Quick Reference	by Scott Palmer	1-56884-960-5	$9.99 USA/$12.99 Canada
DESKTOP PUBLISHING / ILLUSTRATION/GRAPHICS			
Harvard Graphics 3 For Windows For Dummies™ Quick Reference	by Raymond E. Werner	1-56884-962-1	$9.99 USA/$12.99 Canada
FINANCE / PERSONAL FINANCE			
Quicken 4 For Windows For Dummies™ Quick Reference	by Stephen L. Nelson	1-56884-950-8	$9.95 USA/$12.95 Canada
GROUPWARE / INTEGRATED			
Microsoft Office 4 For Windows For Dummies™ Quick Reference	by Doug Lowe	1-56884-958-3	$9.99 USA/$12.99 Canada
Microsoft Works For Windows 3 For Dummies™ Quick Reference	by Michael Partington	1-56884-959-1	$9.99 USA/$12.99 Canada
INTERNET / COMMUNICATIONS / NETWORKING			
The Internet For Dummies™ Quick Reference	by John R. Levine	1-56884-168-X	$8.95 USA/$11.95 Canada
MACINTOSH			
Macintosh System 7.5 For Dummies™ Quick Reference	by Stuart J. Stuple	1-56884-956-7	$9.99 USA/$12.99 Canada
OPERATING SYSTEMS / DOS			
DOS For Dummies® Quick Reference	by Greg Harvey	1-56884-007-1	$8.95 USA/$11.95 Canada
UNIX			
UNIX For Dummies™ Quick Reference	by Margaret Levine Young & John R. Levine	1-56884-094-2	$8.95 USA/$11.95 Canada
WINDOWS			
Windows 3.1 For Dummies™ Quick Reference, 2nd Edition	by Greg Harvey	1-56884-951-6	$8.95 USA/$11.95 Canada
PRESENTATION / AUTOCAD			
AutoCAD For Dummies™ Quick Reference	by Ellen Finkelstein	1-56884-198-1	$9.95 USA/$12.95 Canada
SPREADSHEET			
1-2-3 For Dummies™ Quick Reference	by John Walkenbach	1-56884-027-6	$8.95 USA/$11.95 Canada
1-2-3 For Windows 5 For Dummies™ Quick Reference	by John Walkenbach	1-56884-957-5	$9.95 USA/$12.95 Canada
Excel For Windows For Dummies™ Quick Reference, 2nd Edition	by John Walkenbach	1-56884-096-9	$8.95 USA/$11.95 Canada
Quattro Pro 6 For Windows For Dummies™ Quick Reference	by Stuart A. Stuple	1-56884-172-8	$9.95 USA/$12.95 Canada
WORD PROCESSING			
Word For Windows 6 For Dummies™ Quick Reference	by George Lynch	1-56884-095-0	$8.95 USA/$11.95 Canada
WordPerfect For Windows For Dummies™ Quick Reference	by Greg Harvey	1-56884-039-X	$8.95 USA/$11.95 Canada

Order Center: **(800) 762-2974** *(8 a.m.–6 p.m., EST, weekdays)*

12/20/94

Quantity	ISBN	Title	Price	Total

Shipping & Handling Charges

	Description	First book	Each additional book	Total
Domestic	Normal	$4.50	$1.50	$
	Two Day Air	$8.50	$2.50	$
	Overnight	$18.00	$3.00	$
International	Surface	$8.00	$8.00	$
	Airmail	$16.00	$16.00	$
	DHL Air	$17.00	$17.00	$

*For large quantities call for shipping & handling charges.
**Prices are subject to change without notice.

Ship to:

Name _____

Company _____

Address _____

City/State/Zip _____

Daytime Phone _____

Payment: ☐ Check to IDG Books (US Funds Only)

     ☐ VISA   ☐ MasterCard   ☐ American Express

Card # _____ Expires _____

Signature _____

Subtotal _____

CA residents add
applicable sales tax _____

IN, MA, and MD
residents add
5% sales tax _____

IL residents add
6.25% sales tax _____

RI residents add
7% sales tax _____

TX residents add
8.25% sales tax _____

Shipping _____

Total _____

Please send this order form to:

IDG Books Worldwide
7260 Shadeland Station, Suite 100
Indianapolis, IN 46256

Allow up to 3 weeks for delivery.
Thank you!

IDG BOOKS WORLDWIDE REGISTRATION CARD

RETURN THIS REGISTRATION CARD FOR FREE CATALOG

Title of this book: Visual Basic 4 For Windows For Dummies

My overall rating of this book: ❑ Very good [1] ❑ Good [2] ❑ Satisfactory [3] ❑ Fair [4] ❑ Poor [5]

How I first heard about this book:

❑ Found in bookstore; name: [6]

❑ Advertisement: [8]

❑ Word of mouth; heard about book from friend, co-worker, etc.: [10]

❑ Book review: [7]

❑ Catalog: [9]

❑ Other: [11]

What I liked most about this book:

What I would change, add, delete, etc., in future editions of this book:

Other comments:

Number of computer books I purchase in a year: ❑ 1 [12] ❑ 2-5 [13] ❑ 6-10 [14] ❑ More than 10 [15]

I would characterize my computer skills as: ❑ Beginner [16] ❑ Intermediate [17] ❑ Advanced [18] ❑ Professional [19]

I use ❑ DOS [20] ❑ Windows [21] ❑ OS/2 [22] ❑ Unix [23] ❑ Macintosh [24] ❑ Other: [25]_____ (please specify)

I would be interested in new books on the following subjects:
(please check all that apply, and use the spaces provided to identify specific software)

❑ Word processing: [26]

❑ Data bases: [28]

❑ File Utilities: [30]

❑ Networking: [32]

❑ Other: [34]

❑ Spreadsheets: [27]

❑ Desktop publishing: [29]

❑ Money management: [31]

❑ Programming languages: [33]

I use a PC at (please check all that apply): ❑ home [35] ❑ work [36] ❑ school [37] ❑ other: [38] _____

The disks I prefer to use are ❑ 5.25 [39] ❑ 3.5 [40] ❑ other: [41]_____

I have a CD ROM: ❑ yes [42] ❑ no [43]

I plan to buy or upgrade computer hardware this year: ❑ yes [44] ❑ no [45]

I plan to buy or upgrade computer software this year: ❑ yes [46] ❑ no [47]

Name: _____ Business title: [48] _____ Type of Business: [49]

Address (❑ home [50] ❑ work [51]/Company name: _____)

Street/Suite#

City [52]/State [53]/Zipcode [54]: _____ Country [55]

❑ **I liked this book!** You may quote me by name in future IDG Books Worldwide promotional materials.

My daytime phone number is _____

IDG BOOKS

THE WORLD OF COMPUTER KNOWLEDGE

☐ YES!

Please keep me informed about IDG's World of Computer Knowledge.
Send me the latest IDG Books catalog.

COMPUTER
BOOK SERIES
FROM IDG